ANGLO NOSTALGIA

EDOARDO CAMPANELLA
MARTA DASSÙ

Anglo Nostalgia

The Politics of Emotion
in a Fractured West

OXFORD
UNIVERSITY PRESS

Oxford University Press is a department of the
University of Oxford. It furthers the University's objective
of excellence in research, scholarship, and education
by publishing worldwide.

Oxford   New York

Auckland   Cape Town   Dar es Salaam   Hong Kong   Karachi
Kuala Lumpur   Madrid   Melbourne   Mexico City   Nairobi
New Delhi   Shanghai   Taipei   Toronto

With offices in

Argentina   Austria   Brazil   Chile   Czech Republic   France   Greece
Guatemala   Hungary   Italy   Japan   Poland   Portugal   Singapore
South Korea   Switzerland   Thailand   Turkey   Ukraine   Vietnam

Oxford is a registered trade mark of Oxford University Press
in the UK and certain other countries.

Published in the United States of America by
Oxford University Press
198 Madison Avenue, New York, NY 10016

Library of Congress Cataloging-in-Publication Data is available
Edoardo Campanella and Marta Dassù.
Anglo Nostalgia: The Politics of Emotion in a Fractured West.
ISBN: 9780190068936

Printed in the United Kingdom by Bell and Bain Ltd, Glasgow
on acid-free paper

To Costanza and Nina

CONTENTS

FOREWORD

This book stems from an attempt to understand the emotional roots of today's geopolitical disorder. Nostalgia is not the kind of topic you would expect an economist and a political scientist to address. However, in the aftermath of the Brexit vote and the election of Donald Trump, it became clear that the present is increasingly becoming a source of discomfort for large sections of the population (particularly in the West) and that nationalist leaders are keen to resort to nostalgic arguments to mobilize their citizens. In February 2017 we started to explore the idea of nostalgic nationalism applied to the Anglo-Saxon world in an article for *Foreign Affairs* entitled "A Future of the English-Speaking Peoples". We are grateful to Kathrin Allawala Salam, then an editor at the journal and now at *Foreign Policy*, for accepting it and making it readable. The article triggered some interesting intellectual reactions, and we were provided with opportunities to discuss its rationale at a number of conferences organized by Aspen Institute Italia, Chatham House, the Instituto per gli Studi di Politica Internazionale (ISPI), and the European Council on Foreign Relations.

From our conversations with scholars and policymakers we immediately realized that everyone (including ourselves) was taking for granted the concept of nostalgic nationalism. In the press too, nostalgia began to be increasingly associated with the major political disruptions that were turning the global order upside down. In reality however, nostalgic nationalism had not received a clear and coherent definition—except in a few important books on nostalgia itself. Was it really a new form of nationalism in its own right? How does nostalgia infect the political debate? And, more importantly, why was nostalgia spreading so quickly across the whole world?

The time was ripe to analyse in greater depth an emotional syndrome that will probably shape domestic and international politics for many years to come. This is exactly what induced Michael Dwyer, managing director at Hurst Publishers, to accept our proposal for a book about the changing landscape of emotions and ideas in Western politics: Brexit was the perfect test case. We are immensely grateful to him for this opportunity.

The book focuses on the link between nostalgia and nationalism. Demographic, economic and technological forces are spreading the disease of longing at an impressive pace. Older people are struggling to keep up with a world that is changing too fast. Globalization and technological progress disrupt traditional industries, creating job opportunities for a small elite of highly qualified professionals. And immigration destabilizes self-contained local communities, questioning the traditional values that keep them together. These forces, being structural in nature, are producing a generalized sense of insecurity that jingoist leaders are addressing by promising to "take back control" at the national level—as in an idealized past.

At the heart of today's nationalist narrative is a promise to turn the clock back. Of course, memories of bygone eras are emotionally and historically biased. But that is how nostalgia works. It is selective by nature.

To improve our understanding of the phenomenon, we crossed the boundaries of a number of fields, well beyond our comfort zones of international relations and economics. We turned to psychology, anthropology, cultural studies, and history. We came to the conclusion that nostalgic nationalism is indeed a new form of nationalism—rather than a simple populist revolt. But only in the United Kingdom, given its historical legacy, was this phenomenon so ripe that it contributed to a highly temporally regressive decision such as Brexit. The tiny majority of the highly polarized British population who voted Leave and were brainwashed with nostalgic national myths of past glories did not just want divorce from Brussels. They wanted to return the United Kingdom to a time when the country was fully sovereign and simulta-

FOREWORD

neously able to play a global role. That is why this book refers in detail to the debate over the Anglosphere as a geopolitical alternative to the European Union.

Our Anglo-Saxon interlocutors were intrigued that two Italians had dared intrude on their debate and delve into what many perceive as a highly emotional topic. Our bet is that two outsiders, while strongly connected to the Anglo-American world through a number of policy, academic, and corporate connections, could provide an interesting perspective on these issues.

Along the way, we benefited from the expertise of a number of collaborators. Ph.D. candidates Niccolò Serri and Edoardo Andreoni provided excellent research assistance for some of the historical chapters. The journalist Hannah Roberts improved our understanding of the nostalgic flavour that characterized the United Kingdom in the years leading up to the Brexit referendum. At Hurst, we are indebted to Lara Weisweiller-Wu for her patience, competence, and steadfastness, as well as to the rest of the editorial and marketing staff. We are also grateful to Gyneth Sick and the team at the journal *Aspenia* for running an editorial on nostalgia. Edoardo also had the opportunity to write a long essay on a related topic for Project Syndicate. He is grateful to Ken Murphy, Romand Frydman, and Nicolas Chatara-Morse for supporting this idea.

A number of friends and colleagues commented on part of the draft or the entire manuscript: Pramit Pal Chaudhuri (Rhodium Group), Stephanie Flanders (Bloomberg Economics), Timothy Garton Ash (Oxford University), Christopher Hill (Cambridge University), Ivan Krastev (*The New York Times* and Centre for Liberal Strategies in Sofia), Charles A. Kupchan (Council on Foreign Relations), Walter Russell Mead (Bard College), Roberto Menotti (Aspen Institute Italia), Larry Summers (Harvard University), George Tsarouchas (Dialectica). We are also very grateful to two anonymous reviewers whose comments and suggestions contributed greatly to improving the book.

On a more personal level, we would like to thank our relatives for putting up with our frequent "detours" from our family lives throughout the project. Edoardo would like to thank Margherita for continuing to be a source of unconditional support and for reading every word of his writings, even the most boring. The article in *Foreign Affairs* was published the day after Costanza's birth, and she has since been the best source of distraction from his Anglo-Saxon ruminations. Marta wishes to thank the Aspen Institute Italia for having enabled her to work on a book largely focused on topics that are central to the Aspen network, as well as thanking her own family, starting with Gianluca and Otti, for being patient and supportive.

The book is dedicated to Costanza and Nina.

INTRODUCTION

"Remembrance of things past is not necessarily the remembrance of things as they were"

Marcel Proust

The world is marching backwards into the future. More and more countries are becoming trapped in a past that no longer exists—and probably never really existed at all. Millions of people, particularly in advanced economies, believe that life was better fifty years ago: job opportunities abounded, local communities were intact, and the pace of technological change was under control.[1] A majority of Russians still mourn the Soviet Union. Hardline Brexiteers yearn for the days when the British Empire ruled the waves, while a significant portion of the American population longs for the power and influence that the United States used to enjoy during the Cold War and its immediate aftermath. Even Mao Zedong has been rediscovered, with hordes of Chinese descending each year on his rural home town, Shaoshan, to pay homage.[2] It is a sense of loss that is fuelling this epidemic of nostalgia—a lost global status, a lost socio-economic prosperity, a lost cultural integrity. Ordinary citizens no longer project their aspirations onto utopian visions of an idealized future. They prefer to look back to a time when national borders were less porous and governments supposedly did a better job of protecting their citizens. Nostalgia offers relief from socio-economic angst. Yesterday is associated with progress; tomorrow with stasis or regression.

From a purely psychological point of view, nostalgia represents a coping strategy for dealing with moments of deep uncertainty and radical discontinuity. It removes its victims from an unpleasant present and throws them into a familiar past, reinforcing their self-esteem and the self-confidence needed to navigate periods of sustained stress. Collectively, it strengthens bonds with those who reminisce about the same idealized time—thus drawing a clear line between competing groups in a highly exclusionary way, particularly with respect to new-comers and immigrants. With the world on the cusp of massive geopo-litical, demographic, and technological transformations, there is no shortage of reasons to be nostalgic. The denouement of American lib-eral hegemony is creating opportunities for post-imperial powers such as China, Russia, and Turkey to reassert their lost status on the world stage. Reviving moments of past glory helps motivate a nation, and shows that reshuffling the global order is possible, and somewhat legiti-mate. At the same time, the employment threats posed by globalization and exponential technological change induce workers, particularly in the West, to long for the economic security and the social mobility enjoyed by their parents. And the ageing of the population in Europe, North America, and parts of Asia psychologically compounds all these factors. Older people are the most likely to fall victim to nostalgia.

Far from being innocuous, this infatuation with a mythicized past, which is usually remodelled at will, is shaping our politics in risky ways. Collective anxieties weaken the ties of civil society, give rise to tribalism, and splinter civilizations into warring factions. Not only does nostalgia blur the past, present, and future, it also induces citizens and governments to find comfort in a time when national borders were still rigid—a pre-globalization era in which each nation was (supposedly) in control of its fate. This is why nostalgia and nationalism are inti-mately interlinked.

Nostalgia becomes an emotional weapon in the political debate that can be used either defensively or offensively. To those who reject a cosmopolitan world and yearn for the socio-economic opportunities enjoyed by older generations, nationalism promises a source of identity and security: a return to full sovereignty will supposedly stem the global forces responsible for today's uneasiness. Solidarity is then restricted to small clans, and nostalgia acts as a self-defence mecha-nism. Equally, to those who aspire to restore the national glory of the past, nationalism provides a means to gain influence to the detriment of other nations. Here, nostalgia is deployed aggressively to fuel tension among states, leveraging fractures generated by ethnic, cultural, or historical factors and making cooperation on global issues impossible. The logical endpoint of these trends is a Hobbesian world characterized by conflict. Nostalgia can only rarely be employed in a cooperative way. This occurs when nations share special cultural, religious, or historical links (like the Anglo-Saxons). But national interests might diverge even between similarly nostalgic countries, inevitably leading to tension. Cooperative nostalgia, in other words, is the exception that confirms the rule.

The age of nostalgia has begun. It is an age of false myths, unparalleled political miscalculations, and rising tensions between nations—a time of regression and pessimism. Jingoistic leaders are increasingly activating and harnessing nostalgia for their own ends.[3] They do not simply view the past through critical eyes, recognizing that, even though some things have been lost, much has been gained along the way. They want instead to start over, rebuild the lost home, and restore the past as it was; turning the clock back to face the challenges of the future with the strength of the past. This is the most toxic form of nostalgia.

Chinese President Xi Jinping calls for the "great rejuvenation of the Chinese people". With 5,000 years of continuous civilization, China is re-emerging as a global economic and political power. For his part, Donald Trump was elected President of the United States with a clear mandate to preserve and restore Washington's primacy and "Make America Great Again". Turkish President Recep Tayyip Erdoğan harbours neo-Ottoman ambitions, while Japanese Prime Minister Shinzo Abe's political lodestar is the nineteenth-century Meiji Restoration, which laid the foundations for an expansive Japanese empire. In other cases, nostalgic leaders reject their countries' historical reversals of fortune. While Hungarian Prime Minister Viktor Orbán still regrets the Kingdom of Hungary's territorial losses after the First World War, Russian President Vladimir Putin has described the collapse of the Soviet Union as "the greatest geopolitical catastrophe" of the twentieth century. Nostalgia is animating all the far-right nationalist or populist movements that are currently fracturing Western Europe, from the League in Italy to the National Front in France and the Danish People's Party in Denmark.

But it is Brexit that epitomizes our new age of nostalgic nationalism in its purest form. It captures the economic pain of the left-behind, the social disruptions generated by immigration, and the geopolitical ambitions of a once glorious empire. During the referendum campaign, and in the aftermath of the vote, nostalgic arguments have been used defensively against the European Union, offensively to boost Britain's global influence, and cooperatively to strengthen ties with its former colonies. Brexit, as argued by the distinguished political scientist Albert Weale, was a "triumph of nostalgic democracy".[4]

Only in the United Kingdom is it possible to clearly identify the three moments of a periodizing nostalgic narrative: the "golden days"; the "great rupture"; and the "present discontent".[5] The golden age is represented by the imperial era, during which the United Kingdom held sway over "one continent, a hundred peninsulas, five hundred promontories, a thousand lakes, two thousand rivers, ten thousand islands".[6] It was a multi-faith, multi-lingual, and multi-ethnic maritime imperium, with no rivals in terms of vastness and richness. Global maritime, commercial, and political links turned this offshore island into, first, an "Atlantic nation" and eventually into the centre of a worldwide network of trade, culture, and politics. The rupture came not only with the slow demise of the British Empire, but also with the United Kingdom's decision to join the European project in 1973. The present discontent is caused by the unwillingness of many Britons to come to terms with Britain's transformation into an ordinary nation-state. In the eyes of a hardcore Eurosceptic, the European Union represents an abrupt break from the uninterrupted history of continuous progress that has characterized the United Kingdom since the introduction of Magna Carta. Brexit was supposed to close this nostalgic cycle by bringing Britain back to its golden era—not just immediately before the infamous decision to join the European Economic Community, but possibly to a more distant glorious past. No other country has yet made a comparable leap backward.

Such an apparently irrational and masochistic choice took place in a country that has, over the last five centuries, created and developed the most growth-friendly institutional setting in the world.[7] This is the nation that nobody would have expected to fail—in the sense of deliberately making economically harmful decisions. The Brexiteers spoke masterfully to the gut of their fellow citizens and leveraged their emotions to overcome the terrifying messages of "Project Fear" (which was unusually associated with mainstream parties), denigrating the experts, deriding their gloomy predictions, and keeping up the morale of their crew with dreams of a past that they promised to restore—at least to some extent. The Brexit debate, as former Prime Minister John Major put it, had turned into a "battle between economics and emotion".[8]

Post-empire melancholy—as well as an eagerness to regain full control of the law and the borders—completely altered any rational cost–benefit analysis about the economic consequences of a historic decision of this kind. But this is how nostalgia works. It projects its victims two or three generations back and two or three generations ahead, heavily discounting short-term costs and massively overstating long-term benefits. The warnings of academic and commercial economists about the negative-growth spillovers of a divorce from Brussels were simply ignored. The Organization for Economic Cooperation and Development (OECD) published a report ahead of the referendum stating that by 2020 and 2030 GDP per household would be, respectively, £2,200 and £3,200 lower.[9] But Britons simply did not care. This indifference was not only a by-product of the generalized distrust of experts that was spreading across the world at that time.[10] Brexiteers were to some extent aware that their grand strategy of restoring full sovereignty could not be implemented overnight. It would clearly be costly and painful, but was worth pursuing.

From the perspective of the Leave camp, Brexit provided an opportunity to regain control of Britain's past and future, allowing it, once freed from European constraints, to take advantage of all the great economic opportunities that the world could offer to a global power rediscovering itself. But, as Vince Cable of the British Liberal Democrats puts it, "Too many were driven by nostalgia for a world where passports were blue, faces were white and the map was coloured imperial pink."[11] With their minds completely obfuscated by questionable myths of national glory, nostalgic Leavers ignored the greed, depredation, and cruelty at the heart of British imperialism. That, after all, is how nostalgia works. The negative emotions associated with our memories tend to dissipate more quickly than the positive ones.

However, these imperial inclinations are also associated with a key feature of British nostalgia: the lack of a proper British nationalism. There are Scottish, Welsh, and Irish national identities that have developed in reaction to a stifling English imperial identity, but not a truly collective British identity.[12] The English first built a land empire by expanding from the south of the British Isles to the north-west. They then created an overseas empire, the first in the Western Hemisphere, in North America and the Caribbean, and then in the East, in India and Southeast Asia. The "inner empire" was clearly a creation of the English. But the "outer empire" was, despite the many contributions of the Welsh, Irish, and Scots, also de facto considered an English endeavour. After all, it was English Common Law, the English Parliament, and the English monarchy that supplied the key institutions to the two empires. It was this outer empire that allowed the different national identities of the United Kingdom to converge and merge into a common British identity. Once the empire dissolved, only the English were left without a traditional national identity. But they remained a "post-imperial" people, and Brexit deluded them with Anglosphere fantasies aimed at restoring their imperial past—at least to some degree.[13] The empire was in fact a recurring, but not exclusive, theme in the nostalgic rhetoric of hardcore Brexiteers that possibly also influenced the voting decisions of moderate Leavers who cared very little about it, but needed a source of strong inspiration to ditch Brussels. They swapped what they perceived as a mediocre future within the European Union for a glorious past.

When one looks at the geography of the Brexit vote, these contrasting views manifest themselves plainly. Excluding London, England voted to leave the European Union by 55.4 per cent to 44.6 per cent, whereas 62 per cent of Scots and 55.8 per cent of the Northern Irish voted to remain.[14] As the writer Anthony Barnet put it: "It was England's Brexit."[15] London, instead, is in a class of its own, thanks to its melting-pot of languages, religions, ethnicities, and nationalities. But the truth is that never in recent history has the United Kingdom been as divided as it is today, with political and economic divides cutting across cities, regions, and social groups. Using the jargon of journalist David Goodhart, there are, on the one hand, the "Somewheres", who are rooted in a specific place and are often less educated, and on the other there are the "Anywheres", who are footloose, urban, and socially liberal. These fault lines characterize the whole of the West. But it is in Britain that tensions between these two groups have manifested themselves in the most dramatic way.[16]

* * *

Those who campaigned for Brexit did not propose an amorphous future outside the European Union. There was certainly a lot of confusion and inconsistency in the arguments put forward by the Leavers. They all shared a desire to free their country from the tight fetters of a rule-imposing Brussels; but they had confused ideas as to how to turn their aspirations into reality. Ultimately they believed that a divorce from Brussels would allow Britain to regain "control", first of all of external borders, and even rejoin its true "kith and kin"—that is, English-speaking countries that are committed to common law, democracy, and free markets. "Global Britain" was meant to strengthen its relationship with the United States and the old Commonwealth, while also establishing new trade ties with countries in the Far East. Hardcore Brexiteers, a minority within the Leave camp, clung nostalgically to the idea that Britain would find her right place within a renewed Anglosphere—namely, Australia, New Zealand, Canada, the United Kingdom, and the United States; that it would go from being an ordinary European Union member state to a modern version of the old imperial Mother Country. In addition, within this core group of English-speaking countries, Leavers overemphasized the special relationship with America that was instrumental to easily navigating any post-Brexit adversity. After all, the most enthusiastic Eurosceptic sees in the American Empire the natural evolution and continuation of its British predecessor.[17]

The debate concerning Great Britain's global role is nothing more than the culmination of an intellectual dispute that has lasted for more than 150 years—since the late Victorian era when the British Empire's global pre-eminence was slipping as a result of combined internal and external fractures. It all started in 1873 at the Oxford Union, with a debate on how to reorganize and modernize *Pax Britannica*.[18] Since then, plans have differed in detail, but they have all sought to unite the Anglosphere behind a common purpose. Some have called for the creation of a British imperial federation or a multi-national common-wealth, while others would have liked to see a more formalized Atlantic Union, or even a new Anglo-American state. Hardcore Brexiteers simply continued this project. All the institutional arrangements proposed over the years were intrinsically nostalgic and utopian. They attempted to creatively preserve a past that was falling apart by promoting Britain's political and economic interests to the detriment of increasingly more assertive colonies. Not surprisingly, none of these proposals has ever amounted to anything. Nostalgia, which tends to oversimplify reality, hardly makes for enlightened politics and effective policies.

To be sure, only a minority of Leave voters truly yearn for a revival of their imperial past. In a way, only a few eternally nostalgic people, such as the leading Brexiteers Boris Johnson or Jacob Rees-Mogg really believed in the restoration of a sort of modern empire. According to a poll taken by Lord Ashcroft Polls, only 6 per cent of Leavers wanted to expand British economic and trade opportunities outside the European Union.[19] But even if the Anglosphere was not the chief concern of a dissatisfied British electorate, the legacy of a globe-spanning empire acted as an ideological construct that sugared the Brexit pill. Away from Brussels, but without an Anglo-Saxon alternative, the United Kingdom would have enjoyed more political and policy freedom, but its economic prospects would have been grim. The Anglosphere created the illusion of preferential access to a trading area that was expected to provide more commercial opportunities than Europe—despite the fact that the continent is still Britain's largest market for its exports. This was the offensive and cooperative side of nostalgia in the Brexit debate: the eagerness to regain global influence, while leveraging ancestral global connections. In political jargon, it coincided with the idea of Global Britain.

Most Brexiteers were probably more pragmatic and somewhat more realistic. They primarily wanted to regain control of their borders and laws. Taming what was perceived as an out-of-control immigration process and pushing back an intrusive Brussels were their most pressing priorities. Nearly half of the Leave voters believed that decisions about the United Kingdom should be taken in the United Kingdom, and 33 per cent wanted to regain control over immigration.[20] But even these issues were heavily tinged with nostalgia in its defensive form.

INTRODUCTION

The empire fuelled a sense of exceptionalism that makes the United Kingdom uncomfortable when in a position of equality rather than leadership. This is especially true when it comes to sharing power with other countries, such as France and Germany, which are not even part of the Anglo-Saxon clan; or when a supranational actor such as the European Union undermines sovereignty from above, betraying the democratic principles that the United Kingdom has upheld for centuries. From the very beginning, Britain had joined the European project with a chauvinistic otherness that nourished the expectation of deserving special status. As Margaret Thatcher put it: "God separated Britain from mainland Europe, and it was for a purpose."[21] But the many "optouts" that were offered to the United Kingdom never proved enough to secure its full engagement. For almost fifty years, nostalgia for a time when Westminster was fully in charge of British affairs has provided a rallying cry against external intrusions.

An additional manifestation of defensive nostalgia emerged in the years leading up to the Brexit debate. Fear of foreigners triggered by the intensification of migratory flows from Eastern Europe and the dislocation generated by globalization and technological progress pushed many British citizens (although the phenomenon is widespread in the West) to look back to a past when their governments (supposedly) had the political power and the economic tools to stem these global forces. Due to its lack of steadfastness, the European Union represented an obstacle to addressing these public concerns. Both forms of defensive nostalgia (against Brussels and against globalization in all its different forms) correspond to the idea of a Little England, even if no one really likes this branding, which finds its lifeblood in the myth of the island nation—an insular geography that shapes the character of its people.[22]

In no other place in the world is nostalgia so multifaceted as to be used as a political weapon defensively, offensively, or cooperatively, depending on the circumstances. In the United Kingdom, nostalgia is an emotion that is both inward and outward looking, generating conflicting worldviews: that of Global Britain and that of Little England (two nostalgic terms themselves with roots in the political debate of the late Victorian era). Moreover, Englishness itself has a distinctive nostalgic feature that sets it apart from any other national identity.

Yearning for the past is somewhat intrinsic to the English way of being, and this mindset is compounded, although not outright created, by the demographic, geopolitical, and economic forces that are spreading this epidemic of nostalgia across the globe. It feels as if the United Kingdom has produced such a surplus of history that it can still be consumed decades later. Some say that "Englishness inevitably appears tinged with nostalgia and consistently evokes pictures of an older, more tranquil England, an England of times gone by".[23] Others say that the English are "chronically nostalgic".[24]

In a way, it is possible to speak of "Anglo Nostalgia": a state of mind that induces the British (and particularly the English) to constantly look back to their glorious history to confront the present, usually ignoring the changes that have occurred in the meantime, and often aspiring to restore the past altogether.[25] As stated by the historian David Edgerton: "The past is appealed to as an explanation of the present, for this and that policy, the place where a true national essence is revealed."[26] This also reflects Britain's continuous and painful search for its own national identity since the end of the Second World War.[27] Until the 1940s, the United Kingdom was liberal, cosmopolitan, capitalist, and anti-nationalist, at the heart of a European and global web of trade and influence. Then, as its global position eroded, and after the introduction of the welfare state, it quickly became a more circumscribed, but ordinary, successful nation with shared goals and horizons. In the 1970s it reinvented itself again as part of the European project, and in the following decade as a magnet for global financial and human capital. Since then, under the pressure of these external forces, Britain has struggled to be a nation.

* * *

The rhetoric of the Leave campaigners was so filled with nostalgic arguments and historical references that at times it felt as if the United Kingdom was completely removed from the present. Trump went back no further than the 1950s in depicting his ideal of America; Brexiteers, however, dug deep in reminiscing about the British past—all the way back to the introduction of the Magna Carta in 1215. On many occasions it seemed that leading Brexit supporters were living in a different era. Throughout the campaign the former

INTRODUCTION

Mayor of London, Boris Johnson, continuously mobilized his political hero Winston Churchill; Nigel Farage, leader of the UK Independence Party (UKIP), celebrated military victories that only specialist historians still remember; and the MP Jacob Rees-Mogg revived a lost ideal of pure Englishness. Their narrative centred on a sort of atavistic conflict between the United Kingdom and the "old continent". It fleshed out four key elements: imperial pride; the discomfort of being ruled by others; an unparalleled sense of trust among Anglo-Saxon countries; and a pronounced mistrust of foreigners seen as invaders. Brexit was a modern-day Battle of Britain. After having defeated the French and the Spaniards throughout the centuries, after having stopped Wilhelm II, Hitler, and Brezhnev from permanently disrupting the global order, the time had come for Britain to push back Brussels' technocrats. In April 2016, the former Deputy Prime Minister Nick Clegg explicitly accused the Leave campaign of nostalgia during a speech at Princeton University:

> Those campaigning for us to leave the European Union like to evoke a sentimental, nostalgic vision of Britannia, proud and independent, ruling the waves once again. But the truth is, leaving cannot return us to a halcyon age—if such an age ever existed—and may even mean sacrificing the United Kingdom itself.[28]

However, the inclination of some British people to live in the past was not only the fault of the Brexiteers. Thanks to various semi-fortuitous circumstances, the country was especially receptive to nostalgic arguments. Events such as the Royal Wedding, the Queen's Diamond Jubilee, and the 2012 Olympics, or the anniversaries of the First World War, Magna Carta, and Shakespeare's death contributed to create that emotional sense of national pride and belonging which turned out to be key in the United Kingdom's decision to say goodbye to the European Union. Furthermore, the British culture and entertainment industry had unwittingly lent the Leave campaign a helping hand by reinvigorating the "Blitz spirit" related to Britain's military triumphs in the two World Wars and creating a national infatuation with the late Victorian and Edwardian eras. In the years leading up to the 2016 referendum, an outpouring of films, television series, books, and art exhibitions glorified Britain's past and celebrated Englishness as the lost apotheosis of *noblesse oblige*.

This pathological infatuation with the past distorted reality, misleading millions of British citizens about the future of their country outside Europe. Brexiteers mobilized the history of their nation to create myths about the United Kingdom's global role, the uniqueness of the relationship with America, the construction of the Anglosphere, and the uselessness of the European Union. By deploying nostalgia both offensively and defensively, Brexiteers found themselves promoting two inconsistent visions of the United Kingdom: an outward-looking Global Britain and an inward-looking Little England. The former depicts the ambitions of a part of the Oxbridge elite that is against the European Union, while the latter embodies the frustrations of low-skilled workers. As shown by Brexiteers' inability to agree on a shared post-Brexit plan during the negotiations with Brussels, striking a balance between global and insular aspirations is simply a Herculean challenge. The only thing they have in common is the idea of reclaiming sovereignty. But then these two groups would use their regained power to achieve conflicting goals.

This book analyses how nostalgia has infected the political debate globally, and then looks at the United Kingdom as a case study. Coming from outside the Anglo-Saxon world, while being closely connected to it through our professional network, we attempt to provide a balanced outsiders' assessment of the nostalgia phenomenon in the United Kingdom, with no emotional or practical involvement in British politics. The first section is about the psychological biases produced by nostalgia that end up creating national myths (by definition a mix of truth and falsehoods), highlighting the role of history, politics, and the media. Chapter One analyses the global epidemic of nostalgia as a major force affecting both domestic and international politics. Chapter Two emphasizes the link between nostalgia and nationalism, defining the features of Anglo Nostalgia. We will argue that Brexit is the only true example of nostalgic nationalism—a new category of nationalism in its own right. Chapter Three describes the nostalgic atmosphere that characterized the years leading up to the Brexit referendum, and how Brexiteers used it as leverage along with their propaganda machines to create a narrative about bygone glorious times. Chapter Four analyses the history of the intellectual debate surrounding the United Kingdom's role in the world since the Victorian era, all the way to

Brexit. Those who animated this debate tried to preserve a past that was slipping out of their hands.

The second section is a reality check aimed at dismantling the fallacies produced by nostalgic arguments focusing on the three pillars of Britain's foreign policy: the troubled relationship with the European Union, the conflicting relationship with the British Empire, and the special relationship with the United States. Chapter Five emphasizes the gap between electoral nostalgic promises and a complicated political reality when it comes to dealing with Brussels. As a member of the European Union, the United Kingdom used to be "in" but with important opt-outs; now it will most likely be "out" but claim specific opt-ins, with a new variant of British exceptionalism. And it cannot be completely discounted that distortions of reality created by nostalgia could be powerful enough to force Britain to a Breturn. Chapter Six argues that the Anglosphere already exists in many fields, but that it is an invisible political animal, and can hardly be turned into something more institutionalized, as claimed by some hardcore Brexiteers. Chapter Seven describes the nuances of the special relationship between the United Kingdom and the United States, arguing that Britain has always felt the "specialness" more than America has. The final chapter draws conclusions, focusing on the complex interactions between sovereignty and nostalgia.

As the reader will discover, this is not a book about Brexit. Electoral patterns or the socio-economic causes that led to it are not the object of our analysis. By the same token, we do not dare to predict how Brexit will unfold in the end. This would be a pointless, and probably fruitless, intellectual exercise. Attention is instead focused on how nostalgic arguments that fed through the political debate have produced the first visible and shocking crack in Western liberal order. This is a book about the role of nostalgia in driving global politics.[29]

PART ONE

MYTHMAKING

1

A GLOBAL EPIDEMIC

"One is always at home in one's past."

Vladimir Nabokov

In 1884, Greenwich became the clock of the world. With the spreading of the telegraph system, along with advances in railways and shipping, the standardization of time had become a global priority to effectively connect cities, nations, and the world as never before. Gathering in Washington for the International Meridian Conference, delegates from twenty-five nations decided to split the world into twenty-four time zones based on longitude and to divide the Eastern and Western Hemispheres, using the Greenwich Meridian as the zero line. With Great Britain ruling the waves, the choice was inevitable, as was the irritation of its arch-enemy France, which abstained from voting in protest.

France was unwilling to accept the new reality. Sailors had already synchronized time using chronometers set by longitudinal measurements based on the Greenwich Meridian, and two-thirds of the world's telegraph lines belonged to British companies. Setting the time for the whole world did not just represent an enormous privilege and a display of British power. It was also necessary to coordinate all commercial, administrative, and military activities across its globe-spanning dominions. For the first time after four centuries of imperialistic expansion, noon in London would coincide perfectly with dawn in eastern Canada, early afternoon in South Africa, sunset in India and Australia, midnight in the Fiji Islands, and, a day earlier, in Western Samoa. And the sun would always shine on the British Empire.[1]

More than a century later, Greenwich Mean Time remains the world's time standard. But today's Great Britain looks very different from its imperial zenith. In 1921 the British Empire dominated roughly a quarter of the world's population, covered about the same share of the earth's land surface, and had assimilated an unrivalled array of languages, cultures, and religions.[2] Now, however, it accounts for less than 1 per cent of the global population and less than 0.2 per cent of the world's land surface. In just a little more than eighty years, its overseas territories have shrunk to just fourteen scattered islands, such as the British Virgin Islands in the Caribbean and Pitcairn Island in the South Pacific, while the Commonwealth of Nations founded before the Second World War is just a relic of the colonial era. With the liquidation of its dominions, colonies, and protectorates, little is left of Britain's past glory, power, and influence.

The transformation of the United Kingdom into an ordinary nation was probably too swift and too recent for its citizens to ignore and dismiss the imperial experience. The dismantling of the British Empire started in 1947 with the independence of India and Pakistan, at a time when Britain, economically exhausted by six years of war, was revered as the champion of freedom that had liberated Europe from the Nazi threat. Just two years earlier, at the Yalta Conference, when the post-war global order was decided, British Prime Minister Winston Churchill was photographed sitting with the American President, Franklin Delano Roosevelt, and Joseph Stalin, the supreme leader of the Soviet Union. Great Britain was still formally on a par with the two powers that would dominate the rest of the century. But the erosion of its global status continued inexorably with the surrender of the British Mandate for Palestine in 1948, the humiliating withdrawal from the Suez Canal in 1956, and the demand for independence by the Gold Coast (now Ghana) in 1957. Ten years later, in 1967, Britain decided on a hasty withdrawal from Aden: its role "East of Suez" was over by the beginning of the 1970s. The progressive demise of the empire continued with Rhodesia's transition to Zimbabwe in 1980, and culminated with the transfer of sovereignty over Hong Kong to China in 1997. Prince Charles described that moment in his personal diary: "Such is the end of Empire, I sighed to myself."[3]

Like him, any person in Britain over the age of twenty-five has, one way or another, lived in the shadow of the British Empire. Not all regret world domination or the imperial deeds and misdeeds, but many sadly witnessed the empire's relentless decline with the bitter taste of not having lived through the heyday of this successful enterprise. According to a 2014 YouGov poll, 59 per cent of "British people think the British Empire is something to be proud of rather than ashamed of", and one-third of Britons "would like it if Britain still had an empire".[4] The historian Jeffrey Richards, referring particularly to the English, speaks of a retreat "into a nostalgia for an empire which they barely remember and of which they know almost nothing".[5] The legacy of the British Empire has profound personal connotations, especially among the Oxbridge elite. Some of their ancestors were missionaries, imperial bureaucrats, members of the Armed Forces, and businessmen who took advantage of a borderless empire to pursue their ambitions. As admitted by the historian Niall Ferguson, travelling to Australia, Kenya, Canada, or India subconsciously still feels like visiting an imperial province.[6] But even for those critical of the imperial experience, the empire remains a cumbersome presence that, with all its contradictions of openness and closedness, freedom and repression, acts as an ideological construct that affects their way of thinking and shapes their collective identity.[7] This is not a British peculiarity. It is true for most former imperial powers of the recent past. Empires may dissolve, but their ontological legacy lastingly permeates the nations that emerge from their collapse—not least through the grandiosity of their monuments.

During the Brexit referendum campaign, the empire was the elephant in the room, and contributed to the drawing of a clear line between the Remain and Leave camps. Remainers, even the most sympathetic to the imperial experience, believed that the European Union was the future, while the glory of the past could only help Britain exert a stronger influence both inside and outside this club of nations. The empire played instead an important role in the Brexit narrative of the Leavers. For a minority of highly influential Brexiteers it was a fundamental motivation; for the majority of the Leavers it was just another good reason to divorce

Brussels. Imperial glory acted as a source of inspiration for making a difficult decision, and to remind them why the British were different from the rest of Europe—in short, why they were not Europeans.

From the perspective of the most nostalgic hardline Leavers, people such as former London Mayor Boris Johnson, the decision to break away from the European Union was a sort of first step in the construction of a modern version of the British Empire—based on soft power rather than on territorial expansion. In their eyes the European project represented an insult to Britain's glorious history. The concepts of Global Britain and the Anglosphere, which in different ways aspired to put Britain at the centre of a new global order, embodied their neo-imperial ambitions. As discussed in Chapter Three, this small group of hardcore Brexiteers set the tone for the propaganda machine that persuaded slightly more than half of the British population to say goodbye to Brussels.

The average Leave voter, instead, living in rural areas and with fewer connections to the outer world, did not care about the actual or symbolic restoration of the empire—it was something too distant from his daily life. These voters simply believed that the European Union had curbed the ability of a democratically elected government to protect them from the disruptions generated by unfettered global forces. In their minds, a divorce from Brussels represented, rightly or wrongly, an effective way to address globalization and immigration fears, while re-establishing a proper democratic order by taking back Britain's full sovereignty. From their perspective, it would have been enough to go back in time to 1973, right before Britain joined the European Economic Community, when it was still in control of its own affairs— except that the 1970s were years of economic stagnation and declining global status. For this kind of voter the continuous references to imperial history made by hardcore Brexiteers were a reminder of the lasting greatness of the United Kingdom that would have allowed the nation to effortlessly withstand the stifling uncertainty and painful cost generated by a divorce from Brussels. After all, the British Empire remains at the heart of British exceptionalism. This has always prevented Britain from being truly engaged with the European project, conveying the message: "We are still a great country, we can do things our own special way."[8]

This is precisely what connected the two souls of the Leave camp. Although the intensity of nostalgia for the empire markedly differed within it, all Brexiteers agreed that for the United Kingdom, being equal partners with countries in a position to exert real, horizontal influence through a shared membership of institutions was intolerable. It was a betrayal of its long-standing democratic tradition and the global status that it enjoyed less than a century ago. During the Brexit campaign the doctrine of "taking back control" for an "independent Britain" and an infatuation with the utopian plan of a Global Britain spoke to these deep concerns about being led by others. It was Britain that should lead, and assume full responsibility for its own domestic affairs. The concept of British exceptionalism, used in the past to justify British imperial rule, fostered the narrative that the United Kingdom was not suited to become a colony of a new kind of European empire. This uneasiness with Europe's political integration was compounded by the perception that the European dream was actually a Franco-German project: run by Germany and France for their own benefit, whilst sacrificing the national interests of other member states, especially those of Britain.

In the immediate aftermath of the Brexit vote the British government resorted to imperial fantasies to make Brexit more digestible to those concerned with the future of their country outside the European Union—inadvertently making it even more unacceptable to pro-European voters who, instead, tended to remember the gloomiest aspects of the colonial era. The Conservatives proposed recommissioning the royal yacht *Britannia*, which in the past had hosted several American presidents such as Dwight Eisenhower, Gerald Ford, and Bill Clinton.[9] In March 2017, Whitehall officials dubbed the plan for Britain's post-Brexit trading relationship with the Commonwealth "Empire 2.0". With significant historical amnesia, the then Secretary of State for International Trade, Liam Fox, tweeted: "The United Kingdom is one of the few countries in the European Union that does not need to bury its 20th century history."[10] Fox inadvertently vindicated Franklin D. Roosevelt's feeling that imperialism was innate to the British. During a conversation with Churchill in 1941, he said: "The British would take land anywhere in the world, even if it were only a rock or a sand bar. You have 400 years of acquisitive instinct in your blood."[11]

Nostalgia here and there

Brexit represented a sort of new Greenwich moment for the United Kingdom. As in 1884, by voting to leave the European Union, Britain tried to reset the clock—but this time only its own, and not that of the world. It would be a mistake, however, to believe that this pathological obsession with the past is a British peculiarity. Brexit is the most concrete fallout of a more global phenomenon. The world is becoming populated by jingoistic leaders who appeal to past national glory and inhabit a rose-tinted past.

The lexicon deployed by Donald Trump during his presidential campaign clearly pointed to a precise temporal destination: a time when Washington was the undisputed global hegemon. The words "again" and "back" recurred continuously in his speeches and slogans. Trump promised to counter the decline of the United States ("Make America Great Again") and restore its traditional values ("If I'm elected … we're all going to be saying 'Merry Christmas' again").[12] He kept promising to bring back almost anything that had been lost along the way: bring back manufacturing jobs, bring back the steel industry, bring back national pride, bring back citizens' security. But Trumpism is not only about a return to the past. It is also about freezing the present and stopping the process of societal change. Building a border wall with Mexico symbolizes determination to contain immigration; banning Muslims from the United States demonstrates a resolve to remove any source of social contamination and defend American national identity as historically framed by the white, Anglo-Saxon Protestant culture.

Looking at China, President Xi Jinping's call for a great revival of the Chinese nation is aimed at restoring its former pre-eminent place in the world order that was put on hold by the century of humiliation (1849–1949), during which Western powers inflicted successive defeats on the Chinese empire. The rejuvenation narrative is built on China's "indelible contributions" to world civilization. It evokes memories of the Middle Kingdom that used to collect tributes from the rest of the world; it exalts China's ingenuity that led to the invention of gunpowder, paper, printing, and the compass. It also celebrates the country as an expansive, outward-looking power that during the Ming dynasty sent Admiral Zheng He to explore the Red Sea and the east coast of Africa with a naval fleet of over 300 ships. The Maritime Silk Road, which is part of the Belt and Road Initiative, is intrinsically nostalgic, as a sort of homage to Zheng's expedition. The rejuvenation of the country serves to set the economic and geopolitical aspirations of the Chinese, as well as to cement their identity. Xi equated this process with the "Chinese Dream", rooted in collective values, as opposed to the individualistic American Dream: "a dream of the whole nation, as well as of every individual".[13]

In a parallel vein, Japanese Prime Minister Shinzo Abe draws inspiration from the nineteenth-century Meiji Restoration, which turned Japan into the leading Asian power through a swift process of modernization and industrialization. In 1868 a group of Samurai and sympathetic merchants overthrew the feudal rule of the Tokugawa Shogunate, ended Western influence over Japanese domestic affairs, and restored the Emperor Meiji to power. Their motto was "revere the Emperor, expel the barbarians".[14] They secured the tradition of imperial rule and limited the presence of foreigners, while pushing for the adoption of foreign and advanced modes of conducting business. They struck a difficult balance between modernity and history, openness and closedness. Abe increasingly sees himself as a latter-day Meiji figure, ready to restore Japan to its former greatness.[15] Similarly, Indian Prime Minister Narendra Modi idealizes India's Hindu past in his attempt to modernize the Indian economy.[16] In 2017, Modi even appointed a committee of scholars to prove that today's Hindus directly descend from the land's first inhabitants many thousands of years ago and to make the case that ancient Hindu scriptures are fact, not myth.[17]

Shifting attention to the Middle East, nostalgic nationalism is deluding Turkish President Recep Tayyip Erdoğan with neo-Ottoman ambitions. Erdoğan has openly criticized the 1923 Treaty of Lausanne, which created the borders of modern Turkey, as having made the country "unfairly" too small.[18] He has claimed, for example, that Mosul, Kirkuk, and portions of northern Iraq were seized illegally from the Ottoman Empire by the British at the end of the First World War, and should be returned to Turkish sovereignty. Similar assertions have been made about the Dodecanese Islands, currently controlled by Greece, and for portions of the Turkish–Syrian borderlands. Erdoğan's party, the AKP, has promoted the glorification of the Ottoman heritage in a number of ways—such as, for example, the adoption of traditional Ottoman dress for a ceremonial military brigade or the revival of traditional Ottoman military band music.[19]

Nostalgia for a time when the Soviet Union competed with the United States for global hegemony has characterized Russian President Vladimir Putin's twenty-year rule. Putin has rehabilitated the figure of Joseph Stalin and reinstated the Soviet national anthem—personally chosen by Stalin in 1944—as Russia's national anthem.[20] In addition, he has employed a nostalgic style of rhetoric to justify his revisionist goals in the former Soviet sphere of influence. In 2014 he used a biased version of Russian history to brainwash his people and justify the country's ethnic chauvinism at the time of the annexation of Crimea and the Ukrainian crisis:

> Everything in Crimea speaks of our shared history and pride. This is the location of ancient Khersones, where Prince Vladimir was baptised. His spiritual feat of adopting Orthodoxy predetermined the overall basis of the culture, civilisation and human values that unite the peoples of Russia, Ukraine and Belarus. The graves of Russian soldiers whose bravery brought Crimea into the Russian empire are also in Crimea. This is also Sevastopol—a legendary city with an outstanding history, a fortress that serves as the birthplace of Russia's Black Sea Fleet. Crimea is Balaklava and Kerch, Malakhov Kurgan and Sapun Ridge. Each one of these places is dear to our hearts, symbolising Russian military glory and outstanding valour.[21]

Within the European Union, far-right parties such as Italy's League, Germany's Alternative für Deutschland (AfD), and the French Rassemblement National (formerly the National Front) utilize controversial historical claims to legitimize their sovereignist Eurosceptic agenda, often exalting the pre-Euro and pre-Schengen eras. In Germany, Frauke Petry, former co-chair of the AfD, called for the destigmatization of the German word *völkisch*, which signifies a people characterized by a specific race—a word that carries heavy connotations from the Nazi era.[22] Hungarian Prime Minister Viktor Orbán has tried to rehabilitate Miklós Horthy, the authoritarian and anti-Semitic leader of the interwar years, by erecting statues across the country. Horthy was an ideologue and proponent of a "Greater Hungary", believing that it would one day reclaim the territories lost during the

First World War. Even the election of a mainstream politician such as Emmanuel Macron has revived old sentiments of French greatness. Physically, he reminds one of the young general Napoleon Bonaparte, who between 1803 and 1815 disrupted the *ancien régime*, leading Paris to temporary domination of the continent. Despite already having experienced considerable internal opposition, Macron has used his charisma to reinvigorate the solemnity and grandiosity attached to the French presidency since de Gaulle, promoting the vision of a strong leader who nurtures a troubled nation's recovery.[23]

A global malaise

Despite its romantic flavour and ancient Greek roots, nostalgia is actually a malaise—and should be treated as such.[24] The word has nothing to do with poetry or philosophy: it comes from medicine. In his *Dissertatio Medica de Nostalgia, Oder Heimwehe*, published in 1688, the Swiss physician Johannes Hofer coined the term by merging the word *nostos* (homecoming) with *algos* (pain). The disease was similar to paranoia—except for the fact that the sufferer was obsessed with longing, not perceived persecution—and to melancholy, but specific to an object or place. Hofer identified this disease by observing Swiss soldiers who, after long, arduous, and often miserable military campaigns abroad, were susceptible to nostalgia triggered just by listening to a particular Swiss milking song, "Khue-Reyen". This lullaby reminded them of the Alpine landscapes of their childhood. Just listening to this melody was enough to bring tears to their eyes, or to make them lose focus or fall sick. For this reason, playing this song was punishable by death in the army. Emotionally, these mercenaries were detached from the present, and thus represented a potential threat to their comrades-in-arms.

Hearing voices or seeing ghosts were the earliest symptoms of a disease that afflicted the imagination and incapacitated the body. Longing for home exhausted vital spirit, becoming a persistent obsession for the infected that made them incapable of distinguishing the past from the present. Nausea, loss of appetite, pathological changes in the lungs, and brain inflammation were some of the most common manifestations of the disease. Hofer noted that the desire to return to one's native land produced erroneous representations that caused the affected to lose touch with the present. But the disease was believed to be curable to some extent. Leeches, warm hypnotic emulsions, opium, purging the stomach, and, more importantly, a physical return to the beloved motherland usually calmed the symptoms.

In the case of Hofer's patients, homesickness was the chief cause of nostalgia. At that time, when European countries were continuously at war with one another, physical distance from home characterized the life of a large portion of the population. In the following centuries, especially after the emergence of Romanticism, nostalgia continued to be viewed as a European disease and cases of this illness in the American army were rather limited. And while Hofer believed that this malaise was actually an expression of love for freedom and for the homeland, American doctors argued that it manifested a lack of manliness and progressiveness.

Later on, in the twentieth century, psychologists classified nostalgia as a form of mental illness that could degenerate into depression.[25] In Freudian terms, nostalgic feelings were the result of a traumatic separation from the pre-Oedipal mother, just as excessive exposure to a foreign environment affected Swiss soldiers. Meanwhile, the concept of nostalgia acquired an additional temporal dimension, besides its original spatial one. Nostalgic minds do not just look back to a specific place, but to a specific era—such as a particular stage of their lives or a glorious moment in the history of their country. A cure for this kind of malaise was proposed by the nineteenth-century French doctor Hippolyte Petit: "Create new loves for the person suffering from love sickness; find new joy to erase the domination of the old."[26]

The current epidemic of nostalgia has little to do with a pure form of homesickness, and is more focused on the idealization of the past. The late sociologist Zygmunt Bauman, in his intellectual testament *Retrotopia*, published immediately after his death in 2017, argued that we take refuge in the past because it can be "remodeled at will", thus providing the "blissful omnipotence lost in the present".[27] Many people long for a time when their country was less diverse, communities were more homogenous and self-contained, and one's immediate surroundings largely defined their experience of the world. Nostalgia acts as an adaptive tool to deal with the psychological trauma caused by major changes taking place in the world. It acts as a self-defence mechanism to maintain resilience, cultivating what psychologists call "self-continuity"—that is, a person's ability to maintain their identity and sense of self through the vicissitudes of life.[28] Human beings, according to Bauman, no longer project their aspirations into utopian visions of an idealized future. They abandon the search for Utopia, and take instead refuge in an un-dead past, a "retrotopia". Job insecurity, falling incomes, rising inequality, and a lack of social mobility induce people to long for a past when the world was less flat and governments could protect their citizens from external threats.

Across the West, individuals yearn for those elements of the social contract that positively defined the lives of the previous generations. Europeans dream of the economic stability and prosperity enjoyed by their parents; Americans reminisce about the socio-economic dynamism and mobility that for decades allowed the sons and daughters of humble families to climb the social ladder. In 2016, the Public Religion Research Institute revealed in its annual American Values Survey that 51 per cent of the population felt that the American way of life had changed for the worse since the 1950s.[29] Furthermore, seven out of ten likely Donald Trump voters said that American society had become worse since that idealized decade. Similar perceptions are widespread across Europe and South America.[30] When in 2012, on the occasion of the sixtieth anniversary of the reign of Queen Elizabeth II, YouGov asked Britons whether their country had changed for better or worse since her accession to the throne, 43 per cent thought that Great Britain had become worse, as opposed to 30 per cent, who argued the opposite.[31] Many of those who voted for Brexit desired to disengage from the wider, threatening world and to control immigration, reverse globalization, and restore national greatness. Broad sections of the Russian population also tend to have rather positive memories of the Soviet era. In their view, unlike the current liberal environment, the centrally planned economy of their fathers promoted social cohesion and economic stability, providing steady employment, adequate wages, and reasonable access to broad social services. In their eyes, even corruption was less widespread than today.[32] What is more surprising is that, in 2014, despite an impressive economic performance in the aftermath of the financial crisis,

24 per cent of eastern Germans believed that it would have been better if the Berlin Wall had stayed up.[33]

But nostalgia is not only fuelled by economic insecurity, social immobility, or immigration fears. Especially among post-imperial powers, it is related to claims concerning a lost global status. The Chinese, the Russians, the Turks, and the British (or at least some of them) long for the power and influence that their countries used to enjoy when they ruled large portions of the world. When in 2017, the Turks voted—albeit by a tiny majority and in a heavily manipulated referendum—in favour of the constitutional reform that gave sweeping powers to the President, they de facto signed up for the introduction of a sort of neo-sultanate that in theory would leave Erdoğan in office until 2029. According to some commentators, Turkey's shift from pro-Western democratization to Islamist rule derives much inspiration from the late Ottoman Empire under Abdülhamid II, who reigned for more than thirty years in the late nineteenth and early twentieth centuries.[34] Looking at Turkey's neighbouring former Soviet countries, a recent Pew Research Center report found that in most of Central and Eastern Europe there is solid public support for "a strong Russia" to counterbalance "the influence of the West".[35] This sentiment is most evident among Orthodox Christians, confirming the role played by religion in identity politics. It is quite surprising that not only do most Russians view the breakup of the Soviet Union in 1991 as "a bad thing", but also that people in Georgia, Armenia, and Moldova are more likely to have a more favourable opinion of Stalin than of Gorbachev.

Historical amnesia

Like most psychological disorders, nostalgia is usually accompanied by amnesia. It depicts the past in such an idealized way that some details, often not irrelevant, are lost. Human beings tend to view historical evidence through a filter that selects the rosier part of the process, ignoring what does not fit their preconceptions. Every single bit of information that corroborates these positive feelings is collected, while the rest is discarded. In other words, people see what they want to see. Behavioural economists call it "confirmation bias".[36] At the same time, the negative emotions associated with our memories tend to dissipate more quickly than the positive ones. In other words, we are more likely to remember the good things from our distant past than the bad ones, and our past constantly shifts to accommodate our present, reframing personal histories to fit into a greater life period. This is what psychologists call the "fading effect bias".[37] Evolutionary adaptation is behind this mental process: dismissing the painful parts of one's past provides the psychological resilience needed to survive natural selection. After all, photographs, which are the quintessential way of recalling bygone times, allow people to arrange their lives in such a way that painful or unpleasant aspects are systematically erased.[38]

Returning to the American Values Survey, Americans recall the joyful lives of their parents in the booming 1950s, consciously ignoring the fact that they now live longer, more healthily, more comfortably, more opulently, and in safer cities. For their part, the Turks forget that the collapse of the Ottoman Empire was largely precipitated, among other things, by its internal political decay, power abuses, and systematic violations of human rights that dramatically eroded the foundation on which it was built. The Russians overlook the fact that for four decades during the Cold War, their dominant role as one of only two superpowers was guaranteed by mutually assured nuclear destruction, while standards of living were much lower than those enjoyed in the West. The 17 million Chinese, who in 2015 made pilgrimages to Mao's home town probably forgot the cruelties of his regime, and the eastern Germans regretting the Berlin Wall ignore what it meant to live in the days of the Stasi.

The positive attitudes towards communism observed in several post-communist countries are illustrative of how our biased memories come to light. Living under a certain economic and political regime affects the way citizens form their preferences. In order to survive, even the most authoritarian and repressive political system must exert some positive influence on its citizens—at least on a small fraction of the population. Take East Germany.[39] From 1945 to 1990 Germany was split into two parts for reasons that had nothing to do with its people's desire for separation. The division was purely exogenous. It is well documented that the forty-five years of communism in East Germany affected individuals' attitude to market capitalism and the role played by the state in providing welfare and the reallocation of resources from the rich to the poor. East Germans still tend to favour redistribution and state intervention more than their fellow citizens in the former West. They became accustomed to highly interventionist governments, and they still assess their living conditions using the communist years as a benchmark. It will probably take forty more years to have a full convergence of preferences between the two parts of the country—by which time all the people in the East will have been born after Germany's reunification. In short, the past, in all its biased versions, is filtered through today's eyes, in the sense that the present is compared to a sweetened version of the past; but the present is also filtered through the eyes of the past, in the sense that it is interpreted with the set of values that a person develops early on in life.

Among other things, the intensity of historical amnesia depends on whether a country feels that it was on the right side of history. In Germany the sense of collective guilt for the atrocities committed during the Second World War remains extremely strong.[40] The British art historian Neil MacGregor defines Germany as possessing "a history so damaged that it cannot be repaired but, rather, must be constantly revisited".[41] In the United Kingdom, however, the gloomiest aspects of the British Empire have been forgotten faster than its brightest ones, as its dismantling started not after a catastrophic military campaign, but after having contributed to liberating Europe from Nazism. One in three British citizens think that the empire has left its colonies better off.[42] In the mind of the average Englishman, imperialistic expansion was not driven by greed, adventurism, or a lust for power; it was a sort of divine mission aimed at bringing law, order, and free trade to benighted corners of the world. As George Bernard Shaw complained: "The ordinary Britisher imagines that God is an Englishman."[43]

There is certainly also some positive heritage. The British Empire invested in infrastructures, installed institutions, collected taxes, supervised the police, oversaw public works, advanced agriculture, promoted health, and built schools. On average, ex-British colonies tended to be more prosperous than French and Spanish ones because of the economic and political institutions inherited from Britain that enabled innovative energy to emerge, allowing a process of sustained economic growth.[44] Nevertheless, by looking at the past through biased lenses, the British overlook the atrocities associated with the imperial age. British colonial rule ended up extracting resources, neglecting famine-struck populations, subjugating peoples on the basis of race, and destabilizing countries. The opium wars, the slave trade, and the use of poison gas against "uncivilized tribes" (as Churchill put it) are telling examples of imperial brutality.[45] When in 2015 Jamaica called for Britain to pay billions of pounds in reparations for slavery, Sir Hilary Beckles, chair of the Caricom Reparations Commission, wrote an open letter to the then Prime Minister David Cameron stating:

> You are a grandson of the Jamaican soil who has been privileged and enriched by your forebears' sins of the enslavement of our ancestors. ... You are, Sir, a prized product of this land and the bonanza benefits reaped by your family and inherited by you continue to bind us together like birds of a feather. We ask not for handouts or any such acts of indecent submission. We merely ask that you acknowledge responsibility for your share of this situation and move to contribute in a joint program of rehabilitation and renewal. The continuing suffering of our people, Sir, is as much your nation's duty to alleviate as it is ours to resolve in steadfast acts of self-responsibility.[46]

To be clear, historical amnesia is not only a spontaneous psychological process. It is often induced by well-orchestrated governmental propaganda. In the case of East Germany, nostalgia for the Berlin Wall, particularly among older people, is partly due to the indoctrination that for decades was produced by the government's control over schools, the press, and television.[47] In Turkey, fashion shows, art exhibitions, university seminars, television series such as *The Magnificent Century* or movies such as *Conquest 1453* are reviving the Ottoman brand that was lost nearly a century ago.[48] More recently, Japan, Russia, and China have taken steps to indoctrinate their citizens, fuelling dangerous forms of competing nationalisms by re-writing their own history.[49]

The recently re-designed National History Museum in Beijing focuses strongly on the massacres perpetrated by Western colonizers and the Japanese, but is silent about the Chinese victims of famine caused by Mao Zedong's Great Leap Forward in the 1950s. Equally, Xi's nostalgic rhetoric about the grandiosity of Chinese civilization omits to mention that while China boasted the largest economy in the world in the nineteenth century, its global influence was hampered by its technological backwardness when compared to Europe—a gap that contemporary China is progressively closing, with the country projected to be a major technology superpower by 2030.[50] In Japan, Abe has complained that Japanese history is taught in a "masochistic way"— although textbooks usually downplay crimes such as the Nanjing Massacre of 1937 or the use of sex slaves by the Japanese imperial army. Putin recently observed that several schoolbooks denigrated the Soviet people's role in the struggle against fascism. Eastern Europe, in his view, was not occupied by the Soviet Union; it was liberated from the Nazis.

In the United Kingdom too, the government has, since the 1950s, purposely created a positive image of the imperial era by systematically destroying or hiding thousands of documents that detailed some of the most shameful acts and crimes committed by the British Empire. Some of these papers fortuitously came to light a few years ago in a secret Foreign Office archive in Hanslope Park, creating significant embarrassment for Downing Street.[51]

Structural causes

Today's nostalgia phenomenon is too synchronous and too global to be happening by chance. It feels as if all over the world people are looking at the present with scepticism and to the past with melancholy. Brexit and Trumpism are just the two most virulent symptoms of the disease in the West. While country-specific factors are creating fertile ground for the spread of nostalgia, a combination of economic, demographic, and political factors, which are reinforced by the heavy legacy of the Great Recession of 2008, is structurally contributing to this global epidemic of nostalgia. These forces are overwhelming, disruptive, and revolutionary. The changes they are creating are so radical that they induce people to find comfort in a highly malleable past. Exploring the different channels through which the malaise spreads and propagates is key to predicting the direction that the world might take in the future.

First of all, the tectonic geopolitical shifts that are transforming the international system have major collective psychological implications. The unipolar global order that has prevailed since the fall of the Berlin

Wall in 1989 is giving way to a non-polar system.[52] The West no longer rules unchallenged, the East is asserting itself, and non-state players compete for global influence as never before. With the roles within the system being continuously re-defined and re-assigned, this structural change is creating opportunities for emerging powers, while putting pressure on the incumbent: the United States. Once-powerful countries want to seize the moment to reaffirm their roles in the global arena, and nostalgic arguments are often powerful ways of gathering popular support. In order to revive an otherwise declining power, Vladimir Putin refers to the breakup of the Soviet Union as "the greatest geopolitical catastrophe" of the twentieth century—something that must be reversed.[53] Brexiteers want to pull out of a crisis-ridden European Union in the hope that Britain will regain its place as leader of the English-speaking world. Xi's call for the "great revival of the Chinese nation" serves to motivate its citizens and remind the rest of the world that the subordinate role played by China with respect to America is merely a historical aberration. China can legitimately claim the status of global power on a par with the United States. In reaction to these attempts to reshuffle the global order to the detriment of the United States, Trump's "America First" doctrine is aimed at weakening its emerging competitors before it is too late. During a rally speech in Ohio, Trump stated: "We're going to bring back our jobs, bring back our wealth, and we are going to bring back our dreams, and we are going to bring back, once again, our sovereignty as a nation."[54]

Under these circumstances, nostalgic nationalism creates paradoxical situations. Xi's China looks to the future with a good dose of optimism and pretends to be a status-quo power as far as the current international system is concerned, while Trump's America is plagued with pessimism and acts as a revisionist power. When, in January 2017, Trump was attacking his main trade partners, Xi presented himself at the World Economic Forum in Davos as the leader of the liberal economic order.[55] Despite the fact that he leads the most protectionist, mercantilist, and predatory major economy in the world, that so far has lacked true leadership on several global issues, Trump's nostalgic rhetoric, instead, has explicit sovereignist connotations. Nostalgia is intimately connected with a return to a past in which governments were in full control and national borders still acted as the last bastion of defence against threats coming from outside. Fair trade (as opposed to free trade) and immigration control (as opposed to the free circulation of people) has become the new mantra of a post-liberal order.

The ageing of the population in the West and parts of Asia reinforces geopolitical nostalgia. Between 2005 and 2015, the percentage of people aged sixty-five or older within the European Union rose from 16.6 to 18.9, and is expected to get close to 30 per cent by 2050.[56] China, Japan, and Russia are also ageing fast. These demographic patterns matter because nostalgia obviously has a stronger pull on older adults—a phenomenon that psychologists call the "reminiscence bump".[57] In middle and late adulthood people tend to remember their youth better than any other period of their lives—years that contributed to shaping their identities and are usually associated with happy moments and youthful thoughtfulness. You yearn for the best memories of your past and distrust the novelty of the present. At the time of the Brexit vote 59 per cent of pensioners wanted to leave the European Union, as opposed to 19 per cent of those aged between eighteen and twenty-four.[58] When British retirees were young the empire was still alive, albeit crumbling, and being part of the European Economic Community was not yet an option. Equally, almost nine out of ten Russians over the age of sixty have a strong sense of loss for the collapse of the Soviet Union, while only 27 per cent of those between eighteen and twenty-four feel the same way.[59] In Italy, which according to a recent study is the most nostalgic country within the European Union, 80 per cent of the fifty- to sixty-five-year-olds think the world used to be better in the past—and if the survey had focused on the very old too, the percentage would likely be even higher.[60]

Each generation's worldview owes a great deal to early life experiences and the foreign-policy issues that dominated their childhoods. Take, for example, the United States across generational lines.[61] Millennials grew up at the time of the dissolution of the Soviet Union, the increase in speed of globalization, and the geopolitical fallout from the 9/11 terror attacks. Compared to previous generations, they perceive the world as something less threatening, are more inclined to support international cooperation (including when it comes to China), and less supportive of military interventions (especially after the failures in Iraq and in Afghanistan). By contrast, American non-millennials tend to see the relationship with Russia through the prism of the Cold War as if they were still stuck in that era.

When it comes to the economy, older generations look back to the past with good reason. Since the fall of the Berlin Wall the world surrounding them has changed dramatically—and not always for the better, at least from their perspective. An untamed globalization process has caused the displacement of millions of jobs, the collapse of traditional industries, an explosion in income inequalities, the squeezing of the middle class, and an increased vulnerability to external shocks. With urbanization, migration from small towns has left desolation behind it, whereas immigration has disrupted local communities. The socio-economic stability and dynamism of the Roaring Fifties and Sixties has become a mirage. In the United States over the last fifty years a child's chances of out-earning his or her parents have fallen from almost 90 per cent to 50 per cent.[62] The Pew Charitable Trust has found that "43 per cent of Americans raised at the bottom of the income ladder remain stuck there as adults, and 70 per cent never even make it to the middle".[63] Making it to the top requires social and financial capital to invest in high-quality education—something that is a prerogative of a self-perpetuating elite.

Similar patterns can be found throughout the West. The social contract looks broken, the best days of many nations seem gone forever, and a sense of decline pervades both those at the top and at the bottom of the social ladder. Older people resent the system not only because their future is more uncertain than it seemed in the past, but also because the economic prospects of their offspring are often so grim as to force them to leave their birthplaces and migrate somewhere else within the country, if not abroad. Thus, it is not surprising that the strongholds of Trump and Brexit are rural areas where the perceived losses associated with the globalization process seem to outweigh the benefits. Almost two-thirds of rural and small-town American voters chose Trump, while a similar proportion in large cities chose Hillary Clinton. In the British countryside 55 per cent voted for Brexit, while cities as varied as Bristol, Glasgow, Cardiff, Liverpool, and London decisively voted Remain.[64]

Demographic forces also nourish nostalgic sentiments via race. In India for instance, Hindus are projected to remain the dominant majority by far; there are expected to be 1.3 billion Hindus by 2050, compared to the Muslim minority, which will number just 300 million. Nevertheless, India will by then be the largest Muslim nation in the world. In addition, even if the Hindus continue to outnumber the Muslims, the latter will grow faster because they have a lower median age and a higher fertility rate. In 2010, the median age of Indian Muslims was twenty-two, compared with twenty-six for Hindus. Likewise, Muslim women have an average of 3.2 children, compared with 2.5 for Hindu women. These demographic trends might explain why Modi is so eager to dig into the racial past of his country.[65]

Similarly, in the United States non-white births exceed white births, and each year more whites die than are born. By 2044 non-Hispanic whites will become a minority.[66] These demographic shifts also hide a wide—and growing—optimism gap that has opened up between poor and middle-class whites and their counterparts of other races. The highest costs of being poor in America come not only in the form of material goods or basic services, but in the form of unhappiness, stress, and lack of hope. What is most surprising, though, is that the most desperate groups are not minorities that have traditionally been discriminated against, but poor and near-poor whites.[67] These groups are contraposed to the "coastal elites", which can be seen as a market-dominant minority—a group that steers the socio-economic system in its favour, creating huge fractures in the society.[68] Part of Donald Trump's electoral success has to do with his ability to understand the concerns of the white community and leverage its fears by harking back to a past in which white Americans largely enjoyed unchallenged economic and cultural dominance. His "Make America Great Again" campaign overtly relied on rhetoric and imagery designed to appeal to white Christian America. From blanket accusations against Mexicans, to banning Muslims, and singling out Christian Americans as deserving of special respect and protection, Trump has constantly drawn a line between those who belong to his "Great" America and those who do not. In other words, Trump ran on a platform of restoration—of old values, identities, industries, and jobs.

Fear of foreigners and concerns about the social disruption created by immigrants have been consuming issues in the European political debate as well, but for reasons different from that in the United States.

According to a variety of metrics, Europe is the least culturally and ethnically diverse region in the world—meaning that, unlike America, immigration has not so far altered the socio-economic structure of the continent.[69] Immigration flows, measured against the population of the European Union, remain rather limited—with the exception of the 2015 crisis, when more than a million refugees and migrants entered Europe. And yet, public perception of the importance of this phenomenon—linked most of all to structural demographic and economic unbalances between Africa and Europe—depart significantly from current reality.

In an emotionally loaded political context, the migration issue has been producing a disruptive impact on the political discourse in Europe, favouring re-nationalization and Eurosceptical parties and exposing the inability of European governments to share the burden of integration.[70] In short, this is primarily a European political crisis, rather than a migration crisis.[71] In continental Europe, from north to south, the issue has mainly to do with migration flows from sub-Saharan Africa and the Middle East; in the United Kingdom, however, the problem is immigration from other European Union members, particularly from the east. Seventy-one per cent of Britons believe that immigration has made the communities where migrants have settled more divided.[72] Those in the north of England are the most hostile to immigration, with 53 per cent regarding it negatively, compared to 30 per cent of Londoners.[73]

Mass movements of people from one region to another undoubtedly have a lasting impact on the receiving communities. They force the host communities to adapt and accept cultural diversity; polarizing debates about national identity and the role of Islam in Europe are evidence of the related difficulties. Immigration, moreover, fuels competition between insiders and outsiders to seize power and resources from central and local government. Residents are inevitably tempted to look back to a past in which communities were smaller, more homogenous, and more integrated. In 2015, at the peak of the refugee crisis, the Migration Fear Index—a synthetic index created on the basis of indicators of migration-related policy uncertainty—reached unprecedented historical levels in Germany, France, and the United Kingdom.[74] And jingoist leaders took notice. During the Brexit campaign the UKIP leader Nigel Farage commissioned a highly controversial election poster showing a queue of mostly non-white migrants and refugees with the slogan "Breaking point: the EU has failed us all".[75]

Moving forward, innovation is likely to replace globalization, geopolitics, and even immigration as the main source of nostalgic feelings, particularly within fast-ageing societies. Technological change has accelerated sharply, following an exponential trajectory. Each industrial revolution has taken fewer years to produce its effect than the preceding one, while also affecting a larger number of industries.[76] According to the Law of Accelerating Returns, developed by the futurist Ray Kurzweil, the years between 2000 and 2014 saw progress equivalent to that of the entire twentieth century, and another twentieth century's-worth of progress will occur in half that time, by 2021. Ordinary citizens struggle to adapt, with older workers being the most vulnerable, whereas regulators are slow to react to new technologies, and are usually taken by surprise. A widely cited study by the University of Oxford points out that 47 per cent of employment in the United States is at risk from automation.[77] In 2017 the International Monetary Fund (IMF) argued that about half of the decline in the labour income share over the past four decades is attributable to the impact of technology, while only a quarter is due to globalization.[78] A major backlash against technological progress could emerge when populists realize that innovators, not immigrants or imported goods, are the greatest threat to the well-being of their voters. And this will further compound nostalgic sentiments, particularly among the older members of the population, who are more vulnerable to these radical changes. After all, nostalgia can be seen as "the search for continuity amid threats of discontinuity".[79]

New technologies will nourish this infatuation with the past through another channel as well. The internet in general, and digital platforms in particular, give us unprecedented access to our memories. The click of a mouse is enough to connect with people, places, experiences, and narratives of our past lives. Facebook constantly reminds us where we were and what we did at a specific moment in time, carefully selecting the friends or experiences we might be more attached to. The website Ancestry allows people to retrieve information about distant ancestors, but it also gives access to the more than 250,000 pages of Sears catalogues from 1896 through 1993. Using this database, it is possible to track the evolution of consumption habits in the United States and see when some of the most revolutionary goods in the history of American capitalism made their appearance. But entire new industries are springing up by focusing on the commercialization of "nostalgia on demand".[80] It can be your favourite song, movie, museum, or country. There will always be an app ready to dig into the past, projecting one into a different temporal dimension. The risk will be of living more in the past than in the present.

2

NOSTALGIA AS AN EMOTIONAL WEAPON

"You can suffer nostalgia in the presence of the beloved, if you glimpse a future where the beloved is no more."

Milan Kundera

This is not the first time that nostalgia has played a defining role in the political debate. Revolutions, whether political or technological, often trigger outbreaks of nostalgia. The French Revolution, the Russian Revolution, and the "Velvet" revolutions in Eastern Europe were all accompanied by political and cultural manifestations of longing. The degree of adaptation imposed by an uprising is such as to induce a large proportion of the population (usually the losers in the new system) to praise the normalcy and stability of the disrupted status quo. The French Revolution was a product of the *ancien régime* as much as the *ancien régime* in the form we remember it today was a product of the French Revolution. During the Victorian and Edwardian eras, Great Britain experienced a spike in nostalgic sentiments as a reaction to the socio-economic disruption generated by the first and second industrial revolutions.[1] In the 1980s both Ronald Reagan and Margaret Thatcher employed the language of restoration and lost values as core elements of their "revolutionary" political strategies.[2]

And yet our understanding of the politics of nostalgia is fairly limited. So far, the study of nostalgia has been primarily confined to psy-

41

chology, anthropology, and sociology. Past episodes of collective long-ing were usually short-lived, restricted to specific geographical areas, and caused by temporary factors—although its implications were not always negligible, as in the case of the French Restoration. Today, the socio-economic terrain seems fertile for nostalgic sentiments to crys-tallize and proliferate across the most important regions of the world.

Craving for bygone times is far from being politically innocuous behaviour, as it crosses boundaries between public and private spheres.[3] When deployed in political debate, collective nostalgia becomes an emotional weapon, capable of mobilizing a nation towards a common goal. Well-orchestrated nostalgic attitudes create a desire for restora-tion when the temporal distance between the present and the idealized past is wide, but still close enough to nourish such yearning; or for preservation when an unsettling future is transforming a pleasant pres-ent that is rapidly vanishing. In order to induce people to prefer the way things were, jingoistic leaders tend to recollect memories of ear-lier eras in a sentimentally, as well as historically, biased way, polarizing the debate and exacerbating distrust between ordinary citizens who are concerned about the present, and elites who are overly optimistic about the future.[4] Nostalgia then becomes a psychological tool that is used to manipulate a nation's perception of the present by pushing for abrupt political and economic transformations.

Of course, for a nostalgic discourse to be politically effective, the targeted audience needs to be receptive. In other words, the effective-ness of longing depends on where "the speaker stands in the landscape of the present".[5] Evoking even the greatest historical achievements of a country or the splendour of affluent eras might not be enough for a nostalgic narrative to take hold in a country. If individuals are substan-tially happy with the direction that their lives and countries are taking, then the political forces promoting nostalgic narratives will be accused of being bigoted and retrograde. In such cases the past will indicate a path that must be avoided, or simply ignored. In extreme situations the past will even be rejected altogether if its legacy seems to be too con-straining to thrive in the future.

Nostalgia and anti-nostalgia are in fact the two sides of the same coin. They are intrinsically related to the way in which individuals relate to the future in general, and to progress in particular.

Homesickness, in both its temporal and spatial dimensions, prevails when socio-economic transformations unchain a future that upsets unprepared citizens. As argued earlier, today's exponential technological changes and a fast-ageing population are creating fertile ground for these kinds of feelings. The greater the collective discontent with the present, the stronger the appeal of the past.

With a certain degree of generalization, it is fair to argue that the Leave campaign was intrinsically nostalgic, while the Remain one was anti-nostalgic. According to the commentator Tony Barber, emphasis on the exploits of individuals such as Sir Francis Drake, who in the sixteenth century carried out the second circumnavigation of the world in a single expedition, explains why "Brexiters" acquired an extra "e" and became "Brexiteers", as in "buccaneers" and "privateers".[6] And take the role played by the empire's legacy during the Brexit debate—which was only one of the many nostalgic elements used by the Leave propaganda. When in February 2016, one of Brexit's most vocal advocates, Michael Gove, set out the reasons for leaving the European Union, he argued that the United Kingdom had "exported to nations like the United States, India, Canada and Australia a system of democratic self-government that has brought prosperity and peace to millions".[7] Clearly, reference to the imperial past was exclusively meant to emotionally motivate a highly divided people in favour of Brexit: resigning from Theresa May's Cabinet in July 2018, Boris Johnson stated that the Brexit dream was "not to build a new empire—heaven forefend—but to use every ounce of Britain's power, hard and soft, to go back out into the world in a way we had perhaps forgotten over the past forty-five years". The dream was a "Global Britain", like in the past, unchained from European constraints.

Those who campaigned against Brexit, on the other hand, took the opposite tack by either dismantling the myth surrounding the historical imperial experience or by playing down its importance. Former Deputy Prime Minister Nick Clegg, for instance, warned that Britain would be left with "no empire, no union and no special relationship".[8] Newspaper headlines of the kind used by the *Financial Times*— "Brexiters are Nostalgics in Search of a Lost Empire"—or *The Guardian*—"Colonial Nostalgia is Back in Fashion, Blinding us to the Horrors of Empire" were rather common in the mainstream anti-

Brexit media.[9] The Remain camp also used the imperial nostalgia argument to prove that the Brexiteers had no real plan and that restoring the British Empire was simply wishful thinking. Eloise Todd, leader of a group campaigning for a second Brexit referendum, said: "Putting their fingers in their ears while singing 'Rule Britannia' is not how adults negotiate."[10] What many in the Remain camp did not realize in time, however, is that, once nostalgia is ingrained, its victims no longer see reality in an objective way; the politics of emotion itself becomes a source of instability, able to induce sudden change. As the political scientist David Runciman notes in a fascinating book, "Politics means too little most of the time, and then for a few moments it means too much."[11]

Two different forms of nostalgia

What makes the politics of nostalgia such a complex phenomenon is that nostalgia itself is a multifaceted concept that leads to contrasting political outcomes (see Figure 1). It is not just a matter of positively relating to the past. In *The Future of Nostalgia*, former Harvard professor Svetlana Boym explains why nostalgia is not necessarily a source of gloom and doom. She makes a distinction between two types of homesickness. Reflective nostalgia, which "dwells in *algia* (aching), in longing and loss, the imperfect process of remembrance", is the benign form of the malaise. It looks at the past through critical eyes and recognizes that something might have been lost, but that much has been gained along the way. Restorative nostalgia, instead, which "puts emphasis on *nostos* (returning home) and proposes to rebuild the lost

Fig. 1: The Weaponization of Nostalgia and Brexit

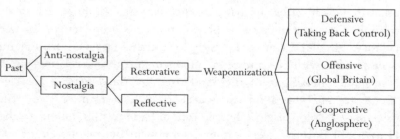

home and patch up the memory gaps", is the malign form.[12] As Boym states, "While restorative nostalgia returns and rebuilds one's homeland with paranoid determination, reflective nostalgia fears return with the same passion."[13]

From this perspective, nostalgia is more a state of mind than an emotion in itself. Depending on circumstances it can be nourished with positive feelings of hope and faith in a bright future, or with negative ones such as fear and anger. In the face of an unstable present, nostalgic individuals may aspire to return to a stable past. Alternatively, in the face of a present that seems overly static, they might desire a past in which things could be put into play, opened up, or moved about.[14] Restorative nostalgia looks back in search of absolute truths; reflective nostalgia puts them in doubt. The former is about the reconstruction of monuments and symbols of the past; the latter lingers on the ruins of past monuments and on the patina of time, speculating about the possible courses that history could have taken. The erection of new statues of Mao in China, Stalin in Russia, and Horthy in Hungary are literal examples of this unreflective, restorative tendency. By contrast, although mainstream political forces in Europe (as much as their populist counterparts) might regret the power and sovereignty that their nations used to enjoy before joining the European project, they are aware of the benefits that a highly imperfect European Union has brought to the continent after two World Wars. In short, they approach the past with critical eyes, without wishing to recreate it, but simply to leverage it.

The 2017 French presidential election is an interesting reference point: it exemplifies how the same nostalgic icon can be deployed to trigger the two forms of nostalgia and achieve opposite political goals.[15] Charles de Gaulle, who was president from 1959 to 1969 and still has a strong influence on the imagination of the French population, became the fetish of aspiring presidents during the electoral campaign. In case of victory, far-left candidate Jean-Luc Mélenchon promised to pay his own electricity bills at the presidential palace, just as de Gaulle had done six decades earlier; while the leader of the far-right National Front, Marine Le Pen, defended her vision of the French economy by calling it "the vision of de Gaulle"; and Emmanuel Macron, launching his cross-partisan movement En Marche, shared a video of de Gaulle explaining why France is neither right nor left wing.

Thus, the same nostalgic political symbol, de Gaulle, was mobilized by leaders like Mélenchon and Le Pen on the extreme left and right of the political spectrum as well as by a semi-technocrat and semi-populist policymaker such as Macron, who positioned himself at the centre. In his official presidential portrait, Macron displays de Gaulle's memoirs and two iPhones on his desk—de facto presenting himself as a link between past and present.[16] Unlike his competitors, he promoted a reflective version of France's bygone heyday. The past is something to be proud of, but the country needs to focus on its present, which is often created somewhere else (as the iPhone reminds the French). It is also interesting to note the presence in the picture of an old clock. This is a metaphor for the time-setting power of the president—anchored to the past, but clearly projected into the future.

The problem is that the world is now primarily dealing with a toxic restorative nostalgia used for political ends. Ordinary citizens struggle to adapt to the disruptions imposed on them by global forces that are out of their control, inducing them to find comfort in historical eras when life was easier, slower, and less coloured by uncertainty. They look back at a pre-globalization era in which national borders were less porous, time flowed gently, and each person was (supposedly) in control of his fate. People recall a time of restrained global forces, insulating domestic policies, and, possibly, world dominance. They aspire to be ruled by fully empowered national governments, if not even by strongmen who can truly and credibly push for rapid and swift change. Restoring the past represents a Herculean task that only rulers with full powers can accomplish. That is why nostalgia and nationalism are intimately interlinked.

Offensive, defensive, or cooperative nostalgia

Restorative nostalgia has two core elements that are key to understanding the actions of most nationalist movements and the manner in which they "weaponize" nostalgic sentiments in political debate: the conspiracy theory and the restoration of origins. The conspiracy narrative exemplifies how nostalgia can be used defensively: to promote the interests and instances of one dominant group against the others, with the premise of "taking back control". It is usually based on a mythical battle between good and evil that ends with the scapegoating of a clearly identified enemy. External forces (such as greedy bankers, global elites, or desperate immigrants) are blamed for having broken a socio-economic equilibrium that benefited the majority of the population. Fears over immigration, globalization-related job insecurity, concerns about the preservation of a nation's racial purity, or the rejection of a cosmopolitan world define clear group boundaries: natives vs. foreigners, masses vs. elites, whites vs. non-whites, urban vs. rural, and so on. In the end it is a matter of identity, which requires full sovereignty in order to be protected. As Samuel Huntington stated: "Identity, it appears, is like sin. However we may oppose it, we cannot escape it."[17]

According to the logic of identity politics, those who do not have access to shared common memories are excluded or marginalized, while social cohesion is tied to cultural or ethnic factors. Donald Trump tries to vindicate the prior claims of white Americans (in the most extreme restorative forms of nostalgia, nativism is a key factor), while Narendra Modi works to further boost the influence of the Hindus. In the trope of "imagined natality"—a weaker concept than nativism—sovereignty is depicted as the source of an exclusive national–cultural tradition which "cannot be delegated, preceded or brushed aside, and that has propelled a given society on an irreversible path of preserving its unique properties in the face of continuous challenges".[18]

It is particularly in the debate about immigration, which has deeply divided the European Union since 2015, that the concept of sovereignty goes beyond the idea of spatial control over territory and acquires a temporal dimension of "we were the first, so we decide". From this perspective, both the temporal and spatial dimensions of nostalgia are combined, as is typical of nationalist movements. Many nationalist politicians in the Netherlands, for instance, both from mainstream and populist parties, see their country as a single house that "is being taken over by foreigners". An increasingly large part of the native population yearns for a time when it was "just us".[19] Similar claims about "home feelings" can be found across Western Europe, including Sweden, where the Democrats have rebranded the concept of "People's Home" (*Folkehemmet*) along ethnic lines. From their perspective, the Swedish golden age coincided with the 1950s, when an advanced welfare state guaranteed a comfortable lifestyle for everyone. The Swedish socio-economic model was so attractive that too many outsiders have tried to take advantage of it, undermining its sustainability. Therefore, fighting immigration becomes a way to defend the national home: a modern form of patriotism.[20] Similar views are expressed by the League in Italy, where socio-economic problems and migration pressures combine to justify rising Euroscepticism in one of the founding members of the European Union.

However, the conspiracy theory is not only about ethnic homogeneity. It labels as "enemies of the people" all those groups that for one reason or another prevent the country, or a specific political movement, from pursuing its own agenda. Expertise, for instance, is blatantly distrusted and continuously attacked by those political leaders who want to turn the system on itself. In 2016 the Brexiteer Michael Gove publicly said: "We are sick of experts." He insisted that they had got it wrong so many times in recent years that they had lost their credibility. Just before the Brexit referendum, UKIP's leader, Nigel Farage, suggested that the "experts" were on the take, working for the British government and in the pay of the European Union itself.[21] Similarly, Donald Trump, while campaigning in 2016, stated: "The experts are terrible."[22]

The second aspect of restorative nostalgia, the restoration of origins, is associated with offensive attitudes. In many cases, current nationalist leaders are not just reclaiming full responsibility for their borders, their laws, and their policies. They want to regain control of time itself, bringing their countries back to a moment in history when they played a dominant role, if not globally, at least regionally. Jingoistic politicians are prone to idealizing the past with myths of a lost paradise that assume a reassuring narrative pattern of order/disorder/order.[23] Today's world looks chaotic when compared to the stability that the *Pax Britannica* or the *Pax Americana* (which is perceived to have passed its peak) used to guarantee to their citizens. Therefore, nostalgic arguments serve to motivate a nation to achieve the ambitious goal of re-establishing a bygone (and more favourable) international order: nostalgia is in this case used as an offensive, rather than a defensive, emotional weapon. In the Brexit context, the concept of Global Britain captures the ambitions of those Leavers who want to place the United

Kingdom at the centre of the world map once again, making London the fulcrum of an intricate network of commercial, political, and financial relations.

In the "weaponization" of nostalgia—the political use of nostalgia, with defensive and offensive variants—classifying British Euroscepticism is particularly complex. In theory, the whole idea of reclaiming sovereignty back from Brussels should be seen as a form of defensive nostalgia. Britain would like to unchain itself from external intrusion in its domestic affairs. And in principle its withdrawal from the European Union, even in its hardest form, has never been explicitly aimed at damaging the European project as a whole and replacing it with something different. However, while the daunting costs faced by the UK in re-negotiating a partnership with Brussels might dissuade other countries from following in its footsteps, Brexit is also contributing to the spreading of "sovereign-first" movements across the continent. Their nostalgic narratives and political agendas might differ; but they all share the same eagerness to envisage a highly weakened European Union. In this sense, defensive nostalgia becomes offensive.

Restorative claims are not only about managing national borders in a more effective way. Especially when reinforced by narratives of "us" against "them" (which is the case with Turkey, for instance, in its relationship with Western democracies, notwithstanding the common partnership in NATO), they destabilize the international system, fuelling tribalism and splintering civilizations into warring factions. This is the darkest side of global nostalgia. With different degrees of acrimony, Turkey or Russia (just to cite a couple of examples) believe that they are at a disadvantage in today's international system—something unacceptable when compared with the influence that they enjoyed decades or centuries earlier. The Russians look at the global liberal order as a straitjacket that clashes with their values. The Chinese believe that the world is not paying due respect to their history. And the Americans feel that their allies are, particularly within the context of the NATO alliance, freeloaders. Turning the global order upside down, in different ways, becomes a priority for all. But in a world of competing nationalisms, where identifying a common global good is not possible, each dissatisfied actor will try to push for unilateral changes. One of the consequences, connecting Brexit to Trumpism, is that these pressures are helping to fracture the West from within.

But there is an exception to these gloomy scenarios. In theory, nostalgic attitudes could reinvigorate bonds between countries with ancestral relations, leading to cooperative outcomes. According to the Brexiteers, the decline of the historical West (built up after the Second World War under the cover of the *Pax Americana*), combined with the fragmentation of the European Union, could lead to a more coherent Anglo-Saxon sphere. In this sense, the Anglosphere represents a fine example of a culturally homogeneous area that transcends national borders. This regional grouping stretches from the Atlantic to the Indian and Pacific Oceans, and in its narrower line-up includes Australia, Canada, New Zealand, the United Kingdom, and the United States. Legal systems of Common Law, democratic principles, English as first language, common business practices, and traditional support for free trade are the glue that holds together such geographically dispersed countries. From the point of view of the Brexiteers, the Anglosphere looks de facto like a modern form of the British Empire, based on soft and not hard power. But one caveat, which the Leavers tend to ignore, is warranted. While culturally kindred nations might find common ground more easily in addressing transnational challenges, any cooperation would have to be in the form of a genuine convergence of national interests that is far from guaranteed—not even, as we will see, between the United Kingdom and the United States. For this reason, restorative nostalgia in its cooperative form is mostly a subset of the offensive version.

Nostalgic nationalism

Nostalgia and nationalism appear to be strongly intertwined. But nuances are needed: while reflective nostalgia can lead to a rediscovery of patriotism, restorative nostalgia is more often combined with sheer nationalism. This difference must be well understood: as George Orwell wrote in 1945, in his "Notes on Nationalism", patriotism is "devotion to a particular place and a particular way of life, which one believes to be the best in the world, but has no wish to force on other people".[24] For most Leavers, even those with restorative ambitions, this was exactly the meaning of Brexit: Britain taking back control of its own national destiny, allowing it to rediscover itself. Brexit was not designed to inflict a fatal blow to the European Union.

What is unclear, however, is whether the current epidemic of restorative nostalgia is also giving rise to unprecedented new forms of nationalism. Political scientists usually make a broad distinction between civic and ethno-nationalism. The former states that "the nation should be composed of all those—regardless of race, colour, creed, gender, language or ethnicity—who subscribe to its political creed".[25] This form of nationalism is intrinsically democratic. It envisages the nation as a community of equal, rights-bearing citizens who are united in patriotic attachment to a shared set of values. The glue that holds them together is the law and not ancestral roots. Ethnic nationalism, however, is based on the idea that "an individual's deepest attachments are inherited, not chosen. It is the national community which defines the individual, not the individuals who define the national community."[26] Since it upholds the interests of the ethnic majority, this form of nationalism is usually accompanied by more or less extreme manifestations of authoritarianism. Although any given moment in time can contain both ethnic and civic nationalistic elements within the same country, the world risks shifting again from "universal, civic nationalism" towards a "blood-and-soil, ethnic sort".[27]

Both forms of nationalism draw heavily on history in order to set the nation apart, to justify its existence, and forge a national identity. But its ethnic manifestation has a more voracious appetite for nostalgic arguments. Looking at the European case in particular, the medieval historian Patrick J. Geary has argued: "As a tool of nationalist ideology, the history of Europe's nations was a great success, but it has turned our understanding of the past into a toxic waste dump, filled with the poison of ethnic nationalism, and the poison has seeped deep into popular consciousness."[28] Of course, nationalists do not hold out for the historical accuracy of their claims and for the attention paid to the details of what really happened centuries earlier. The construction of "imagined communities" is inevitably the result of a biased and emotional selection of historical facts.[29] The past is reduced to a single narrative of good and evil that erases the complexity and ambivalence of history, thus oversimplifying the present as well.

Nostalgia, which is intrinsically biased in the way it searches for those elements of the past that comfort troubled souls, turns out to be an effective rhetorical tool in building national myths. As argued by

Boym, nostalgia "tends to confuse the actual home with an imaginary one. In extreme cases, it can create a phantom homeland, for the sake of which one is ready to die or kill."[30] Yearning for a home that no longer exists, or that has never existed, is central to narratives of nationhood and social belonging. In particular, a sense of decline from a "golden age" provides the impetus to recall and replicate examples of former great ages and the heroic deeds of illustrious ancestors. From this perspective, most of today's symptoms of nostalgic malaise are expressions of standard forms of ethnic nationalism. In particular, the growing intolerance of immigration across Europe, with its many nuances, is a reaction to the perception that a sort of "barbarian" invasion is threatening the very foundations of Western societies—while their economic models are simply too outdated to deal with many of today's challenges.

As in the nationalist movements of previous eras, the return to the "lost home" is purely metaphorical and rhetorical. In other words, it is a return in spirit. Regardless of the reasons behind his or her nostalgic reminiscences, no nationalist leader truly wishes to bring back to light the historical periods he or she idealizes. Narratives of a golden age are a source of moral guidance in a decaying present ("Make America Great Again") or in a present rich with opportunities that is also perceived as very challenging (China's great rejuvenation).[31] By symbolically returning to "how the nation used to be", these representations provide direction to construct a better (otherwise doomed) future. There is not a real temporal rupture with the unpleasant present. A sense of historical progression seems to predominate. The Japanese are expected to adapt the Meiji spirit to their own age; Xi Jinping celebrates the ideal of continuity in Chinese history, linking imperial and communist China; Donald Trump wants to consolidate the global role of the United States by freeing the American superpower from the constraints of the very alliances and rules created by previous American presidents. It is probable that the infatuation with the past experienced by leaders such as Putin or Erdoğan is more genuine, but only because of the enormous gap between reality and their aspirations. Clearly, each nation deliberately picks its own "golden age", frozen in time, as a historical reference.

What makes Brexit unique is that the temporal element is not just a rhetorical stratagem, but has a tangible political valence. As discussed in the Introduction, only in the United Kingdom is it possible to clearly identify the three moments of a periodizing nostalgic narrative: the "golden days", the "great rupture", and the "present discontent". Brexit was indeed meant to create a historical discontinuity that, at least in its hardest form, could have literally returned the country to the past, addressing the pervasive sense of dissatisfaction that characterizes part of the British population. At a minimum, a real divorce from Brussels would have brought Britain back to 1973, when it joined the European Economic Community.

This abrupt, and probably only attempted, reversal of history makes Brexit the symptom of a pure form of nostalgic nationalism that can be seen as a political category in its own right. Through the Brexit lens, the United Kingdom seems to identify itself as something "temporally"— not just ethnically, culturally, or historically—different from the rest of the world. As the next chapter will show in detail, Britain seems to project itself as if in a different era when relating to other countries. It has approached the Brexit referendum and its aftermath by leveraging a global status that it enjoyed decades, if not centuries, ago. Nostalgia for a glorious past is so widespread within the political debate and the entertainment industry that a significant proportion of the population seems to have lived in a parallel temporal dimension for quite some time. This is the natural consequence of the Anglo Nostalgia phenomenon, and partly affects even those members of the establishment who voted Remain but are deeply attached to the glories of the past.

Instead of quietly digesting the dissolution of the British Empire and fully accepting its new role in the European Union, which respectively implies a loss of global status and a loss of national sovereignty (two key elements of the Brexit vote), Britain has always tried to creatively restore the influence of a bygone era. For hardcore Brexiteers, the loss of empire and the loss of sovereignty in favour of the European Union are two historical aberrations that need to be reversed. For more moderate Leavers, only the latter really matters, in the false hope that a truly sovereign government would better protect its citizens from threatening global forces. For the Remainers, by contrast, the past represents an important guide, but only to inspire a better future.

This tendency to find comfort in the past also disguises a deeper insecurity about British national identity. As the historian David

Edgerton argues, the emergence of Britain as a nation was late compared to most of Europe.[32] It coincided with the first fifty years of the past century; until then the United Kingdom, exceptionally open to the rest of the world, was not a self-contained political and economic entity. Was it England? Was it England and Wales, or just Great Britain? Or was it perhaps the United Kingdom of Great Britain and Northern Ireland? And what was the role of the British Empire? Two World Wars, the gradual demise of the empire, the building up of the welfare state, and even the introduction of protectionist measures in the end produced a sense of belonging within a well-defined and circumscribed national community. From a historical perspective, the idea of the British nation is therefore a relatively recent and fragile construct. This helps explain why membership in the European Union has always been perceived, by large sectors of the British elite and population, as a potential risk to national identity. The results of the June 2016 referendum—largely unexpected by the Conservative Party, internally fractured and patently detached from an even more divided British society—become more easily understandable against this background.

All this does not mean that nostalgic nationalism will remain a peculiarity of the United Kingdom. Structural forces that are globally fuelling the current epidemic of nostalgia suggest that in the future other countries might follow suit. Britain was the first victim because of its tendency to long for the past that is intrinsic to its culture (particularly in England). To guess what kind of shape nostalgic nationalism might take elsewhere in the future, it is important to understand how a nostalgic narrative is created, and to clearly identify those elements that temporally set a nation apart from the rest of the world. It is not just a matter of pride in the history of the country, or a predisposition to look backwards instead of forwards. It is also a matter of skilfully using a sophisticated propaganda machine. The Brexiteers were simply masters at that.

3

CONSTRUCTING A NOSTALGIC NARRATIVE

"He [Churchill] mobilized the English language and sent it into battle."

John F. Kennedy

Historical details are easily lost in the mists of time, especially when they concern the founding of a nation. Once a certain temporal threshold is crossed, history and myth become indistinguishable. In *Our Island Story: A Child's History of England*, which was published in 1905 and immediately became a bestseller, the writer Henrietta Marshall bravely mixed up truth and lies while recounting British history from its beginnings to the reign of Queen Victoria. Rather than starting the book with a historically accurate account of the Celtic peoples who populated the British Isles before Roman colonization, Marshall traced the foundation of England to the mythical stories of Albion, the fourth son of the giant Neptune—king of the sea.[1] When Albion became old enough to take on royal duties, Neptune called a great council of advisers to assign him an island. Albion was his favourite son and deserved "a beautiful gem in the blue water". It took great efforts for the council to find something that could please the king. When he saw a little island that had no rivals in terms of beauty, he stated: "This is the island of my love. Albion shall rule it and Albion it shall be called."[2] Many years after Albion's death the island had changed its name to Britannia, but Neptune still loved it. When he grew too old to rule, he gave his sceptre to Britannia so that she could rule the waves herself.

Our Island Story was written when the United Kingdom was still the undisputed global hegemon. Its goal was to glorify the British Empire, resorting to narrative exaggerations in order to engage demanding young readers. It went out of print in 1953, but made a comeback in 2005. Since then, and quite surprisingly, given its deliberate historical inaccuracies, it has helped to shape the political debate of the United Kingdom in many ways. In 2014, when the Scots were about to vote in their independence referendum, the then Prime Minister David Cameron, while pleading with Scotland to stay in, confessed that Marshall's book had been his favourite childhood reading, as it told "the great, world-beating story" of the United Kingdom.[3] A few years earlier, Education Secretary Michael Gove indirectly and nostalgically referred to the book while discussing Britain's history curriculum: "the current approach to history denies children the opportunity to hear our island story".[4] In reaction to the history section of Gove's new national curriculum presented in 2013, Oxford professor David Priestland said that it was a "depressingly narrow ... resolutely insular ... politicized and philistine document. We are firmly back in the land of the Edwardian bestseller *Our Island Story*."[5]

Marshall's book revolved around the myth of the island nation—a geography that shaped the character of its people, determined its fate, and epitomized its uniqueness. The idea of an island encapsulates the defining features of the United Kingdom: internal unity, military security, global reach, and continental separation.[6] To paraphrase Shakespeare's *Richard II*, "a precious stone set in the silver sea" turned itself into a citadel, a bastion, and the heart of a globe-spanning empire. The sea insulated it from the chaotic events that repeatedly tormented the continent. While European powers were busy fighting each other, Britain developed parliamentary government, religious toleration, and common law. The island is a symbol of openness and closedness, independence and resilience. Great Britain was, and is, both stubbornly inward looking and relentlessly international. It became a "world island", while intrinsically remaining an "island world".[7] The myth of insularity appealed to both the Leave and Remain camps. Depending on how you want to see it, the concept of being an island encapsulates equally the essence of both Global Britain and Little England: far enough from the technocratic tyranny of Brussels, but too small to really matter globally.

Two other meta-myths—master narratives that encompass large and long tracts of the history of a country—descend directly from the idealization of the island nation.[8] Britain's isolation has led to its exceptionalism: not only does it stand apart geographically from a crowded continent, it also stands out historically. The Whig interpretation of English history is basically a national myth of continuous progress, an inevitable progression towards ever-greater liberty and enlightenment, culminating in modern forms of liberal democracy and constitutional monarchy.[9] The British pride themselves on an exceptional history of continuous freedom, self-government, and the rule of law. As argued by the historian Jeremy Black, "the British have a genius for the appearance of continuity"—where appearance is a key word.[10] Continuity in national identity creates a sense of proximity to decades and centuries gone before—like a continuous creature "which stretches into the future and the past", in the words of George Orwell.[11] This is the elect nation that has honoured its civilizing mission by spreading its democratic institutions to the rest of the world. It has exported freedom, the rule of law, and representative government. From this self-glorifying perspective, as a Brexiteer would put it, the legal and institutional alignment imposed by the European integration process represented a contamination of British institutional purity (even if Britain's influence in shaping the legal framework of the European Union was far from negligible).

Geographical isolation—and this is the third meta-myth—also implies that the Anglo-Saxons have emerged as something different from their continental peers. In many ways the idea of a unified West is a political construct of the Cold War era. It disguises almost two millennia of fratricidal wars between European powers, but it also overlooks at least three centuries of military confrontations between the Anglo-Saxon world and continental Europe. Every time would-be European or Eurasian hegemons—from Charles V, Philip II, Louis XIV, and Napoleon to Wilhelm II, Hitler, and Brezhnev—threatened to disrupt the global balance of power, the Anglo-Saxons intervened to restore order.[12] Or at least this is the way many people in the English-speaking world look back on their own past.

Culturally, they like to consider themselves the heirs of the democratic tradition that started in ancient Greece, continued with the Romans, inspired the British Enlightenment, and ended up legitimizing

NATO's self-defence against communism.[13] But politically they interpret their history as a long battle against continental powers—a battle between good and evil, freedom and slavery, with God always on their side. Conflicts such as the English Civil War or the American Revolution are subtly presented not as internecine conflicts that took place within the Anglosphere itself, but as events that reaffirmed the idea of Anglo-Saxon exceptionalism. As Margaret Thatcher put it in her famous speech at the College of Europe in Bruges in 1988, when discussing Britain's special contribution to the European project: "Had it not been for that willingness to fight and to die, Europe would have been united long before now—but not in liberty, not in justice."[14]

National myths per se are not dangerous, even when they are factually false (as is usually the case). These three meta-myths obviously underestimated all the positive interactions that throughout the centuries have brought Europe and the United Kingdom together.[15] "The act of forgetting, and I would even say historical error, are an essential factor in the creation of a nation," said the philosopher Ernest Renan during his lecture "What is a Nation?" delivered at the Sorbonne in 1884.[16] By highlighting the origin and purpose of an imagined community, myths contribute to forging a national identity and motivating people within the same community to live together, claiming that the spirit and the strength of the past have not been lost. The problem is not so much the content of the national myth as the way it is interpreted and the political goal it is used for. A myth is not just an entertaining story, but an energizing and mobilizing device. As the philosopher Georges Sorel argued, "myths are not descriptions of things, but expressions of a determination to act".[17] When a nation is at a crossroads, for example before a war or an existential referendum, the glories of the past can be of inspiration to take one path rather than another.

It is this mobilizing power that is of concern, as it might be used to foster tension and conflict both within and between nations. Given its intrinsic malleability, the same national myth can be deployed to achieve different goals, and can be seen through different eyes. Ethno- and civic nationalisms give a symbolic interpretation to the mythical past of a country, using it to project the nation into the future. Clearly, ethno-nationalism has a more voracious appetite for fabricated history. Past, present, and future are intimately interlinked and seen as elements of a process of continuous development. The past predicts what comes next, and the future implies a continuation of what came before. Nostalgic nationalism, instead, tends to take national myths literally, in the hope of bringing history back to life. It instils the idea that at some point in time this process of incessant progress was interrupted, forcing the country to experience a sort of historical regression. To repair the misconduct, the whole nation has to travel in time.

In the conservative narrative of British history, for instance, joining what would later became the European Union marked a discontinuity with a glorious imperial past and with a future in which the United Kingdom could continue to act as protagonist, and not as a bystander.[18] By recounting national myths with a nostalgic touch, jingoistic leaders of this type produce a desire to return to the golden era to correct mistakes. For them, this return to the past is something real; for a more traditional nationalist, however, it is symbolic. David Cameron and the majority of the moderate Eurosceptic Conservatives were openly critical of the European Union, but they genuinely opposed Brexit. They wanted to reform it from within, while continuing to promote the values of the island nation such as democracy, freedom, and tolerance. "The British don't quit," said Cameron in his Downing Street speech just before the referendum. "We get involved, we take a lead, we make a difference, we get things done."[19] By contrast, nostalgic leaders create the illusion that the past can still fit the present. The myth gives the temporal destination: 1973, in the case of Brexit. Nostalgia shows the shortest route to get there: a "Yes" vote in the referendum. Forget that the world has changed in the meantime. A nostalgic person would not notice it.

The propaganda machine

The Brexiteers mobilized (and monopolized) the myth of the island nation in all its variations: Britain was presented as David who deployed resilience against a Goliath would-be invader. They conceived a form of patriotism capable of magnifying the twentieth century, obfuscating the loss of an empire and reducing the process of European integration to a historical aberration. Throughout its glorious history, Great Britain had always defeated the evil forces produced by Europe, ranging from

French absolutism, Napoleonic imperialism, and Prussian militarism to Nazi expansionism and Soviet communism. The time had come for it to face its new continental enemy, the European Union—certainly less bloodthirsty than those of the past, but equally threatening—head on. The latter was depicted as the sort of pan-European superstate that Hitler had wanted to establish. It was accused of being an empire that was reducing the once mighty United Kingdom to a simple colony.[20]

Brussels was the scapegoat for a British elite's frustrations with global aspirations, as well as for the unease of a working class demanding government protection from immigration and globalization. To escape European geography, European engagement, and European constraints, the British had to rediscover the spirit of self-sacrifice and the sense of community that had allowed them to defeat the continental evils of the past. Since all these conclusions logically derived from a national myth that is so entrenched in British society, the Remain camp was short of effective arguments to dismantle the Brexit narrative, and unable to borrow the myth of the island nation for its own ends.

But the Leave camp did not simply follow a standard ethno-nationalist playbook, using a combination of national history and myth to mobilize its fellow citizens. The Brexiteers went a step further. As thoroughly discussed in the rest of the chapter, they activated a strong form of restorative nostalgia by depicting a past that still existed, subtly suggesting a rose-tinted future, breaking temporal barriers and creating a sense of historical continuity. Nostalgia served to show the path and the direction, but also to distort reality and confuse voters. Their rhetoric was imbued with historical references going back to Magna Carta in 1215, which on its 800th anniversary was defined by the Eurosceptic Daniel Hannan as "the Anglosphere's *Torah*: the text that sets us apart while at the same time speaking universal truths to mankind".[21]

Leavers presented the United Kingdom as incarnating a story about the present, told for the living. They stayed on message. Their meta-myth of an island nation was corroborated with specific historical events that logically led to the conclusion that Brexit was inevitable, implicitly setting Britain against the continent. From the perspective of this myth, it is not easy to make a case in favour of the European Union, even when one exalts its peace-making role in a war-prone continent. The wars of the past caused death and destruction, but also contributed to exalt the British character and establish the idea of British exceptionalism. And Britain never caused any of these conflicts. It always intervened to stabilize the situation. If someone needed to be part of the European Union, it was the troublemakers: Germany and France, Italy and Spain. Nevertheless, since all these countries are now well-established democracies, a European architecture is redundant. Democracies do not go to war. Alliances are enough.

The Leave.EU campaign, which was directed by the former leader of the UK Independence Party (UKIP) Nigel Farage, used nostalgia more heavily than the official Vote Leave side (which grew from the Conservative and libertarian establishment).[22] The former was more focused on the Little England side of the campaign, while the latter was more concentrated on the Global Britain one. Quite interestingly, 40 per cent of all citizens felt that the Leave campaign was more focused on restoration than on the future, as opposed to 14 per cent of the Brexit voters.[23] This is a symptom of how nostalgia distorts reality.

In conveying their nostalgic messages the Brexiteers counted on the support of a number of newspapers: *The Sun*, *The Daily Telegraph*, the *Daily Mail*, and the *Daily Express*.[24] Even though it is declining, the role of the press in shaping public opinion should not be underestimated—especially considering the importance that older people, as well as the most nostalgic citizens, tend to attach to it. The *Daily Mail* sells 1.5 million copies a day, and MailOnline is the most visited English-language newspaper website in the world, with around 15 million readers a day. Just days before the referendum, *The Sun*, which boasts a readership of 1.7 million, published a front-page lead article head-lined "BeLEAVE in Britain", with the Union Jack in the background.[25] These media outlets helped spread war-related slogans about Brexit such as "Independence Day" or "modern-day Battle of Britain", or dis-seminate the spirit of the Blitz and Dunkirk. The post-Brexit political jargon has become imbued with references to the Second World War. Politicians wishing to engage with Europe are denounced as "appeas-ers" or "quislings", and a "war cabinet" is overseeing the withdrawal process from the European Union.[26]

Besides the support of sympathetic newspapers, Brexiteers bene-fited from the rather nostalgic atmosphere that characterized Britain at the time of the referendum. Inadvertently, the culture and entertainment industries lent a helping hand to the Leave camp in nationalizing the history of the United Kingdom and in propagating nostalgic feelings for a time when it was the fulcrum of the world. In the years ahead of the Brexit referendum there was a proliferation of films, TV series, books, and art exhibitions that showcased Britain's glorious past and celebrated Englishness in its purest form. With their visual gorgeousness, they contributed to the idealization of bygone times, primarily showing the positive aspects of eras that were no less chaotic and destabilizing than the current one. To be sure, this cultural infatuation with the past was not deliberate. The film industry was almost unanimously against Brexit, and openly campaigned in favour of Remain, even if in many instances it unintentionally conveyed the opposite message.[27] Market dynamics and some fortuitous circumstances created this favourable convergence towards certain kinds of cultural products.

As discussed in Chapter One, an ageing and dissatisfied society struggling to keep up with a present that is moving too fast is inclined to idealize the past and select those historical events that reinforce its convictions. The culture industry simply satisfied the demand for Englishness coming from the older generations. Research by the British Election Study found a very strong correlation between thinking that things in Britain had deteriorated and voting Leave.[28] At the same time, events such as the Royal Wedding, the Queen's Diamond Jubilee, and the 2012 Olympics, or the anniversaries of the First World War, Magna Carta, and Shakespeare's death, provided great excuses to further boost this kind of production, creating an emotional sense of national pride and belonging that turned out to be key to the United Kingdom's vote to say goodbye to the European Union.

This was not the first time that the British entertainment industry stepped up to create a form of patriotism based on devotion to royalty, worship of national heroes, and pride in imperial endeavours. In the first half of the past century, imperial propaganda resorted to any cultural and artistic means to instil loyalty to the empire—even in the man in the street, who cared more about what was happening in his immediate surroundings than about life in some faraway dominion. Packaging, postcards, music hall, cinema, boys' stories and schoolbooks, exhibitions, and parades emphasized the Britishness of the empire and conveyed the message that it was an adventure, an ennobling responsibility for all the people of the British Isles and the symbol of a shared destiny.[29] From its inception, the British Broadcasting Corporation (BBC) gave a helping hand. Programmes stressed that the empire represented a happy union of peoples and benefited the colonized by exposing them to Western science, denying the role of violence in the acquisition of empire, while emphasizing trade and exploration.[30] Talking about imperial geography in 1928 during the show *Keynote of Empire*, the broadcaster Francis James Montgomery Collinson stated:

> Let me remind you that the British Empire was not won by fighting. Australia is ours purely by settlement. New Zealand was handed over to us, of their own free will, by the Maoris. South Africa was bought from the Dutch and in Canada the only part that was conquered was Québec.[31]

The difference between now and then is that no film or TV series in the years leading up to the Brexit vote was produced on request from the government, directly or indirectly. The nostalgic atmosphere that has emerged was not the result of a deliberate, systematic, and conscious propagandistic process. It happened mostly by chance, and people such as Alex von Tunzelmann, the screenwriter of *Churchill*, publicly distanced themselves from the Brexit outcome, making it clear that their projects were commissioned well before the 2016 referendum.[32] In the nineteenth century, by contrast, there was a proliferation of imperial propaganda agencies such as the Empire Marketing Board, the Imperial Institute, the Royal Colonial Institute, and the British Empire League. Moreover, at that time the propaganda machine wanted the nation to look to the future with hope and optimism, taking advantage of the great opportunities provided by a globe-spanning empire. Brexiteers, instead, promoted nostalgic feelings that were inevitably stuck in a time that no longer existed and was carefully filtered.

With no intention of being exhaustive (and taking advantage of a neutral perspective as "non-Britons"), our effort now is to reconstruct the nostalgic national myth that emerged from the fortuitous interaction of different cultural and political forces at the time of the referendum. Good storytellers structure their stories in ways that allow them to achieve their narrative goals. The Brexiteers scrupulously built their

own nostalgic myth, paying attention to its credibility, idealizing a specific historical era, and creating strong links between Brexit and
Britain's history. In the end, past, present, and future were so intertwined that it was impossible to distinguish them. Britain's past golden
age was suddenly seen as its new beginning. What follows is a step-by-
step description of the fabrication of a nostalgic national myth as
inferred from the British case.

Step 1: anchored to reality

To be credible, a nostalgic national myth needs to be anchored to reality—at least to some extent. With their imaginative rhetoric,
Brexiteers persuaded their fellow citizens that restoring the past was
possible. The slogan "Take back control", which appealed to both the
supporters of the "Global Britain" and "Little England" visions discussed
in the Introduction, was intrinsically nostalgic and forward looking at
the same time. It gave a sense of a better future "wrapped in the Union
Jack".[33] The word "back" implied a return to full sovereignty and the
revival of a lost global status. The term "control" spoke particularly to
those British who felt deprived of their agency in directing lives that
were shacked by unpredictable external forces. Establishing 23 June as
Britain's "Independence Day" allowed Brexiteers to clearly put an end
to a shameful period in British history and to start over.

Equally, the slogan "Global Britain" emphasized the restoration of
the United Kingdom's trade pre-eminence, which was possible thanks
to its preferential relations with its "true kith and kin"—the Anglosphere, or the Commonwealth more generally. It was a tangible and, at
least on the surface, non-utopian project. In an article backing Brexit,
The Daily Telegraph wrote: "There is a world beyond Europe that the
Remain camp simply ignores. A world that offers enormous opportunities for Britain to be a global player once more."[34] Brexiteers claimed
to see their future in an alternative model of international cooperation,
where market relations are predicated on emotional ties, patterns of
migration rely on historical memory, and economic cooperation is
defined by cultural affinities.[35] In addition, a national myth that brings
together geographically distant nations implicitly provided an exit
strategy for the United Kingdom outside the European Union. Britain

would not be alone in an increasingly complex world. It could count on the active support of its cousins, including the strongest economic and military power on earth: the United States.

Global Britain obviously rested on the United Kingdom's imperial past, which is temporally close enough for Britons to yearn for it and for Brexiteers to leverage it without sounding too foolish. Although the imperial architecture was dismantled decades ago, its foundations have substantially survived the caprices of history through a dense network of institutional, economic and financial links. After all, this is not the Roman Empire that permanently collapsed centuries ago. Not surprisingly, the British Empire was always in the background of the referendum campaign and supplied a horizon of possibility, even if it played a subordinate role to Vote Leave's focus on immigration control and increased social-security spending. But, in a way, the whole idea of "taking back control" disguised a sense of nostalgia for the centuries during which Britain was the undisputed global rule maker—and not just sovereign in its domestic affairs. Only the hope of partly re-establishing the splendour of past glories could push millions of voters to bear the costs of a divorce from the European Union. Synonyms of Global Britain, such as Greater Britain, Britannia, or Empire 2.0 became part of the jargon used by Brexiteers, both before and after the vote, painting an overly optimistic future for the United Kingdom outside Europe. Just a few days before the referendum, Boris Johnson urged his fellow citizens to back Brexit in order "to take the chains off the giant unshackled Britannia and let the Lion roar again" and win "the battle for British democracy".[36] In a similar fashion, the historian David Starkey compared Brexit to Henry VIII's break from Rome, arguing that the Reformation presaged the "expansion of England" and implying that Brexit may see another age of empire.[37]

The empire was openly used to polarize the Brexit debate in the summer of 2016—just a few days before the vote. The glory of the empire and Britain's naval prowess is commemorated every summer at the last night of the BBC Proms, the final night of a two-month series of classical and orchestral music concerts at the Royal Albert Hall, in a patriotic musical sequence that includes "Rule Britannia" and "Land of Hope and Glory". In contrast to previous proms, on the last night the "Prommers", as they are known, are encouraged to sing along while waving Union Jack flags and banners. A few days before the 23 June vote, Farage's Leave.EU tried to use the name "Last Night of the Brexit Proms" for a pop concert, but was forced to cancel it as the BBC took legal action over the name, and most of the performers due to play pulled out when they realized that it was to become a political rally. And in September 2016, on the occasion of the official Last Night of the Proms, activists handed out 2,500 EU flags to the audience in order to express solidarity for the European Union. In response, Arron Banks, a multimillionaire who helped bankroll Brexit, hit back with 10,000 Union Jack flags.[38] In the Brexit narrative, the Union Jack is a key symbol for a nation with global aspirations. Brexiteers, rightly or wrongly, argue that in the Overseas Territories the flag is not seen as a colonial flag, but as a "purposeful connection" with the United Kingdom. For these countries it is a reminder that they have a sort of dual nationality and multifold identity.[39]

In 2016, evoking bygone imperial glory was no longer anathema, as would have been the case a couple of decades earlier, when the "White Man's Burden" was still weighing on Britain's controversial past. To be sure, the British intellectual elite is still split on the assessment of the imperial experience. But the Brexiteers could count on the partial rehabilitation of the empire that had probably started with the popular work of the historian Niall Ferguson, who glorified the empire in the homonymous PBS documentary and bestselling book.[40] In 2005, former Labour Prime Minister Gordon Brown stated: "The days of Britain having to apologize for its colonial history are over. We should move forward."[41] After the return of Hong Kong to China in 1997 the empire was no longer a relic of the past, but a historical achievement everybody had to be proud of. Ten years later, in 2015, Channel 4 aired one of the most popular television series of the last few years, *Indian Summers*, which celebrated the Raj lifestyle as it followed the adventures of colonial officials in the old summer capital of Shimla, in the foothills of the Himalayas.

An emblematic example of the superficiality and blindness with which many in Great Britain approach their imperial past comes from Oxford. In 2015, while hosting a debate on reparations for slavery, the Oxford Union sold a cocktail called Colonial Comeback, which contained brandy, peach schnapps, and lemonade, for just £2.50 instead of the standard price of £3.33. To add insult to injury, the drink was advertised on a poster featuring a picture of black hands in chains, triggering a wave of protest among the ethnic minorities at British universities. Ironically, it was at the same conference that the Indian politician Shashi Tharoor launched his harsh attack against Britain's colonial wrongdoings in India that provided the inspiration for his subsequent bestseller *Inglorious Empire*. Also that same year, Rhodes Must Fall, a campaign to remove statues of the imperialist Cecil Rhodes, was quashed by the Oxford University leadership, having spread from South African universities. There was no appetite to root out a controversial figure like Rhodes even in educated British society. Actually, Rhodes was somewhat rehabilitated by the extension of the prestigious scholarship to study at Oxford that is named after him to any student from across the globe, and not just from Anglo-Saxon countries. Both controversies, which attracted extensive press coverage at the time, did not induce Brexiteers to backtrack from their imperial fantasies.

Step 2: temporal destination

Within the Brexit narrative, the British Empire is important for another reason. Not only does it project the nation in to the future, it also projects it into the past. It identifies the temporal destination that a successful nostalgic myth needs in order to be convincing. Just as ethno-nationalism tends to idealize the strength and character of a specific race or nation, nostalgic nationalism exalts the moment in history to which a country is supposed to return. Brexit automatically leads to 1973. For Little England supporters this is probably the end point of their intertemporal trip, but for the Global Britain supporters it is more likely to be the starting point. The late 1960s and early 1970s do not represent Britain's golden days. The economy was stagnant, the empire was collapsing, Europe was coming together, and Britain was slowly moving to the margins of the international system. Had a (hardcore) Brexiteer to choose where to travel back in time, he would probably opt for the late Victorian and Edwardian eras, when the empire was at its apogee. They epitomize Englishness in its purest form.

Of course, no one in the Leave camp was so naïve as to openly state this. But some of its leading figures acted and spoke in ways that might evoke that past and revive its memories within the population.

Consciously or not, they leveraged what psychologists call "rosy retrospection"—that is, our desire to bring back a way of life that existed in a highly idealized historical moment.[42] The leading Brexiteer Jacob Rees-Mogg, who was dubbed "the honourable member for the eighteenth century", speaks in sonorous old-style English, is unfailingly courteous, and seems to live in another era. He called for Somerset, the county containing his constituency, to be allowed to set its own time zone, as it could before all British times were harmonized in the 1840s. In the House of Commons he once asked: "What greater pleasure can there be for a true-born Englishman [than] to listen to our national anthem ... to listen to those words that link us to our sovereign who is part of that chain that takes us back to our immemorial history?"[43] The *Economist* labelled him "the blue passport in human form, the red telephone box made flesh, the Royal Yacht *Britannia* in a pinstripe suit".[44] Equally, at the end of the referendum campaign, Boris Johnson was so immersed in the past that the journalist John Crace wrote in *The Guardian*: "Can the prime minister invite him to return to the twenty-first century?"[45] As odd as it may sound, some Leave voters took Brexit-induced time travel seriously: "We're going back to the Victorian times," one said. "Victorian times had it better than what we have."[46]

The late Victorian and Edwardian eras had recaptured the collective imagination of the United Kingdom well before Brexit, fostering great nostalgic feelings for a time when England was "the country other nations wanted to imitate".[47] It was a "long summer afternoon", a short interlude of peace, prosperity, and progress between the Boer War and the Great War.[48] It was an era of transformative socio-economic change that saw the widespread diffusion of electricity, the advent of the motor car, the invention of the aeroplane, and the rise of department stores, hotels, and seaside resorts. It was the time of the suffrage movement and the introduction of the first forms of the welfare state. It was a golden age of lavishness, strict social etiquette, and glamour, of debutantes' balls and country-house parties. Popular, mainstream television series such as *The Forsyte Saga, Parade's End, Mr Selfridge, The Village*, and *Downton Abbey* have immortalized this effervescent atmosphere.[49] *Harry Potter* itself is essentially a fantasy of an Edwardian public school. And the series *Titanic*, which was released in 2013, almost coinciding with the centenary of the sinking of the passenger liner, essentially focused on the contrasting lifestyles of the classes on board, rather than on the tragedy itself.

Of all the costume dramas of the last few years, *Downton Abbey* is probably the most successful and popular.[50] Set in a great house on an English country estate in the early twentieth century, its characters, both family and servants, inspired great affection, especially thanks to their quintessentially English qualities. By stretching the true meaning of *Downton* a bit, one can decode some masked pro-Brexit messages. It helped to produce an uncontrolled fascination with an era in which the global influence of the United Kingdom was undisputed. Europe was usually associated with war and death, as opposed to America, which is depicted as a source of inspiration. One thing is certain. Its creator, Julian Fellowes, who won an Oscar for the screenplay of a film with a similar theme and sits in the House of Lords under the title Baron Fellowes of West Stafford, openly favoured Brexit. He once said: "History has for hundreds of years been moving towards government that is answerable to the people and suddenly we have done an about-turn and we've gone back to the Austro-Hungarian Empire. I don't think that's the right direction."[51]

Instead of riding the nostalgic wave for these eras as the Brexiteers were to do a few years later, in 2010, at a memorial service held for Keir Hardie, the founder of the Labour Party, David Miliband tried to awaken his fellow citizens from a nostalgic torpor for an era that was far less glamorous than popular culture suggested:

> The first of these is nostalgia, and the temptation to view his life and times as not simply better than our own, but to ignore the poverty, the exploitation of the insanitary housing, the illiteracy, the dangerous pits, the precariousness of the lives of working people at that time.[52]

Politically, the lack of understanding of the economic and political forces behind the cultural fascination with these eras clearly backfired for the Remain camp. The Great Recession, disruptive technological change, and the power shift from the West to the East have made our present and future uncertain, frightening, and unpleasant. Viewers want to watch something that comforts them, gives a sense of optimism, and provides an imaginary escape. They prefer to look back at a time when things were apparently less complicated, and savour the innocence of the years immediately preceding one of the greatest tragedies in the history of humankind. The empire was battered, but it was still ruling the waves. The daily lives of ordinary people were changing for good and for all, albeit at a different speed depending on one's social class. Ten per cent of the British population controlled 92 per cent of the country's wealth, but a servant could still hope to move up the social ladder.[53] The infant mortality rate was high at 150 per 1,000 births, but medicine was advancing massively.[54] Women were discriminated against and marginalized, but their emancipation was in the making. Ireland was in a ferment to achieve its independence, but the kingdom was still intact. Trade unionism was picking up, but society was not fractured yet. All these nuances appeared in these period dramas. But the hardships of that era remain in the background. The focus is on the aesthetics of the past. Brexiteers simply leveraged this kind of infatuation to make the leap less hazardous and relied on the fading affect bias (wherein the mind overstates the rosier parts of the past) discussed in Chapter One. Many Britons try to forget that the Edwardian era paved the way for the First World War and was the beginning of the end of Pax Britannica. It is not really the moment in history that hardcore Brexiteers should hope to revive, unless one filters out the unpleasant parts of it.

Step 3: temporal proximity

For a country to return to an idealized past, voters need to be offered a sense of temporal proximity to the most defining moments in the history of the nation, such as wars or revolutions or to the most celebrated national heroes. This is important in order to create a sense of urgency, give the impression of a never-ending fight, and revive the character of a people in order to face unprecedented challenges. Clearly these moments in history do not have to coincide with the ideal temporal destination. Nobody would like to go back to the time of the two World Wars, but anecdotes about those events recalled the spirit of an island nation that stood alone in many instances, always emerging victorious. Brexiteers succeeded in this sense, and even created the illusion that the past had, well, not passed at all. Boris Johnson claimed that Churchill would have joined him on his campaign bus. Equally, David Davis, who was initially in charge of Brexit negotiations with Brussels, rejected suggestions that the civil service did not have the resources to negotiate Brexit, saying: "Our civil service can cope with World War II, they can easily cope with this." The use of the present tense, "can", was hardly a grammatical mistake. It created the feeling that the war was still ongoing. The Nazis were about to cross the Channel and Britain was taking care of the problem. Equally, David Cameron's negotiated deal with Brussels was likened to Chamberlain's non-aggression pact with Hitler.[55] The comparison was absurd, but it helped break a temporal gap between two distinct eras. The Remainers struck back two years later, in 2018, with Mid-Norfolk MP Keith Simpson saying: "Calm down Boris, you're no Winston in our darkest hour."[56]

To create this sense of temporal proximity and transport their voters back in time, Brexiteers also resorted to musical stratagems—which in the psychology of nostalgia are considered to be very effective in engaging large-scale neural networks across the brain and in evoking vivid memories of the past.[57] For example, as it toured the country, Farage's "battle bus" played music from the 1963 war film *The Great Escape*, which featured the mass escape of British Commonwealth prisoners of war from Stalag Luft III and summed up the bravery of the Allied forces during the Second World War. By leveraging the emotions that the film had produced for decades, Farage was clearly providing not only his own version of history, but also his own interpretation of the film. The sons of Elmer Bernstein, who composed the music for the film that propelled Steve McQueen to stardom, openly criticized Farage's musical choice, arguing that their father "would surely say that *The Great Escape* celebrated those who bravely saved Europe from a horrifically racist, nativist and violent regime. He would hardly see UKIP as either a worthy successor of that cause or embodying the spirit of those who liberated Europe from oppression and hatred."[58]

Films are even more powerful than music at triggering nostalgic feelings. Building on the great success of the movie *Dunkirk*, directed by Christopher Nolan and released one year after the referendum, Brexit is now being established as this generation's Dunkirk. Farage urged young people to watch the film, which shows the epic evacuations of Allied soldiers from the north of France in 1940, implying that the spirit of Dunkirk, of the spontaneous armada of small boats working together, will be needed now as never since 1940. By referring to an almost mili-

71

tary catastrophe, Brexiteers implicitly recognize that Brexit, with its tough negotiations and its uncertain transition, will be rather challenging, to say the least. In a piece for *The Daily Telegraph*, Tory minister Penny Mordaunt wrote: "In our long island history, there have been many times when Britain has not been well served by alignment with Europe. ... When Britain stood alone in 1940 after the defeat at Dunkirk, we were cut off and ridiculed. True leadership sometimes does feel isolating. Yet we have never suffered for it. We are resourceful; we are well connected; our brand is strong in the world."[59] In a nutshell, this is how Brexiteers expect the United Kingdom to be in the future: proudly isolated, independent, and "strong in the world".[60]

Leavers also leveraged the First World War massively, creating a direct link between it and Brexit. As in all European countries, the First World War holds a particularly sentimental place in British history, but only recently has its popular remembrance come close to inappropriate celebration and distasteful partisanship. Each November, in the run-up to the annual Armistice Day and Remembrance Sunday ceremonies, politicians, television stars, sportspeople, and ordinary citizens wear paper poppies in memory of the battle of Ypres—the Belgian city where the German and Allied armies fought each other on five occasions between 1914 and 1918. There is a rising militancy regarding the tradition of wearing poppies. In recent years public figures forgetting to wear a symbolic poppy in the run-up to the ceremony have experienced censure. Around a third of British people believe it should be compulsory, according to research by Consumer Intelligence, while one in ten oppose the tradition, which they believe glorifies war.[61]

However, it was in 2014, on the occasion of the centenary of the beginning of the Great War, that this ceremony fuelled unprecedented patriotic feelings and caused controversy. Paul Cummins and Tom Piper's commemorative art exhibition 'Blood Swept Lands and Seas of Red' inundated the Tower of London with 888,246 ceramic poppies to represent the fallen British soldiers in the conflict. Jonathan Jones condemned the memorial in an article for *The Guardian*, depicting it as a xenophobic monument that fuelled an inward-looking UKIP-style mood by celebrating only the soldiers of Britain and its colonies, while ignoring those of other nations.[62] Indeed, the Leave.EU campaign took advantage of the commemoration to tweet a photo of a Chelsea veteran examining the ceramic poppies in the grounds with the comment: "Freedom and democracy. Let's not give up values for which our ancestors paid the ultimate sacrifice. #LeaveEU."[63]

The Remainers, who were more parsimonious in their use of historical references, struggled to bring history back to life. In a sixty-second video from their campaign, one veteran says: "For me, Britain is stronger in Europe because it reflects the values my generation fought for in Europe during the Second World War."[64] Although highly emotional, the video's message hardly resonated with a large part of the population (probably the majority) who have never experienced a continental war. This narrative about the European project partly reflects an outdated vision of Europe that belongs to a distant past. In recent years the European Commission itself has tried to reframe the narrative of the European integration process in a more appealing way, especially for younger generations.[65] Rightly or wrongly, peace in Europe is now almost taken for granted. There might be overlapping existential crises in Europe, but the risk of all-out war looks rather unrealistic. It is no coincidence that Cameron's claim that Brexit would lead to a third world war backfired and was ridiculed.[66]

When it became clear that history was playing against the Remain camp, Cameron tried to "hire" Churchill for his own campaign. With his steadfastness, courage, wit, and defiance, Churchill embodies Britain's self-perceived national character. In 2002, thirty-seven years after his death, BBC television viewers voted Churchill the greatest Briton of all time, ahead of Shakespeare, Diana, Darwin, and the Queen, citing his resolve in taking on the Nazis against heavy odds.[67] Both before and after the Brexit vote, the production of Churchilliana has been intense, often (but not always) celebrating Churchill as an unparalleled statesman and national hero. Two movies in particular, *Churchill* and *Darkest Hour*, contributed to cement the figure of Churchill in the immediate aftermath of Brexit.[68] At least in the intentions of its creators, *Darkest Hour* had nothing to do with Europhobia or the nationalism that was gathering momentum, although it ended up fuelling post-Brexit fantasies, with audiences reported to have clapped and cheered at the end of the "We shall fight them on the beaches" speech.[69] Conscious of Churchill's political attractiveness, at some point during the referendum campaign Cameron stated:

At my office, I sit two yards away from the Cabinet Room where Winston Churchill decided in May 1940 to fight on against Hitler—the best and greatest decision anyone has made in our country. He didn't want to be alone, he wanted to be fighting with the French and with the Poles and with the others, but he didn't quit. He didn't quit on Europe, he didn't quit on European democracy, he didn't quit on European freedom.[70]

But it was too late. Churchill was already the prey of the Brexiteers. Boris Johnson was probably the one who leveraged his legacy most persuasively. With his book *The Churchill Factor*, published in 2014 when he was still Mayor of London, he was not too subtle in implicitly drawing a parallel between himself and the wartime leader. John Kampfner wrote in *The Guardian*: "The reader is invited to see the two men as supreme orators, literary masters and slayers of spineless Conservatives and perfidious foreigners."[71] The book provided an opportunity to equate the European Union with a crushing of the British spirit, and supplied Johnson with a variety of themes that he deployed in the run-up to the referendum. In a comment piece for *The Sun*, when he unexpectedly announced his intention to join the Leave campaign, he argued that the European Union was "stifling" the democracy that Churchill fought so hard for, adding that the wartime Prime Minister believed in self-determination for all, and fought against the dictatorships in Europe "not just for British survival, but for the right of the people to choose who makes their laws, and to kick them out at elections".[72]

In fact, Churchill's attitudes towards Europe ebbed and flowed. In 1930 he wrote an article in the *Saturday Evening Post* saying: "We see nothing but good and hope in a richer, freer, more contented European commonality. But we have our own dream and our own task. We are with Europe, but not of it. We are linked but not compromised. We are interested and associated but not absorbed." And in 1942 he wrote a letter to his Foreign Secretary, Anthony Eden, saying that "hard as it is to say now, I look forward to a United States of Europe, in which the barriers between the nations will be greatly minimized and unrestricted travel will be possible".[73]

As if Churchill was not enough, the Brexiteers also invoked William Shakespeare—the undisputed symbol of Britishness. Leaving the European Union was a Hamlet-style dilemma, after all. In 2011 the think tank Demos conducted a poll in which the Bard beat the pound, the monarchy, the BBC, the Beatles, and Parliament as the symbol that gives Britons a sense of pride. Luckily for Brexiteers, the 400th anniversary of his death fell in 2016, and the year was punctuated with events celebrating his life and work, including concerts, radio readings, and performances. Whether Shakespeare involuntarily provided messages consistent with the idea of Brexit is more than questionable— actually, it is a futile intellectual exercise. But what mattered for the Leave campaign was to pretend that the most celebrated writer in British literature was on their side, at least in their nationalistic spirit. Brexiteers used the "scept'red isle", a quote from Shakespeare's *Richard II*, to express the concept of Britain as a uniquely blessed land, inhabited by a superior people chosen to rule the world. A sceptre is a symbol of royal authority, and a "scept'red isle" is an unforgettable image of a sovereign England owing allegiance to no outsider.[74]

Boris Johnson was even writing a biography of Shakespeare, which was supposed to come out in time for the anniversary in October 2016, but the book was shelved after the vote, presumably because of his ministerial commitments. In a speech made at Chatham House in 2017, Johnson produced a mash-up of Shakespeare quotes from *Macbeth, Hamlet*, and *Julius Caesar*. "I suggest humbly to our friends and partners in Brussels now is the time to get on with it. Let's not let 'I dare not' wait upon 'I would', or let the native hue of resolution be sickled o'er with the pale cast of thought—or whatever. There is a current in the affair of men—they should grip it and get on with it and start talking about the future."[75] But Shakespeare was anything but inward looking: many of his greatest plays, including *Hamlet*, *Othello*, and *Julius Caesar*, are set in Europe, with foreign characters, which demonstrate great depth and humanity. Often stories were drawn from French and Italian sources that he may have read in the original. Arguably, Shakespeare's plays often showed the folly of nationalism.

Step 4: historical continuity

The final key element of a successful nostalgic narrative is the creation of a sense of historical continuity. By regaining full control of its economy, its borders, and its sovereignty, the United Kingdom would return to the path of uninterrupted democratic and economic progress that its ancestors had traced before it undertook the short detour caused by the infamous decision of 1973 to join the European Economic Community. Joining the European project was a historical rupture. Brexit, instead, symbolized a historical conjuncture. King Henry VIII blazed the trail more than five centuries ago. As the political scientist Adrian Pabst put it: "If you ever wondered about the origins of English Euroscepticism, look no further than the Protestant Reformation."[76] When Henry VIII broke with Rome and became the head of the Church of England, he turned his country from a member of a huge, medieval, cross-channel European empire into an independent sovereign nation-state, free from the authority of any foreign potentate, in particular the Pope. In addition, Britons were induced to think of a brave action such as Brexit as part of a recurring theme in the history of their country. Right before the referendum vote, the leader of UKIP Wales, Nathan Gill, stated:

> Thank heavens Captain Cook didn't heed any advice not to take his great voyage of discovery because it was a leap into the dark. … Scott, Hudson, Drake, Livingstone, Riley, all helped shape the modern world we live in today, by taking giant leaps into the dark. … We are a people who have always taken brave leaps.[77]

More generally, Leavers presented Brexit as the final act of an uninterrupted sequence of battles that had pitted Britain against the continent for centuries. They cast back into history, to the victory of Agincourt against the French army at the time of the Hundred Years War in 1415, to the defeat of the Spanish Armada in 1588, and to the Battle of Waterloo against Napoleon in 1815.[78] To mobilize Brexit supporters, the leading Conservative MP Jacob Rees-Mogg declared: "This is Magna Carta, it's the Burgesses coming at Parliament, it's the Great Reform Bill, it's the Bill of Rights, it's Waterloo, it's Agincourt, it's Crecy."[79] On 25 October 2015, on the 600th anniversary of the Agincourt victory, the irreverent Leave.EU campaign tweeted: "Britons have always triumphed in the face of adversity. Let's lead the charge once more and #LeaveEU."[80]

Brexit was a continuation of this endless conflict by other means. In 2015, Nigel Farage declared that leaving the European Union "is our modern day Battle of Britain", a struggle to reclaim "the very principles that were fought for seventy-five years ago. If we succeed, not only will our country be a free, self-governing democracy but I believe the rest of Europe will follow too. It is a high prize."[81] After more than forty-five years of battles with Brussels, in 2018, in the midst of Brexit negotiations, Brexiteers proudly announced their intention to establish a Museum of Sovereignty in which they would collect Brexit campaign memorabilia.[82] From having been the fulcrum of the largest empire in the history of humankind, it felt as if London had suddenly turned into the post-colonial capital of someone else's empire. But it was probably Boris Johnson who drew the most extreme line of historical continuity:

> The truth is that the history of the last couple of thousand years has been broadly repeated attempts by various people or institutions—in a Freudian way—to rediscover the lost childhood of Europe, this golden age of peace and prosperity under the Romans, by trying to unify it. Napoleon, Hitler, various people tried this out, and it ends tragically. The European Union is an attempt to do this by different methods. But fundamentally what it is lacking is the eternal problem, which is that there is no underlying loyalty to the idea of Europe. There is no single authority that anybody respects or understands. That is causing this massive democratic void.[83]

Continuity in British history is not just related to an endless sequence of wars with the continent. It is a country that has ruled itself uninterruptedly for centuries. It is the perfect fusion of imperial power, democratic accountability, and monarchical constitutionality. Affection for the royal family, in particular, is closely tied to national identity in the United Kingdom, and having a monarchy in itself differentiates Great Britain from republican France and Germany. In the years leading up to the Brexit referendum, a host of films and television series, such as *The Queen, The Crown, The King's Speech*, and *Victoria*, celebrated and humanized the Royal Family. In 2012, an Ipsos MORI poll of 1,006 British adults found that 80 per cent were in favour of the monarchy, with just 13 per cent in favour of the United Kingdom becoming a republic. And the Brexiteers found in the Queen an unexpected, and probably involuntary, ally. While members of the Royal Family are constitutionally prohibited from expressing political views, the Queen probably cherishes Britain's effort to rebuild its relationship with the Commonwealth that she has helped to maintain. *The Sun* even insinuated, with a front-page story, that the "Queen backs Brexit".[84]

Storytellers vs. liars

As Marshall did in *Our Island Story*, Leavers recounted the history of the United Kingdom not as historians, but as storytellers. The use of these nostalgic tricks certainly reflected a skilled use of emotive linguistic strategies compared to the lacklustre rhetoric of the Remain camp. They enriched the rhetorical arsenal of the Brexiteers, helping them win the battle of words against their ideological adversaries.[85] This is not to say that the deployment of a nostalgic rhetoric was enough to win hearts and minds. But it certainly helped project the country into another era, thanks also to the special nostalgic atmosphere that characterized the United Kingdom in those years. In addition, the heavy reliance on nostalgia also implied a better understanding of the country. As in the rest of the advanced world, the British population is ageing fast and, as discussed in the previous chapter, old people are more inclined to long for the old good days. After all, 60 per cent of people aged sixty-five or older voted to Leave, as opposed to 27 per cent of those between eighteen and twenty-four.[86] The Brexiteers targeted the group that is demographically, and hence politically, more powerful.

The "now and here" strategy adopted by the Remain camp failed for another reason. It was too rational at a time when the electorate was experiencing a highly emotional moment, partly caused by the financial crisis and partly by globalization more broadly. After all, voters, even the most informed and politically aware, often think and act with their hearts. As argued by the psychologist Drew Westen, the "political brain is an emotional brain. It is not a dispassionate calculating machine, objectively searching for the right facts, figures, and policies to make a reasoned decision."[87] Rising inequalities, stagnant earnings, unstable jobs, widespread poverty, and unsettling immigration fuelled negative emotions such as fear, anger, intolerance, and frustration, which led to an apparently irrational decision. The Brexiteers leveraged and reinforced this underlying emotional state by building a narrative that was centred on a sort of atavistic conflict between the British Isles and the Old Continent. With a population prone to reminisce about the past and vulnerable to nostalgic feelings, they monopolized and nationalized British history to convey a message that was consistent with their political agenda.

However, there is a profound difference between Marshall and the Brexiteers. Both lied. But the former openly admitted it; the latter did not. Writers can, politicians cannot. In the Introduction to *Our Island Story*, Marshall warned her young readers to place the book next to their novels, and not their history textbooks. She also added: "Remember, too, that I was not trying to teach you, but only to tell a story."[88] For a professional storyteller, lying has no consequences. Actually, the reader praises it if that contributes to his amusement. A politician, instead, has to live up to his bombastic promises. Brexiteers put themselves in the uncomfortable position of having to turn their story into history, bringing back to life something that no longer exists.

4

BIRTH OF AN IDEA

"The old colonial system is gone. But in its place no clear and reasoned system has been adopted."

J. R. Seeley

A casual glance at the history of the last three millennia reveals a striking pattern. Hegemonic power tends to move westward. The collapse of the flourishing empires of the East, from the Babylonians to the Persians, gave way to the rise of the Greeks, who ultimately handed over the imperial torch to the Romans. Then, for a few centuries, the Spaniards, the Portuguese, the French, and the British fiercely battled each other to seize the dominant role of the global system until Britain gained the upper hand. Eventually, the United States reached the pinnacle of the world. It was in the Middle Ages that theologians elaborated the meta-concept of *translatio imperii*—the idea that the political and cultural legitimacy of a declining civilization was passed on to the rising one in a sort of cyclical and perpetual movement, from classical antiquity to modernity, from a declining power in the East to the dominant force in the West.[1]

In his biography of Winston Churchill, Boris Johnson argued that a feeling similar to the *translatio imperii* probably helped his hero rationalize the looming collapse of empire.[2] Following Hitler's defeat, the United States started to take over Britain's hegemonic role. And Churchill was the man who intellectually, personally, and politically embodied the transition from Pax Britannica to Pax Americana. In his mind, the beginning of American hegemony represented the continuation of the British imperial era in a new guise. He spent almost three decades, from the early 1930s to 1958, giving form to his ideas with the four-volume *A History of the English-Speaking Peoples*. With a traditional Whig approach to the past, the book traced the history of the Anglo-Saxons from the first century to the outbreak of the First World War, magnifying British history as an uninterrupted progress that spread across the globe the concepts of constitutional government, individual liberty, parliamentary democracy, rule of law, and economic liberalism.[3]

Churchill was the quintessential example of a man of the two worlds, probably the first truly Anglo-American. As he wrote to John F. Kennedy after the presidential election of 1960, his special relationship with the United States dated back to the day of his father's marriage. On 15 April 1874 Lord Randolph Spencer Churchill, the son of the Duke of Marlborough, married Jennie Jerome, the daughter of an American millionaire. But his American family connections actually went further back in history: George Washington was a distant relative, and three of his ancestors were heroes of the American Revolutionary War.[4] His upbringing in such an Anglo-American social milieu, with the cultures, the accents, and the traditions of the two countries mixing with one another, helped influence his approach to international politics. He did not just see the English language as a powerful tool that allowed his American mother and his British father to chat easily in the luxurious rooms of Blenheim Palace, the official residence of the Churchill family. English was a powerful means to connect former and current colonies, creating a strong sense of belonging that transcended race, historical grievances, and geographical distance.

He highlighted the importance of linguistic commonality during a speech at Harvard University in 1943:

> The great Bismarck—for there were once great men in Germany—is said to have observed towards the close of his life that the most potent factor in human society at the end of the nineteenth century was the fact that the British and American peoples spoke the same language. That was a pregnant saying. Certainly it has enabled us to wage war together with an intimacy and harmony never before achieved among allies.[5]

This intimacy was key to cementing Anglo-Saxon unity and stemming the tide of illiberalism that was blowing across the globe in the darkest hours of the Second World War and the early stages of the Cold War. At the same time, the construction of a strong relationship between Great Britain and the Dominions—her semi-independent white colonies—was necessary to provide stability to the empire and, after 1949, to the newly enlarged Commonwealth of Nations.[6] It is said that during his last Cabinet meeting, upon leaving office in 1955, Churchill warned his colleagues "never to be separated from the Americans".[7] He believed that the British Prime Minister and the American President should be in constant, symbiotic contact. The fraternal association between the United States and the British Commonwealth would be the backbone of any English-speaking concord and should lead to a common defence, a common citizenship, and even a common currency with the insignia of a pound and a dollar intertwined. When he showed the drawing of the new currency to the son of President Franklin Delano Roosevelt, who was visiting London, the young American asked him what he would call it. Churchill replied: "The sterling dollar." James Roosevelt inquired: "What, Sir, if my father should wish to call it the dollar sterling?" "It's all the same," Churchill beamed. "We are together."[8]

Churchill's emphasis on Anglo-Saxon unity was based on facts, but it was driven by a large dose of political opportunism. Only by jumping on the American bandwagon could Britain hope to retain part of the global influence that was slipping out of its hands. Nostalgia for a time of glory and influence that was about to evaporate forced Churchill to think creatively in order to carve out a new global role for Britain. He had inherited the greatest empire in the history of humankind and was leaving behind him an ordinary nation. But Churchill was not the first to celebrate the concept of Anglo-Saxon solidarity. Since the whole imperial architecture had started to crumble many decades earlier, a number of British intellectuals before him had resorted to this political stratagem to preserve the power that Britain was slowly and inexorably losing.

The debate on the unity of the Anglo-Saxons picked up in the Victorian age and has continued through out our time—with a break in the Cold War era, when the idea of a united West was taken for granted, America was focused on Russia, and Britain was absorbed by its existential crisis with Brussels. Over the last 150 years, proposals have differed in ambition, detail, and rationale, ranging from the creation of a British imperial federation or a multinational commonwealth to the transformation of the Anglo-American relationship into an Atlantic Union, if not even into a world state. In the beginning, British intellectuals stressed the racial factor that kept the British diaspora together; then institutional commonalities and shared values became predominant. The outbreak of a new war, a technological disruption, or a shift in the global order was enough to change priorities, produce new threats, create illusions about what was achievable, and reframe the debate about the future of the English-speaking people in a new fashion. Throughout this long intellectual journey, the messianic impulse that animated the initial proponents of an organized Anglo-Saxon polity in opposition to rising "evil" powers has largely vanished (although in fact the expression "axis of evil", to identify the enemies of the West, still has a place in American foreign-policy jargon). What has survived is Britain's sense of dissatisfaction with playing a marginal role in an increasingly less conquerable world.

The ambitiousness of these proposals grew with the shrinking of empire. The British colonies wanted to enjoy more autonomy, so why not create an Imperial Federation? The United States had replaced the United Kingdom as global hegemon, so why not turn the Anglo-American partnership into an Atlantic Union?[9] The whole empire had collapsed, so why not establish a world government?[10] Not surprisingly, none of these proposals has ever come to anything. With the benefit of hindsight, all of them can be interpreted as ways to cure a nostalgic malaise created by the traumatic implosion of empire. Each territorial loss created a moment of grief that inspired creative institutional proposals to offset its negative spillovers on Britain's influence and leave it unchanged—if not in form, at least in substance. A colony could become independent, but its links with Britain had to be preserved. In this sense, all the proposed institutional arrangements were not only utopian (as they betrayed no form of political pragmatism), but also intrinsically nostalgic (as they were motivated by Britain's unwillingness to accept the hard fact of a diminished influence). Probably, this lack of pragmatism and nostalgia went hand in hand: as discussed in previous chapters, nostalgia tends to oversimplify reality, even if it involves a longing for a relatively close past.

To some extent, the Brexit referendum and the confusion surrounding the future of Great Britain outside the European Union can be interpreted as the continuation, and probably the culmination, of this long-standing debate. If joining the European Community in 1973 was partly designed to find a new global role after the loss of empire, then Brexit resurrects that dilemma.[11] Hardcore Brexiteers anchor their expectations for a revival of their bygone glories to the emergence of a new type of Anglosphere, whose feasibility is discussed in Chapter Six, strictly linked to the United States and with Britain in a central position.[12]

Anglo Nostalgia can be seen as the by-product of this continuous soul-searching process caused by the gradual loss of Britain's privileged imperial status. Two factors have facilitated these post-imperial fantasies up until Brexit. First, the decolonization process was, in many cases, peaceful and amicable. This made it easier to preserve the economic, and sometimes military, relationships in the interest of both the former Mother Country and the ex-colony. Since the beginning of the First Industrial Revolution, technological progress has inspired new ways of reconfiguring the British Empire. When the British Empire still existed, new means of communication and transport induced British intellectuals to advocate for a closer institutional integration between Britain and the other Anglo-Saxon countries, that was less coercive in nature but equally capable of benefiting Britain through continuous inflows of goods, people, and ideas. Nowadays, the promoters of the Anglosphere point to the internet and digital technologies as instrumental to the elimination of geographical barriers and the facilitation of integration among Anglo-Saxon countries.

Second, as highlighted by Hannah Arendt among others, British imperial expansion was more enlightened and far-seeing than, for instance, the French equivalent. France tried to extend its national boundaries through a process of full political and cultural assimilation, building an empire in the old Roman sense.[13] It imposed the use of the French language, the adoption of its own laws, and the influence of the metropolitan culture of Paris upon the colonized people, who were treated as both brothers and subjects at the same time: brothers because the political body of the nation developed into an imperial structure that gave colonies representation in the National Assembly, transforming a nation of 40 million into a global entity with over 100 million citizens; subjects because the ultimate purpose of overseas possessions was to serve the French nation and follow its lead. The British, instead, adhered more to the Greek-based model of colonization. The dispersion of the British diaspora did not expand, but transplanted Britain's political structure, so that the countries assimilated remained closely tied to the motherland, keeping the gates of their domestic markets open to imperial commerce. When a French colony became independent, it rejected French identity altogether; British colonies, instead, remained intrinsically (and happily) British, even after independence.

Looking at the intellectual evolution of this enduring debate, while drawing parallels between past and present, will shed light on today's nostalgic fantasies. This dispute contains all the concepts at the heart of Brexit, in particular the idea of British exceptionalism and the presumption that Britain should be the one to lead, regardless of the way in which the surrounding world is changing. It shows how interest in the establishment of a transcontinental English-speaking polity has always been a British concern, promoted in its own interest, while its Anglo-Saxon cousins never cared too much about it. Finally, it concludes that institutional plans anchored to nostalgic dreams, but de-anchored from practical politics, are likely to remain exercises in cultural and political science fiction. In other words, it feels that a strong sense of nostalgia for the good old days has been present in the British debate for more than a century, and has reached a tipping point with Brexit. But the final outcome is unlikely to be too dissimilar.

Greater Britain vs. Little England

The terms Greater Britain and Little England, which are commonly used to distinguish outward-looking from inward-looking visions for a post-Brexit future, are both intrinsically nostalgic. In the second half of the nineteenth century they were used to identify two different approaches to deal with a crumbling empire. Little Englanders, who primarily belonged to a wing of the Liberal Party typified by William Gladstone and never liked to be known as such, viewed the British colonies as economically burdensome and advocated the granting of self-government as quickly as possible. They favoured nationalism over imperialism, as ventures abroad distracted from the consolidation of power and the economy at home.[14] The idea of Greater Britain—a union between the United Kingdom and its colonies—stimulated the imagination of those who wanted to provide new lifeblood to a declining empire by re-configuring a national consciousness that was losing confidence in British superiority. The geographer Halford Mackinder argued: "We must grow used to the thought that the Empire is no longer based on a Mother Country and her Colonies. ... The new view, acceptable to all the Britons, is that the Empire rests on a group of allied nations."[15]

Just like today's hardcore Brexiteers, Greater Britain proponents did not speak with one voice, but were louder than the Little Englanders. They believed that the British diaspora formed an organic unity. It was a single, transcontinental political community that could act as the guarantor of British supremacy, promoter of democratic principles, and custodian of global stability. As John Robert Seeley, the Regius Professor of History at Cambridge, argued in those years: "If Greater Britain in the full sense of the phrase really existed, Canada and Australia would be to us as Kent and Cornwall."[16] By merging the different national components of the empire into a single polity, Britain would set in motion a process of systematic emigration from the United Kingdom to the Dominions, thus reducing domestic demographic pressures, neutralizing growing democratic requests, and exporting patriots who would be eager to defend the Union from any external threat.[17]

In the second half of the nineteenth century the case for reforming and reinventing the empire was strong. The whole imperial architecture was crumbling under the pressure of both domestic and foreign forces. Abroad, foreign powers threatened Britain's hegemony from different fronts. The geographical vastness of the imperial possessions made their management and control difficult in an age where other colonial powers scrambled for land. The Second Industrial Revolution, based on steel and electricity, had turned Germany and the United States into new global powerhouses, and cross-continental railways boosted the influence of land powers such as Russia vis-à-vis naval ones such as Great Britain—particularly in vast India. The blatant hostility between Britain and Germany made Germany appear to be the biggest rival. In *The Battle of Dorking*, published in 1871, the novelist George Tomkyns Chesney prophesied a German invasion and a British defeat. At that time, the United States was also perceived as an important threat.[18] In his annual address to Congress in 1823, President James Monroe had already declared the exclusive dominion of the United States over the Americas and the Western Hemisphere in order to rebuff the colonial ambitions of European powers. It was in these decades that the idea of Manifest Destiny—the inevitability of American primacy—came to light.[19]

Domestically, the empire was too vast for either orderly internal administration or effective external defence. At home, the rapid industrialization process was leaving behind social tensions, discontent, misery, and poverty. Working-class movements such as Chartism, which advocated broad electoral reform, threatened internal stability. The political revolutions of 1848, after having shaken Europe, trickled over across the Channel, and their influence was felt particularly in Ireland, where it fed into the independence campaign. From 1870 onwards, the Ireland Home Rule movement became a thorn in the side of the British government.

By 1860, with very few exceptions, all colonies in North America, Australasia, and South Africa had achieved the status of responsible government. This arrangement implied discretion about domestic affairs and limited political representation, but subjugation to foreign policy set in Westminster. In the meantime, the British North America Act of 1867 united Nova Scotia, New Brunswick, Québec, and Ontario into the Canadian Confederation, which obtained its own constitution and was granted the status of Dominion—a step closer to independence than responsible government. Later, between 1870 and 1873, Manitoba, British Columbia, and Prince Edward Island were added, laying down the foundation for a confederation that stretched from the Pacific to the Atlantic.[20] Australia, New Zealand, and other colonies also demanded the privilege of Dominion—which would eventually be conceded at the Imperial Conference of 1907. By the end of the nineteenth century only a few colonies such as India, the West Indies, and Fiji were still under full British control.

As anticipated, technological progress lent a helping hand in rethinking the entire imperial architecture. For centuries, the almost 6,000 kilometres separating Washington from London posed an insurmount-able obstacle to the emergence of an Anglo-Saxon federation, making the daily management of any interstate institution unfeasible. But then the Industrial Revolution revolutionized geography, blurred physical boundaries, and turned utopian ambitions into realistic political plans. New technologies—many of which were carefully selected, developed, and promoted by colonial officials for imperial rule—reduced the bar-riers to British control of overseas possessions, making it possible "for a nation to have oceans roll between its provinces".[21] The application of the steam engine to railways and maritime transportation allowed for progressively faster travel by land and sea, to such a point that on the eve of the First World War the price of wheat was almost the same in the United States and Great Britain.[22] The discovery of quinine allowed malaria to be treated and reduced the barrier to imperialism generated by endemic tropical diseases, while the telegraph saved British rule in the 1857 Indian Mutiny by facilitating coordination between colonial bureaucracies.[23] As the historian John Robert Seeley argued in 1883: "Science has given to the political organism a new circulation, which is steam, and a new nervous system, which is electricity."[24]

Similarly, the contemporary impetus for the establishment or strengthening of the Anglosphere came from both external and tech-nological forces, and well before the Brexit referendum. The lifting of the Iron Curtain ushered in a series of technological and political trans-formations that unexpectedly opened a window of opportunity for those utopians who dreamed of an English-speaking union. The fall of the Berlin Wall in 1989 seemed to confirm the superiority of the Anglo-Saxon principles of democracy and freedom, whereas the adop-tion of the euro fuelled (or simply confirmed) fears among British Eurosceptics that the European project was going too far in the direc-tion of an "ever closer" Union.

In addition, within the rest of the Anglosphere, the wind seemed to be blowing in favour of new ties among the English-speaking people. Australian Prime Minister John Howard, after declaring that he refused to put "Australia in any sphere—Anglo or otherwise" and that his coun-try did not have to choose "between its history and geography", clearly worked hard to reinforce ties with the Anglo-Saxon world, particularly with the United States.[25] In Canada, Stephen Harper stated that "the 'little island' and the 'Great Dominion' will be eternally bonded by language, culture, economics and values". Harper was defined as "the most pro-British and pro-American leader in the world". But the most surprising declaration of interest in the Anglosphere came from India. In 2005 the Indian Prime Minister, Manmohan Singh, seemed to engage with the concept, when stating during the acceptance of an honorary doctorate that "if there is one phenomenon on which the sun cannot set, it is the world of the English-speaking peoples, in which the people of Indian origin are the single largest component".[26]

In the meantime, the world was becoming apparently flat (three decades later we can safely say apparently), not only as a result of an accelerated globalization process, but of technological progress as well. The never-ending revolution in transportation and communication had completely annihilated the tyranny of distance in ways that were unimaginable even to an imperial techno-optimist such as Seeley. And the Internet Revolution marked the beginning of a new growth model that was less centred on the production of tangible goods and more on the creation of intangible services, whose shipping across the world would happen with a click. The gradual, but rapid, removal of obstacles imposed by geography made the impossible possible. Bringing together geographically distant countries that were united by the same legal, political, linguistic, and cultural traditions was no longer a mirage. Technology seemed to trump history and geography, reducing the importance of size and place. The moment was propitious for reimagining a common future for the Anglosphere as an alternative to European Union membership.

The final boost came with the overlapping existential crises that plagued the European Union in general and the Eurozone in particular after the outbreak of the Great Recession. From the point of view of the Eurosceptics, the European project did not deliver, and was seen as an obstacle along a brighter, different path. As James Bennett, a leading Anglosphere ideologue, argued: "In the United Kingdom, Euroscepticism is painted as backward-looking and nostalgic; but it's actually very forward-looking. It's about making new links which have more to do with culture and ways of doing things than geographical closeness."[27]

Despite these historical similarities, it is important to highlight a key difference. In the Victorian era the debate about Greater Britain arose from necessity. Rising powers and more assertive colonies were putting at risk the very existence of the empire. In the 1990s and thereafter, Anglosphere fantasies grew out of opportunity. The global order was changing in such a favourable way that it was possible to brush up old dreams of glory. What is striking is the persistence of nostalgia for a glorious past and the idea that technology dissolves geography. In reality, geography still matters a lot. Politically, the national interest of any medium-sized country is primarily defined by its immediate regional surroundings—even if a nostalgic United Kingdom still conceives of itself as a global power. Economically, many studies show that trade between two countries that are not adjacent to each other is half what it could be if they were.[28] Despite what Brexiteers believe, tribal links between Anglo-Saxons can only partially mitigate the constraints of geographical distance.

Utopian proposals

What the debate about Greater Britain and the Anglosphere have in common is the utopianism of their proposals. An unwillingness to accept that the past has passed alters the perception of reality. The Victorians did not realize that the more independent colonies wanted to retain a degree of freedom from Britain that was substantial and not just formal. Equally, the first Anglosphere enthusiasts heavily discounted different national interests among its potential members, and underestimated the difficulty of building up a new trade paradigm for the United Kingdom after Brexit. Utopianism is never inconsequential. More than a century ago, the lack of a realistic alternative to the empire contributed to its gradual dissolution. Now, Brexit is pushing Britain out of the European Union without having a credible alternative in the Anglo-Saxon world.

Within Queen Victoria's ruling and cultural elite there were conflicting views about Greater Britain's institutional structure, and thus about the directions that should be undertaken in the future. Two camps fiercely challenged one another. At one extreme of the political spectrum, the anti-federalists did not perceive the democratization process that was taking place in the settlement colonies as a threat to Britain's authority. In their view, socio-political ties between the Anglo-

Saxon peoples were strong enough to make a formal political structure unnecessary, if not counterproductive. The political enfranchisement of the Dominions allowed the United Kingdom to maintain control over its vast possessions in a less intrusive, but probably more effective way. The most extremist among the anti-federalists were the Little Englanders, who wanted the United Kingdom to simply abandon its imperialistic ambitions and focus on domestic issues. The anti-federalist group could count in its ranks personalities of the calibre of historians Edward Augustus Freeman and Goldwin Smith, the philosopher Herbert Spencer, the jurist Albert Venn Dicey, and statesmen such as Robert Lowe, John Morley, and William Ewart Gladstone.

The most brilliant intellectual contributions from the moderate anti-federalist front came from Sir Charles Dilke, who was a radical politician and Liberal Party member. In 1868 he published *Greater Britain*, an influential travelogue of his voyages across "the English-speaking countries", as the subtitle reads.[29] He placed the races he met on a scale of civilization, arguing that the "gradual extinction of the inferior races is not only a law of nature, but a blessing to mankind". According to Dilke, granting independence to white settler colonies was a historical inevitability. In his view, global colonial unity could rest on the existing Anglo-Saxon bonds without the need to build a more complex constitutional architecture: what "raises us above the provincialism of citizenship of little England", he wrote, "is our citizenship of the greater 'Saxondom', which includes all that is best and wisest in the world".[30] Greater Britain, according to Dilke, would bring freedom across the English-speaking lands, while taming the ambitions of the new Great Powers.[31] Others, who elaborated the idea of common citizenship, or isopolity, echoed his thinking: "reciprocal" citizenship among English-speaking people was enough to secure permanent unity, without the need for federal structures. One can find here the seeds of a recurrent British allergy to federal unions, with all its weight in Euroscepticism.

At the other extreme end of the spectrum, federalists feared that the political empowerment of the Dominions would lead to their full independence and eventually to the complete dismantling of the empire. The North American federal experience, both in the United States and in Canada, provided the institutional blueprint for striking a balance between the autonomist ambitions of local governments and the need to create the critical mass necessary to compete with rising global powers. Granting more independence to the most developed colonies and federating them to Britain was seen as a way to revamp the fortunes of the British Empire. Britain would continue to interfere, albeit with more discretion, in the domestic affairs of its possessions, whereas the Dominions would have a say in the management of the empire. Political integration would lead to economic self-sufficiency and imperial interdependence, especially through the imposition of tariffs on products coming from outside the imperial boundaries. British industrial goods would be exchanged for colonial foodstuffs and raw materials.

But this virtuous circle would have not started spontaneously. It was necessary to set up an appropriate institutional architecture, in order to facilitate cooperation and coordination of the different members of the federation. And on this issue the federalist front was far from being united, given the existence of three competing options: an "extra-parliamentary" federation; a "parliamentary federation"; and "supra-parliamentary federalism".[32] The first proposal was the least intrusive, with the setting up of joint committees providing non-binding advice on imperial affairs. Supporters of the second plan suggested the creation of an Anglo-Saxon Switzerland, with an imperial parliament operating above and beyond the individual political assemblies of the British Empire, including Westminster. The third option implied the construction of a globe-spanning state, with supranational institutions.

These utopian projects stimulated the imagination of Tories, Liberals, and Radicals alike; progressives and reactionaries; free and fair traders. Joseph Chamberlain, Colonial Secretary between 1895 and 1903, and Cecil John Rhodes, Prime Minister of the Cape Colony between 1890 and 1896, were among its most prominent members. Both Rhodes and Chamberlain believed in the racial superiority of the Anglo-Saxons. The former hoped to make "the Anglo-Saxon race but one empire":[33] with the Rhodes Scholarship he hoped to create an imperialist equivalent of the Jesuit order.[34] The latter made several references to the "two transatlantic branches of the Anglo-Saxon race", referring to Great Britain and its North American offspring.[35] Their thinking was influenced by the doctrines of positivism and social Darwinism, which perceived race as part of a strict global hierarchy. Greater Britain was de facto an Anglo-Saxon political space, a racial polity, with the settlement colonies (even the United States) being an extension of the British nation. The concept of an "English race" rested on a combination of cultural markers—historical memories, language, shared values, habitus—circumscribed by "whiteness".[36] Accordingly, India, regarded by many as the cornerstone and "jewel in the crown" of British hegemony, was seen as too unmanageable to remain part of the empire in the long run. But the leading figure of the federalist movement was Professor Seeley, who, in *Expansion of England*, argued:

> If the United States and Russia hold together for another half century, they will at the end of that time completely dwarf such old European States as France and Germany and depress them into a second class. They will do the same to England, if at the end of that time England still thinks herself as simply a European State.[37]

In 1884 the federalists founded their own organization, the Imperial Federation League, whose mission was to "secure the permanent unity of the empire". It numbered more than a hundred MPs in its ranks, with future Prime Minister Lord Rosebery as its long-serving president.[38] Its headquarters were in central London, but it had branches in most white settler colonies such as Canada, Australia, New Zealand, Barbados, and British Guyana. The League advocated for an Anglo-Saxon federation with a central representative authority to manage foreign policy and military affairs and enforce colonial authority over those possessions, such as India and non-white-dominated countries, which were not regarded as constituent parts of the Anglosphere.[39] The London branch of the League disseminated its ideas and influenced the political debate by publishing its own journal, *Imperial Federation*; by managing its educational organization, the Imperial Institute (today's Commonwealth Institute); and by creating a network of private and official contacts between the core and the periphery of the empire through its different branches.

Moving the clock ahead, the intellectual debate about the Anglosphere that started about thirty years ago has certainly been less fervent than the one on Greater Britain we have just briefly recalled—and its supporters certainly lacked an organization like the Imperial Federation League to propagate their ideas. The debate on the Anglosphere opened at the end of last century, and was restricted to a minority of intellectuals and politicians, primarily from the Tories' liberal wing and with a propensity for high-flying speculations. They rejected the quasi-racist elements of earlier discussions about the establishment of an Anglo-Saxon community, while focusing on shared institutional and cultural factors. Actually, the multicultural composition of most of the English-speaking world was praised as an element of strength, which made it possible to include non-white Commonwealth nations. The Anglosphere turned out to be a sort of pathfinder for humanity. What is striking is that the two camps that opposed one another over the best institutional arrangement for the Anglosphere have largely mirrored the two factions—the federalists vs. the antifederalists—of the Greater Britain debate.

In 1999, Paul Johnson and Robert Conquest, two influential figures within the Tory Eurosceptic wing, put forward the most utopian projects. The former envisaged Britain, Canada, Australia, and New Zealand becoming formal member states of the United States and taking up a suitable number of House and Senate seats.[40] Conquest suggested the creation of an "Association of the United States, the United Kingdom, Canada, Australia and New Zealand—as well as, it is to be hoped, Ireland and the peoples of the Caribbean and the Pacific Ocean".[41] The Association would have to be more than an alliance, but less than a union. A few years later, Conquest carefully detailed how the Association should be structured, going beyond what even the most ambitious imperial federalist would have dared envisage.[42] To start with, the American President would be the Association's president while the Queen would become the Queen of the Association.

On the opposite side, American businessman and conservative thinker James Bennett made the most coherent and convincing case for an institutionally underdeveloped Anglosphere. He envisaged the Anglosphere as a network civilization of "nations sharing language, customs, history, legal systems, religions, and other significant values—most specifically trust characteristics".[43] Over time, however, this network would develop various cooperative institutions in areas such as trade and defence. The emphasis was on a variable geometry of different nations opting in and out of cooperative arrangements, depending on their interests. The concept of variable geometry also allowed him to propose a detailed vision of membership. The Anglosphere would be structured as a series of concentric spheres, with the United States and Britain at the core, surrounded by English-speaking Canada, Ireland, Australia, New Zealand, and the English-speaking Caribbean.[44] The "intermediate" sphere would include states where English is one of several official languages, but where primary connections to the outside world are in English. This comprises English speakers in South Africa, Zimbabwe, the non-Islamic former British colonies in Africa, the South Pacific, and parts of Asia. Finally, the outer sphere would comprise English-using states of other civilizations, and might include India, Pakistan, the Arab states formerly under British control, and Britain's former Islamic colonies.

Proposals of this kind, no matter how utopian or simplistic, prepared the ground for the Brexit debate as they provided an alternative setting—outside Europe—for British identity. When leaving the European Union became a concrete prospect, many Anglosphere enthusiasts revised their ambitions, proposing slightly more realistic plans. The Conservative Daniel Hannan, for instance, called for a free-trade agreement between Australia, New Zealand, Canada, the United States, the United Kingdom, Singapore, and Hong Kong. The deal should be based on the principle of mutual recognition and not on common standards—the way trade within the European Union works.[45] Others, such as Bennett himself, the historian Andrew Roberts, and the economist Andrew Lilico, argued in favour of a CANZUK trade deal (Canada, Australia, New Zealand, and the United Kingdom).[46] According to Bennett, these four countries should move beyond free trade to include the free movement of people, a mutual defence guarantee, and combined military capabilities. In addition, he envisaged a confederal entity in charge of investments in common infrastructures and development projects. This new Commonwealth Union, under the aegis of the British monarch, would not replace the existing Commonwealth of Nations.[47] Roberts has argued that CANZUK "would be easily the largest country on the planet, have a combined population of 129 million, the third biggest economy and the third biggest defence budget".[48]

Divided fronts

Brexiteers and their Victorian forebears share an inability to form a common front and frame a coherent plan to give shape to an Anglo-

Saxon polity. Confusion starts with the choice of name for this ideal-ized political community. Leavers speak of Britannia, the Anglosphere, Global Britain, Greater Britain, or Empire 2.0 (a term rarely used but widely derided). Anglosphere probably appeals to all sides. In the eigh-teenth century, newspapers and pamphlets popularized terms such as United States of England, Oceana, Federal Britain, and Greater Britain. Eventually, there was some sort of convergence on Greater Britain, as it conveyed the idea that white-settler colonies were an overseas exten-sion of England. What follows is the membership problem: who should belong to the community? A century ago some intellectuals imagined a political community that spanned the whole empire, India included. Others preferred to invest efforts and energies in a political project that would have involved only the settlement colonies (Canada, Australia, South Africa, and New Zealand), whose populations, eco-nomic power, and strategic importance were rapidly growing. A third group hoped to involve the United States, with its potential as a Great Power. Today, the Anglosphere means different things to different people. Some, as we just saw, would restrict it to the CANZUK, others would include the United States, and a few also look with interest to Singapore, India, and Ireland.[49]

The very name Imperial Federation League was symptomatic of the confusion that characterized the debate. Edward Freeman stated that the "phrase Imperial Federation is a contradiction in terms. What is imperial cannot be federal and what is federal cannot be imperial."[50] A polity defined by domination could not be governed simultaneously by a system of devolved legislative powers and equal representation. The organization was ideologically too divided to have a lasting political impact. Some wanted to establish a military alliance, others aimed for a free-trade area, while the most ambitious pushed for a genuine politi-cal union. These heterogeneous opinions prevented the League from expressing a well-defined line of action. In addition, the national inter-ests of its potential member states did not coincide. Colonial adminis-trators were uninterested in tightening their relationship with Britain at a time when they were trying to carve out a more independent role for themselves. These inconsistencies became apparent at the First Colonial Conference in 1887: on that occasion, Australian and Canadian representatives voted against the creation of a customs and military imperial union.[51]

The greatest failure of the Imperial Federation League came in 1893, when it submitted a federal plan to the government led by the Liberal Gladstone. He ridiculed the proposal, labelling it "chimerical if not a little short of nonsensical".[52] The document suggested the introduction of common citizenship, the development of a common foreign policy and a common defence, a supreme judicial tribunal, and the establishment of a representative assembly. The most important point was probably the introduction of a Council of the Empire with direct representation for Britain, Canada, Australia, and South Africa, and with indirect representation for India and the Crown Colonies. Gladstone rejected both the plan and the suggestion of organizing an ad hoc imperial conference to discuss it. As a consequence, the League collapsed almost immediately.

Today's Brexiteers run similar risks: on applying a reality check (see Chapter Six), the rise of an Anglosphere as the culmination of Brexit sounds quite implausible. Furthermore, the special relationship with the United States (see Chapter Seven) is indeed now becoming not so special. However, all these debates—past and current—on an Anglo-Saxon community clearly define a dividing line between Britain and continental Europe. The Anglosphere is very likely a non-starter as an alternative to the European Union. And yet, the very idea of a different regional cooperation scheme has deepened Britain's identity crisis in Europe. Striking similarities do exist between the discussion on the possible evolution of the Anglosphere (institutions, membership, variable geometries, opt-outs, and so on) and recurrent debates about the future of the European Union. Both, after all, are conceived as regional cooperation or integration schemes. For Leavers, the two are mutually exclusive projects, even if history has proved the opposite. The Anglo-Saxon identity of the United Kingdom cannot co-exist, in their view, with European Union membership.

Not in everyone's interest

While the idea of the Anglosphere has thus been used by hardcore Brexiteers as leverage to propose a vision for Britain's future outside the European Union, the other potential members of the Anglo-Saxon tribe seem to shy away from the project. Canada is torn between its

Anglo and French identities. New Zealand and Australia are primarily Asian nations, with an Anglo-Saxon pedigree. And the United States is too powerful to tie itself to such a regional grouping in the name of a shared historical background. The support that the idea of the Anglosphere enjoyed at the dawn of the twenty-first century was partly due to the fact that at the time a Brexit scenario was unthinkable: musing about a project like the Anglosphere was, for its potential members, inconsequential. In 2016, however, the challenge was much bigger for the European Union as a whole. No leader of the Anglosphere openly campaigned for Brexit. They all tried to dissuade British voters from withdrawing from the European Union. The then American President Barack Obama visited the United Kingdom just a few weeks before the referendum, warning that, should there be a Brexit, Britain would go to the "back of the queue" in free-trade negotiations.[53] Other putative leaders of the Anglosphere, from Canada's Prime Minister Justin Trudeau to New Zealand's John Key and Australia's Malcolm Turnbull, voiced similar positions. Stephen Harper himself campaigned for Britain to remain. Tribal dreams were not enough to obfuscate the costs accruing from the disintegration of the West.

Turning back to history, in the late eighteenth century the outright implosion of the empire would have represented a political and economic debacle for Britain, but its colonies would have gained independence and room for action. British politicians, journalists, and intellectuals tried to emphasize the racial and institutional connections between the United Kingdom and the settler colonies to preserve part of the dissolving imperial status. At the Second and Third Imperial Conferences, held respectively in 1892 and in 1897, Colonial Secretary Chamberlain tried to persuade delegates coming from the most disparate parts of the empire to take steps towards an imperial federation: but settlement colonies, Australia and Canada in particular, strongly opposed any federal arrangement, starting with taxation.[54]

What is interesting is both the persistence over time of British imperial nostalgia and the predictable unwillingness of former colonies to fall prey to it. Despite the debacle of the Victorian federalists, in 1909 members of Milner's Kindergarten[55] organized the so-called Round Table, whose mission was to facilitate the transition from British leadership of the empire to an equal partnership among its members.[56] The

99

organization was the de facto heir of the Imperial Federation League and believed that a supranational entity was necessary to preserve and perpetuate British power encompassing the United Kingdom and all its Dominions. It opened branches in London, Canada, the Union of South Africa, Australia, New Zealand, and Newfoundland. The Round Table had to be seen as a truly cooperative enterprise, and its mission did not have to be perceived as a renewed colonizing attempt by the British. In this sense, they had learned from the mistakes of their predecessors, but it was not enough to realize their plan.

The movement's propaganda tool was the journal *Round Table*, established in 1910 to connect its national branches by publishing contributions provided by influential academics and politicians from both the United Kingdom and the Dominions.[57] But the Round Table was founded with a view to action more than just ideas. Most of the Dominions' Round Tablers believed that it would be impossible to survive as independent nations at a time when Great Power competition was intensifying.[58] For its part, the United Kingdom could no longer bear alone the cost of naval rearmament vis-à-vis Germany. For the Tablers, it would have been possible to contemplate sharing part of the British military burden in exchange for full self-government for the Dominions.[59] But it was too late: despite the military unity displayed in the First World War, the Dominions pushed to free themselves from Britain. It fell to Arthur James Balfour—British Foreign Secretary in the aftermath of the war—to manage the conflicting demands of imperial unity and colonial autonomy. Balfour's guiding policy was that of "absolute equality" between Britain and its Dominions within the empire.

The idea was ventilated first by the Australian historian Duncan Hall in an influential book, *British Commonwealth of Nations*,[60] in which the author envisioned the empire as a "free cooperating society of nations".[61] Balfour took up this principle at the 1926 British Imperial Conference: the conference's official report declared that the "British empire *was* not founded upon negations" and that "every self-governing member of the Empire *was* the master of its destiny".[62] The Balfour Declaration paved the way for the establishment of the British Commonwealth of Nations. It did not, however, solve all the delicate constitutional problems related to the apparent contradiction between the formal autonomy of the Dominions, the indivisibility of the empire, and their common allegiance to the British Crown. Only the approval of the Statute of Westminster, in 1931, solved the conundrum. The Dominions were granted legislative autonomy, and thus, full national sovereignty, but were also compelled to consult one another on matters related to the monarchy.

In the meantime, the role of the United States within any English-speaking union had been evolving dramatically. In the Victorian era, racial but not necessarily racist arguments played a fundamental role in bringing Britain and America, who were "almost destined to be enemies", back together. The Venezuelan crises that took place at the end of the nineteenth century were the catalyst for a rapprochement: Britain acknowledged that its American cousins played an equally powerful role at a global level, and that of a hegemon in the Americas.[63] In Britain, some started to talk about a "race alliance" between the two cousins as the best response to increasingly assertive competitors such as Russia, Japan, Spain, and Germany.[64] Racial identity was key to clearly drawing a line between civilizations that controlled vast swathes of the globe, and to distinguishing friends from enemies. At his Scottish castle, Skibo, the American industrialist Andrew Carnegie flew a flag with the Union Jack on one side and the Stars and Stripes on the other, bearing testament to the unity of the Anglo-Saxons.[65] He believed that if the two nations were to merge, the world would enjoy peace, order, and justice.[66]

After two World Wars, however, the United Kingdom slowly turned into the junior partner of a vastly more resourceful America. Tory Party leader Harold Macmillan argued that after 1945 the English were left as the "Greeks in this American empire". Macmillan's words betrayed a patronizing attitude, but underscored the acceptance that Britain had finally lost its previous standing. With a large dose of arrogance, he added: "You will find the Americans much like the Greeks found the Romans: great, big, vulgar, bustling people, more vigorous than we are and also idler, with more unspoiled virtues but also more corrupt."[67] When it became clear, during the Cold War, that from America's standpoint any specific English-speaking link was largely diluted in the broader Western security arm of NATO, Britain reluctantly embraced the European project.

Now that Brexit has offered the United Kingdom a new opportunity to rethink its global status, the link to America represents a mixed blessing. From the British perspective, the United States is an indispensable ally for thriving in a post-Brexit world. All the proposals of the last thirty years about an Anglosphere include it as a pillar of any such regional grouping. At the same time, such an asymmetric relationship underlines Britain's relative decline.

Stuck in the West

If one takes the theory of *translatio imperii* seriously, then at some point hegemonic power should return to the East—which is in fact happening, in relative terms. But, in its Western-centric variant, hegemonic power is actually expected to remain stuck at the extreme frontier of the West—that is, the United States. Already in the eighteenth century the American revolutionaries, who claimed to be the legitimate heirs of the Greek and Roman tradition, believed that they were about to establish the ultimate empire. By opportunistically stressing shared historical and cultural roots, as Churchill did, the British can still take pride in it and see it as the continuation of the same civilizational mission. Andrew Roberts has even argued that the emergence of an Anglosphere would create such a truly unified civilization that in the future, nobody would bother to make a distinction between the British-Empire-led and the American-Republic-led eras.[68]

From a long-term historical perspective, it is clear that nostalgia for a dissolving, and now dissolved, empire has been a persistent element in the debate about the establishment of an English-speaking union and about Britain's identity in general. For more than a century the British political elite has invested time and energy in creatively trying to reverse the irreversible and in preserving an evaporating global status. From the point of view of Brexit's ideologues, a divorce from Brussels would allow the United Kingdom to regain its "natural" geopolitical position in the Anglo-Saxon sphere. In a sense, the Anglosphere and the European Union could be described as two competing imperial visions—the first dominated by Anglo-Saxon powers, the second by continental ones, Germany in particular. What hardcore Brexiteers seem to ignore is that neither the United States, nor other former British colonies, are particularly eager to join an "Anglosphere".

What has been clear since the Victorian era is that nostalgic dreams hardly ever lead to establishing common fronts, as each person (or each nation) tends to see the past and the future through their (its) own biased eyes. Oftentimes, the lack of objectivity leads to proposals that are simply divorced from reality. In a way, the perseverance of nostalgic attitudes for lost British hegemony has prevented the United Kingdom from playing an effective role in the European Union. The self-perception of British exceptionalism, linked to its imperial legacy, has always worked against the United Kingdom's full engagement in the European project, together with a strong aversion to supranational integration. Euroscepticism, which was a rallying cry of the Labour Party in the 1960s, and then became primarily a Conservative prerogative, has always been tinged with a degree of imperial nostalgia.[69] But it reached its peak after the outbreak of the Great Recession, thanks to the overlapping existential crises of the European Union. For the ideologues of the Anglosphere, the moment could have not been more propitious; they turned a traditional form of nationalism into a nostalgic one. Brexit and the European malaise ended up reinforcing each other.

The European dimension is one of the major differences in the current debate, compared to what the Victorians used to discuss 150 years ago. At that time the fear was loss of influence, not domination by others. Besides this crucial change of attitude, today's dispute about the future of the United Kingdom within the Anglo-Saxon polity seems to be déjà vu.

PART TWO

REALITY CHECK

5

THE FOREIGN POLICY OF NOSTALGIA

"We should not think of our leaving the EU as marking an ending, as much as a new beginning for the United Kingdom and our relationship with our European allies."

Prime Minister Theresa May

Nostalgia freezes the world at a specific point in time, deluding its victims that simple restorative acts are enough to reset the clock at a predetermined moment in history. In the immediate aftermath of the June 2016 referendum, hardcore Brexiteers seemed to believe that the return of the blue passport, the resurrection of the royal yacht *Britannia*, or the expansion of grammar schools would be sufficient to show the world that Britain was back on the world stage.[1] Roughly half of the British population even fantasized about the replacement of the metric system with the old imperial measurements.[2] With a biased interpretation of the relationship between the United Kingdom and the continent through the centuries, Leavers misled their fellow citizens by claiming that a divorce from Brussels, while allowing the country to regain full control of its national sovereignty, would restore part of its lost splendour. They played on Britain's past to inflate its true power and influence. Little does it matter that Britain no longer rules the waves, that a former colony such as India aspires to become a Great Power, that continental Europe is no longer a military battlefield.

Nostalgic arguments distort reality, turning a politically hazardous decision—largely produced by poisonous fights within the Conservative camp—into a historically brave move. During a speech in February 2018 the leading Brexiteer Boris Johnson, at the time Secretary of State for Foreign and Commonwealth Affairs, stated: "Brexit need not be nationalist, but can be internationalist; not an economic threat, but a considerable opportunity; not un-British, but a manifestation of this country's historic national genius."[3] From his perspective, Brexit was the by-product of Anglo-Saxon exceptionalism that linked past, present, and future:

> It is our collective job to ensure that when the history books come to be written, Brexit will be seen as just the latest way in which the British bucked the trend, took the initiative—and did something that responds to the real needs and opportunities that we face in the world today. ... Yes, it was the British people who saw that it was not good enough for Kings and princes to have absolute power and who began the tradition of parliamentary democracy in a model that is followed on every continent. It was also Britain that led the industrial revolution and destroyed slavery and the British people who had the wit to see through the bogus attractions of protectionism and who campaigned for free trade that has become the single biggest engine of prosperity and progress.[4]

However, when it comes to moving beyond symbolic gestures (such as the blue passport or the royal yacht) and grand statements (like Johnson's), the clash between the nostalgic narrative and political reality manifests itself immediately. Nostalgia alters any objective cost–benefit analysis, pushing the longing souls two or three generations back and two or three generations ahead. Brexiteers aspired to reconnect the country to its historical national strength, but they were probably aware that only their children or grandchildren would savour that kind of greatness. They disregarded the short-term cost necessary to perform the transition from the current system to the future one, while excessively emphasizing the long-term benefits of a risky bet. In the end, the supporters of a more independent Britain idealized the past as much as the immediate future, or at least treated it as a secondary concern to be tackled—well, some time in the future.

The politics of nostalgia worked its magic in the context of the Brexit referendum, where a single Yes or No vote was needed to make a difference, but it was hardly enough to manage the post-referendum environment, and it is certainly not a good compass for navigating the twenty-first century's international system. Brexiteers did not lay out a clear, practical, and pragmatic plan leading away from Brussels and towards their idealized temporal destination. They approached the Brexit vote by scapegoating the European Union for a perceived migratory inflow that would ultimately erode "Britishness" and by fetishizing the idea of a Global Britain, that even within the Conservative camp meant different things to different people. During a banquet speech at Mansion House, Boris Johnson argued:

> Global Britain is fundamentally in the interests of the British people because it is by being open to the world, and engaging with every country, that the British people will find the markets for their goods and services and ideas as we have done for centuries in that great free trade revolution that made this City [London] the capital of the world.[5]

This seemingly straightforward assertion is heir to a Thatcherite variant of conservatism that promoted freedom of circulation for capital, goods, and labour in a highly deregulated environment; Britain should become more open, more outward-looking, and more engaged with the world than ever before. But this ideal of Britishness was in conflict with the "social conservative" variant embodied by the May government—something reminiscent of the Little England vision.[6] These two approaches differed as to the ideal balance between domestic state interventionism and international free trade. Little Englanders were more focused on social reform, greater state intervention, and a drastic reduction in immigration flows. Brexit brought this underlying tension to the surface, as Britons expected not just more freedom, but also more protection—whatever that means in practice. In addition, it was unclear whether Global Britain was to reach out to core Anglosphere countries, emerging economies, or the world as a whole. In short, Global Britain was a good rallying cry that hid a plethora of inconsistencies in its policy implications and its true meaning for the Leave camp. Brexiteers represented the fusion of two different socioeconomic groups with different political agendas, but united by the same Anglo-nostalgic myths. This is how the Brexiteers acted: emotions first, rational calculus later.

All the contradictions generated by the politics of emotion came to light when, following the hangover from the referendum victory, the time came to define the details of withdrawal and to creatively redesign a new relationship with the European Union. Since June 2016, Brexiteers have flirted with a variety of proposals. They had no real clue where they were heading, with their options ranging from a "glorious Brexit", a "red-white-and-blue Brexit", a "hard Brexit" to a "soft Brexit", a "clean Brexit", a "jobs-first Brexit", and even the "no-deal Brexit". In July 2018, after over a year of negotiations, the European Union's chief negotiator Michel Barnier sorrowfully stated: "In the Brexit negotiations, there are still too many questions and too few answers. Time is short. We need to have quickly realistic and workable solutions."[7]

That objective was apparently achieved only four months later, in November 2018, with a withdrawal agreement described by Britain's Prime Minister as a "deal that works for the United Kingdom and the European Union".[8] In reality, the withdrawal agreement with Brussels was a hard sell in the United Kingdom, despite its obvious comparative advantage: preventing a disorderly no-deal exit. As largely anticipated, the Agreement was resoundingly defeated in Westminster on January 15, 2019. Two months before the expiration of Article 50, London was left with no working deal. At the time of writing, alternative scenarios are still possible, including a British request promoted by the House of Commons, to extend Article 50 beyond March 29, 2019.

Only the passage of time showed how a past, no matter how glorious, can hardly fit a modern reality. Facing the reality of a costly divorce that greatly differed from previous nostalgic ruminations, and confronted with a united European position, Theresa May embraced a softer Brexit, with its price attached: turning Britain, at least until the end of the transition period, into a rule taker vis-à-vis the European Union—which frankly looks like a loss of sovereignty, not a gain. The November withdrawal agreement envisaged a customs union with the EU as a transitional arrangement, linked to the so-called "backstop" foreseen by the Protocol for Northern Ireland. This proviso was seen by Brussels as a way to avoid a "hard" Irish border, with the likely collapse of the 1998 Good Friday Agreement. For hardcore Brexiteers, however—many of whom decided to leave the Cabinet, starting with Boris Johnson in July 2018—the spirit of Brexit had been lost. In their view, Britain was wasting an opportunity to go back out into the wider world, "to find friends, open markets, promote its [Britain's] culture and values".[9] This was only one of the many illusions, fallacies, and miscalculations caused by nostalgia that have prevented the United Kingdom, hugely divided internally, from carefully and seriously reflecting on a coherent post-Brexit foreign-policy strategy.

Dealing with Brussels

The Brexit referendum was a sort of cathartic moment, a perfect storm in which disparate forces aligned to produce a radical solution to an old problem: that of the British role "in" Europe—because, after all, the United Kingdom remains geographically (but not only) part of the European continent. This should actually be posed as an existential question: how can a post-Brexit Britain be part of Europe and preserve its uniqueness?

Nostalgia created enormous contradictions in the way Brexiteers tried to answer it. Bewitched by their own rhetoric about the lavish economic opportunities that the outside world could offer, they almost came to believe that Europe was superfluous for Britain. Yes, a trade agreement with the continent was necessary. But to fully take advantage of Brexit the United Kingdom had to rediscover the dynamism of Victorian explorers and look somewhere else, rekindling old friendships in the Commonwealth, rediscovering the special relationship with America, and intensifying links with Asian economies. When the empire still existed, Europe was primarily a source of political problems. Britain had to act as a counterweight, while cultivating its true wealth somewhere else. The truth, however, is that Europe is now more important to the United Kingdom than hard Brexiteers want to admit—not only for its direct economic, financial, and cultural links, but also for what they mean in the relationship with the United States and the other Anglosphere members more generally (see Chapters Six and Seven). During its European Union membership, Britain was "half in, half out", a full member of the single market that negotiated opt-outs from other key EU policies (starting with the Monetary Union and the Schengen area). After Brexit, it will probably end up being "partly out", but with a new variant of Britain's perceived exceptional position vis-à-vis the EU. Global Britain or not, there is no way it can be completely detached from Europe.[10]

Immediately after the Brexit referendum, the United Kingdom was ambiguous about the way it wanted to confront the European Union. Nostalgia called for being fully out, pragmatism meant remaining partially in: a non-member, yes, but with a special and unique relationship with the European Union, which was precisely what Brussels was not ready to grant, so as to avoid rewarding exit from the EU. The letter to the European Council that triggered Article 50 of the Lisbon Treaty on 28 March 2017, stated that the British government wanted to "agree a deep and special partnership between the United Kingdom and the European Union, taking in both economic and security co-operation".[11] Theresa May then reiterated on several occasions that Europe's security is Britain's security (if that is the case, then why Brexit?). In parallel, most of her speeches contained a reference to the cardinal principle of Brexit: to take back control "of borders, laws, and money".

No wonder it was hard to strike a balance between such conflicting goals: a deep and special partnership in which security is to all practical effects shared, on the one hand, and taking back control of just about all the attributes of national sovereignty, on the other. On 2 March 2018, Theresa May declared that the new agreement with the European Union

> must be consistent with the kind of country we want to be as we leave: a modern, open, outward-looking, tolerant, European democracy. A nation of pioneers, innovators, explorers and creators. A country that celebrates our history and diversity, confident of our place in the world; that meets its obligations to our near neighbours and far off friends, and is proud to stand up for its values.[12]

While anchoring itself to a proud past, the self-image of the United Kingdom that emerged had well-defined contours: modern, open, outward-looking, tolerant, confident, proud—and "European". From a psychological (or "psycho-political") perspective, such a flurry of adjectives might inadvertently suggest that Brexit has caused (or simply heightened) a sort of identity crisis in the United Kingdom. This recognition is relevant to any analysis of Britain's future. As May's speech laid out, the country "wants to be" all of those things, but the result is far from assured, and other countries or partners will have to provide a great deal of cooperation in this sense. The road is in fact a narrow one, as was openly admitted in the same speech in relation to economic matters: "In my speech in Florence, I set out why the existing models for economic partnership either do not deliver the ambition we need, or impose unsustainable constraints on our democracy." In short, the line separating success and failure is rather thin.

A few months into negotiations, and with the ticking of the clock becoming increasingly loud, reality started to gain the upper hand over nostalgia. Initial ambiguity was replaced by a stronger conviction that the "special partnership" (as defined by London) meant something closer to "partly in" than to "outright out". At times it even felt as if the British government was behaving like an applicant to the European Union: irresistibly attracted by the economic opportunities offered by the single market; eager to be "connected" to the club (albeit in some loose form); ready to find compromises, but not at all costs (since national sovereignty is not incompatible with European integration); well-intentioned, but worried by the technical complexity of Brussels' machinery.

Britain was unique as a member state, and now hoped to be a uniquely close non-member, as shown by the following statement from Theresa May: "As on security, what I am seeking is a relationship that goes beyond the transactional to one where we support each other's interests."[13] Therefore, unlike the politics of the Brexit campaign (emotional, rhetorically aggressive, and divisive), the post-Brexit image that Britain strove to project was calm, rational, and comforting. Even when it became clear that the divorce was indeed a complex, costly, and tricky process, the Prime Minister often emphasized the positive legacy accruing from the United Kingdom's disputed membership: "We have a unique starting point, where on day one we both have the same laws and rules. So rather than having to bring two different systems closer together, the task will be to manage the relationship once we are two separate legal systems."[14]

Of course, it was conceptually challenging to reconcile such a principle with the idea of "taking back control". "Our default", May said, "is that United Kingdom law may not necessarily be identical to European Union law, but it should achieve the same outcomes."[15] In other words, the post-EU legal system that the British government had in mind was, by and large, functionally equivalent to the one adopted by Brussels. How autonomy and sovereignty had to be articulated from a legal perspective was the conundrum that the agreement on exit was supposed to solve. A similar argument was made for regulations—a classical element of legal sovereignty: "We start from the place where our regulators already have deep and long-standing relationships. So the task is maintaining that trust; not building it in the first place."[16] Just as in everyday life, maintaining trust after a stressful divorce is not exactly a simple proposition. Yet it seemed to be the hope that inspired those in charge of taking Britain out of the European Union. It is a curious twist; after all, was it not a fundamental lack of trust in the European Union that had motivated Brexiteers in the first place?

Brussels naturally drew its own red lines. Since Brexit—the first exit ever from the EU—was seen as an existential risk for the European Union as such, Brussels displayed a clear unwillingness to reward the country for leaving the club. There was too much at stake in this precedent, which inevitably affected the trade-offs that the EU was ready to contemplate as it negotiated Britain's withdrawal. In particular, Brussels defended the integrity of the single market (free circulation of goods, services, people and capital) and refused Britain's proposals aimed at free movement of goods while curbing migration flows from other European members. More generally—as rightly observed by Charles Grant, among others—Brussels adopted the principle that no third country can have as close a relationship to the EU as a member state, thus rejecting the case for British exceptionalism.

This same stance was applied—mistakenly in our view (see below)—to cooperation with the UK on internal and external security. From the EU's standpoint, a principled reaction to Brexit was apparently more important in the withdrawal negotiations, than economic or geopolitical considerations (which will reimpose their weight and logic in future scenarios). And for once, the European Union was able to display strong cohesion.

However, it is undeniable that with Brexit, at least one factor has changed dramatically. For the first time since the establishment of the European Economic Community, Europe's future has been seriously put into question. The assumption across the British political spectrum (which has ultimately been decisive in the whole Brexit debate) is that the European Union is much more likely to fail than to succeed. It is not so much that the European Union, as a *sui generis* international organization, is going to dissolve any time soon, but most Britons (even many among the Remain voters) would agree that Europe, in its current shape, is hardly a solution to any of Britain's major problems. Actually, according to this widespread perception, it has been the cause of many of them. This belief has inevitably affected the Brexit negotiations since their start, giving Britain the false impression that it was in a position of strength.

Interestingly, such a pessimistic assessment about the future of the European Union has spread across the continent—as shown by the rise of nationalist and "sovereignist" political parties, even in traditionally Europhile countries such as Italy—creating forms of "pragmatic Euroscepticism". In short, Brexit has shown all the costs of leaving the club and should discourage other exits, but the existential crisis of the European Union is more pronounced than ever. Despite having found an unexpected cohesion in negotiating Brexit, reaching the November withdrawal agreement mostly on its own terms, the European Union cannot pretend to be in good shape. Taking the United Kingdom out of the picture does nothing to facilitate European integration. And it is certainly a cost on many fronts. For Europe, there is the risk of a self-fulfilling prophecy; the underlying expectation of a bleak future for Brussels (economically slowing down and politically fragmenting) affects the way the rest of the world looks at it, making the European Union and its member states even less confident. In this sense, the British malaise is very much a European malaise.

The Singapore of the North

Brexit forces Britain to deal with a number of major challenges from a completely different perspective (alone, and no longer with the shield of the European bloc). The ripples of globalization in a global system no longer dominated by "the West" call for a new social compact as a result of growing internal inequalities, as does the need to strike a reasonable balance between national sovereignty and openness, or between national autonomy and international commitments. The gamble implicit in Brexit was that Britain, once out of the European

Union, would be more—not less—free to exploit its power multipliers on the international stage. In other words, the gamble was based on the additional assumption that the European Union had acted as a drag on the latent—or dormant—dynamism of "Global Britain". Trade was absolutely central to the success of this new experiment. But approaching it from the perspective of a glorious sea-power tradition was not just delusional; it led to major policy and political miscalculations. Since most of these challenges are unprecedented, history can hardly be a reliable guide for dealing with them.

As we will see, the debate on trade between Remainers and Leavers was not centred upon a linear divide between globalism and autarky. The argument was between the defence of a Europe-first line (which prevailed in the withdrawal agreement with Brussels) and the choice for global free trade, plus an updated version of the old "imperial preferences" view, expressed by Joseph Chamberlain as Colonial Secretary.[17]

Although both the institutional and de facto functioning of the European Union are often unnerving, the rest of the world is a complicated and dangerous place, and does not seem to be rolling out the red carpet for Britain. Post-Brexit British business is not going to find a brave new world of open markets, but rather an overlapping set of regional and bilateral arrangements at a time of a crumbling multilateral trading system. There are two simultaneous threats to the trading system, as understood by a prominent anti-Brexiteer and former senior public official Simon Fraser: "When it comes to trade these days, the world hardly seems to be anyone's oyster. Perhaps it is a Chinese oyster—one which President Trump is finding hard to swallow."[18]

The risk is that China's re-emergence as a leading global power, as well as trade tension between China and the United States, might disrupt the international trade system beyond recognition. Both challenges are simply intractable for a mid-size country that is betting its future on the backdrop of a benign economic international environment. Playing it solo and exploiting tensions between other major powers is likely to backfire. A telling example of the European "pull" factor affecting British policy decisions was the informal alignment with France and Germany on the highly controversial issue of tariffs on steel and aluminium imposed by America in early 2018. In dealing with a potentially disruptive American policy turn, Britain looked to the continent in search of support. A more careful and less biased reading of British history might have reminded hardcore Brexiteers that protectionism was a recurring feature in the days of the British Empire, and that miscalculations among rising and established Great Powers had led to the First World War. Pax Britannica had several dark sides that were overlooked during the Brexit debate and would have allowed a more objective assessment of what a divorce from Brussels would imply.

There is a clear paradox here. Many of the grievances at the root of Brexit had to do with structural changes that are global in nature and have little to do with the European Union. Yet it is far from clear how a withdrawal makes it any easier to face such global challenges. If the basic requirement is managing a phase of relative "de-globalization" and uncertainty, then leaving a powerful trading bloc to "go it alone" may be interpreted as an additional step towards a de-globalized world, rather than a bold leap into a new era of economic openness. All this also because the complexity of twenty-first-century economies calls for sophisticated trade arrangements (including property rights, standards, data protection and so forth) rather than *laissez faire* as such. A light regulatory touch and a fundamental faith in free markets is a legitimate and often effective way to address the needs of an advanced economy, but trade agreements and multilateral agencies are precious precisely as tools to guarantee a level playing field in which market forces can produce the best outcomes. More broadly, detailed mutual guarantees and settlement mechanisms are crucial, as a focus on "fair trade" tends to replace the emphasis on pure free trade. In short, rules are important even in a highly liberalized and deregulated economic environment. In this there is another fallacy of any nostalgic narrative. Trade policies of a century ago were only about tariffs. In today's world, non-tariff barriers at and behind borders are the main threat to the free circulation of goods and services.[19]

A consequence of this simplistic way of thinking was the belief within the Leave camp that the United Kingdom should aspire to become a mega-Singapore of the North, a "super-duper Singapore", a nimble global economic actor—minus the empire.[20] But a nation of 66 million citizens only vaguely resembles a tiny island state such as Singapore, and using Singapore as a benchmark is misleading in many ways. The democratic traditions of the two countries are—to say the least—contrasting, with inevitable consequences for the socio-economic model that characterizes them. Singapore has flourished as a trading hub for goods, services, and capital thanks to its low taxes, light regulatory regime, and stable business environment. How can Britain cut taxes for rich people and large corporations since Brexit was triggered by skyrocketing inequalities? How can the United Kingdom restore its credibility as a business-friendly nation after all the chaos imposed by Brexit on manufacturers and the financial industry? How can Britain be truly global when immigration fears are what pushed it out of the European Union? And most importantly, if a well-functioning customs union materializes, other trade options will simply not come to fruition since British freedom of action with third parties will be severely constrained.

With quite an intellectual effort, it is possible to see the City of London as a sort of "Singapore plus"; but then what about the rest of the country? The bitter irony of course is that London itself voted "Remain", not "Leave". So, there is a "global London" that might help the United Kingdom set up new global partnerships, but this will only be possible by exploiting the full potential of a mid-size island state, whose periphery, however, cruises at an exorbitantly slower pace than its core and tends to be more inward looking than outward looking. The complexity of British politics, which has produced Brexit, will affect any diplomatic initiative or negotiation in ways that the policy makers of Singapore—or other small-sized advanced economies—could hardly imagine. At the same time, business—including, of course, British business—will make investment decisions on the basis of its perceived interests, not out of love for "Global Britain" and its proud maritime traditions. In other words, business people, as well as consumers, will look to the future, not to the past.

The Commonwealth: hopes and frustrations

The heart of the nostalgic and emotional argument put forward by Brexit's ideologues both before and after the referendum was the British imperial tradition—which was certainly "global", but was first and foremost British. In the language of twenty-first-century politics, the hard edge of the imperial tradition needs to be smoothed; but there is an obvious candidate in the form of the Commonwealth. As we will show in greater detail in the next chapter, a narrowly defined Anglosphere already exists (albeit in an informal way), working rather well in the intelligence field (the Five Eyes network) and is unlikely to progress much further. But it is the Commonwealth—the main tangible legacy of the empire, with its fifty-three members, spanning five continents and containing almost 2.5 billion people—on which Britain turned its back when it joined the European Economic Community in 1973. As argued by Paul Nuttall, a leading hardcore Brexiteer:

> The Commonwealth today contains fifty-three countries—compared to the EU's twenty-eight. It covers a quarter of the globe's landmass and contains a quarter of the world's people. Whereas the EU's proportion of world trade is shrinking, the Commonwealth's is growing. In 2013 the Commonwealth economy overtook the Eurozone's and by 2019 it will have overtaken the EU's as a whole, contributing 17.7 per cent in terms of global trade compared to the EU's 15.3 per cent. This is because the Commonwealth contains not only some of the most stable economies in the world like Australia and Canada, but also some of the fastest growing, like India, which is projected to be the second largest economy on the planet by the middle of this century.[21]

During the Brexit campaign, the Commonwealth featured not just as an issue, but as a potential constituency.[22] It was presented as an under-utilized business asset. Institutions such as the Royal Commonwealth Society, the Commonwealth Business Council, and the Commonwealth Secretariat suggested that there was a "Commonwealth Effect" that rendered intra-Commonwealth trade cheaper and easier.[23] The official report entitled *The Commonwealth in the Unfolding Global Trade Landscape*, argued that "when bilateral partners are both Commonwealth members, they trade on average 20 per cent more and generate 10 per cent more FDI inflows than otherwise" and "compared with other country pairs, the bilateral trade costs for Commonwealth partners are, on average, 19 per cent lower".[24] It is no surprise that these staggering figures, while highly questionable from a purely methodological point of view, were continuously reported by Brexiteers in their attempt to brainwash their fellow citizens about the opportunities that the wider world could offer them. In addition, the Commonwealth was seen as ideally placed "to play the role of global bridge-builder and ideas-generator", with its members belonging to both the advanced and developing worlds.[25]

When one puts aside the Brexiteers' nostalgic lenses, however, reality looks far less appealing. Economically, the Commonwealth is a very heterogeneous grouping. Today, six Commonwealth countries dominate exports to other Commonwealth countries, accounting for 80 per cent—Singapore, India, Malaysia, Australia, Britain, and Canada. This means that the true beneficiaries of intra-Commonwealth trade are just a small minority. In addition, a country like the United Kingdom has clear commercial interests elsewhere. In 2017, roughly 72 per cent of British exports were delivered to fifteen trading partners—not one of them a Commonwealth member—whereas about 54 per cent of its total exports of goods and services went to the European Union. It follows, then, that the starting point of any serious trade strategy for Global Britain should be Europe—the legacy of European Union membership is after all much more recent than that of the empire. And, although many tend to forget it, this was already the case in the Edwardian era, when Britain used to trade more with countries outside the empire, Europe included, from where it imported food and raw materials.[26]

The Commonwealth accounts for less than 10 per cent of British exports and imports. The United States alone is about twice as important to the British economy (and the European Union, as we have just observed, more than twice the United States). Without India, with which the United Kingdom will have a difficult time negotiating a free-trade agreement (as seen in greater detail below), and excluding Britain, all Commonwealth nations account for less than 3 per cent of global economic output. Building a trade strategy on this is out of the question.[27] Simon Fraser highlights the different relative importance of Britain's trade partners: "If we lost 5 per cent of our trade with the EU, we would need a 25 per cent increase with the BRICS just to get back to square one."[28] In addition, the grouping has not really functioned as a trading area since 1973, and represents more a loose association than a tightly knit bloc, with each country having developed its own trade links across the world and over the decades. The Commonwealth has not been a trade organization since its former incarnation as the British Empire, during which Britain imposed trade on its colonies that largely benefited itself. Its political heterogeneity and geographical size is a problem, not an advantage, as geographical proximity and institutional homogeneity are key factors for the intensity of trade exchanges.

Therefore, putting the Commonwealth at the centre of a trade strategy could turn out to be rather dangerous. Not only might the expected benefits be negligible, but there could also be paradoxical situations. Thirty-two Commonwealth countries, mainly in Africa and the Caribbean, have already entered foreign trade agreements with the European Union.[29] This means that until Britain signs its own trade agreements with these countries, it might end up trading in worse conditions than Brussels. And since negotiating trade agreements is time consuming, it might take years to finalize them. In addition, even when they come into effect, Commonwealth countries might not be ready to offer the United Kingdom the same terms offered to the European Union. The economic and geographical size of a trading partner defines its negotiating power. In addition, unlike Britain, none of the Commonwealth countries experience any form of nostalgia for the empire—if anything, memories of the colonial era are only negative. Even if the United Kingdom likes to depict itself as a benign colonizer, these countries do not want to risk a return to the past.

An additional reason for caution is the fact that trade issues are closely intertwined with the delicate migration issue, and legal access to Great Britain for workers and migrants is of key interest to many Commonwealth members. This became all too clear on the occasion of the London meeting of the grouping's heads of government in April 2018, which was meant to be a grand celebration to re-launch a spirit of partnership. The gathering started with an embarrassing public apology by the British government for the treatment of the so-called "Windrush generation" of Commonwealth citizens—individuals from the Caribbean who moved as workers to the United Kingdom over several decades and have recently been subjected to various forms of government-led pressure from employers and landlords due to their illegal immigration status. The spat that followed ultimately led to the resignation of the then Home Secretary, Amber Rudd. The questions raised on the occasion of the April 2018 summit go well beyond the Caribbean countries, as there are serious admin-istrative concerns in the United Kingdom itself, given that by 2021 the Home Office will be entirely responsible for immigration and border policies. In general, it appears that among the thorniest policy areas in the post-Brexit world this is exactly the question that bedev-illed the United Kingdom as a member of the European Union and directly contributed to the referendum result: immigration and bor-der management.

The view from the rest of the Anglosphere: India as a test case

As Britons contemplate a post-EU identity with a global reach, it would be instructive for them to look carefully at their prospective partners and ask the question: do they share a fascination with the Anglosphere (particularly those that are not part of its core)? And to what extent do they share the broader worldview that led the British to opt for Brexit? The fundamental challenge is that the United Kingdom would no longer be the dominant player in any possible con-figuration of the Anglosphere—even one not including the United States. Looking forward, there are demographic, cultural, strategic, economic, and diplomatic issues that complicate the pursuit of Anglosphere-based partnerships. And perceptions outside Britain reflect all these issues. India, in particular, seems bent on creating its own "sphere", and behaves as a proudly independent actor on the world stage—the demographer Joel Kotkin, for instance, identifies an "Indosphere" as distinct from the Anglosphere, and a potential rival to the "Sinosphere".[30]

What is certain is that India does not want to run the risk of being subordinate to Britain again. When in 1931, sixteen years before the end of the British Raj, Gandhi was asked: "How far would you cut India off from Empire?" His response was: "From the Empire, entirely; from the British nation not at all, if I want India to gain and not to grieve." He then added: "But it must be a partnership on equal terms."[31] Unfortunately, at the time, Britain was not ready for the "equal part-nership" Gandhi sought. Now, especially in a post-Brexit environment, the British might be ready to move in that direction. But for India the offer probably comes too late. While Brexiteers are stuck in a glorious past, the Indians are projected into a bright future. The leverage that Britain had back in the 1930s has almost entirely evaporated.

There are at least two structural reasons for the unique role that India will probably play in the future: first, as a country it is neither racially nor historically Anglo-Saxon; second, its sheer size means that any Anglosphere would struggle to absorb a country whose population is four times the size of all the other members put together. As recently argued by the Indian journalist Pramit Pal Chaudhuri, a number of additional issues emerge when looking at India through the prism of the Anglosphere.[32] First, as shown by different editions of the World Value Survey, in terms of driving values, Indians are closer to Catholic Europeans and Latin Americans than they are to the more liberal English-speaking world.[33] Moreover, India has officially been a socialist economy for much of its independent history, and has only embraced a more favourable view of the market in the past two decades. Even today, India's trade policy is filled with protectionism (and it remains an obstructive participant in the world trading system).[34]

The current status of English as a common language is also somewhat problematic. English is not an official language in India (except in four states), although it is recognized as the country's language of administration and business, serving as a link between its disparate regions.[35] It is true that the English language's association with middle-class membership, secure employment, and upward social mobility has seen demand for the language surging among lower-class Indians in recent years. However, while there is a small elite whose knowledge of English is indistinguishable from the educated middle class of, say, the United Kingdom or the United States, most Indians speak a stripped-down, utilitarian version that has large infusions of local phrases and terms—it has a close resemblance to "Globish" and is quite distant from the language of William Shakespeare and Jane Austen.

In general, ties with the United Kingdom have weakened, as historical and cultural relations atrophied over the past three decades. Since 2000, trade between the European Union and India has grown 300 per cent, while UK–India trade figures have remained largely static. Furthermore, Germany—and not the United Kingdom—is by far India's largest trading partner in Europe. British–Indian investments represent a more vibrant connection, with Indian direct investment in

Great Britain (revenues of over $50 billion) greater than Indian investment in the rest of Europe combined. This certainly nurtures bilateral ties, but the gap between the trade and investment relationship indicates that India and the United Kingdom lack supply-chain linkages, a sign that the two economies remain remarkably unintegrated, despite a long shared economic history.

If we look at immigration as something cementing bonds between countries, this remains important, but it started to decline after Britain joined the European project. Indians are the second-largest migrant population in the United Kingdom, but were overtaken by Polish migrants in absolute numbers a few years ago. A post-Brexit United Kingdom seems bound to raise the drawbridge even higher in terms of stopping foreign migrants, so that while the number of Indians being issued British visas, whether as tourists, students, or temporary workers, remains impressive, the paths through which such visitors can become British citizens have largely been blocked.

India was unenthusiastic about Brexit from the beginning, seeing it as unnecessarily injecting more uncertainty into the global system. It indicated early on that it had no interest in fast-tracking a free-trade agreement with the United Kingdom, at least until the terms of Brexit had been clarified. Boris Johnson, when he was still Foreign Secretary, flew to New Delhi to turbo-charge the relationship between the two countries.[36] But India has become increasingly sceptical of the benefits of bilateral trade agreements in general, especially those without a strong service and immigration component. Indian Prime Minister Narendra Modi and his officials made it clear that a post-Brexit India–UK agreement would require the United Kingdom to open the door wider for Indian immigrants—something that May said was politically impossible for her. Nostalgic attitudes lead to paradoxical situations. Britain left the European Union because of its insistence on the free movement of people, and sought new partnerships with emerging nations that were once under its imperial umbrella. Emerging economies such as India, however, insist on loose immigration rules as a condition for concluding free-trade deals for goods and services.

The most worrisome issue for Britain is in the security realm. What the British government struggled to sell was the idea that India could gain any strategic or military advantages from a post-Brexit United Kingdom. In India, however, Britain continues to be seen as having little or no influence in Asia—the focus of India's foreign and security policies. Despite repeated efforts by British ministers to play up their naval presence in the Persian Gulf and other odd bits of flag-waving, Indian officials are clear that the only European country that is seen as a major player in their region is France because of its territorial and military presence in the Indian Ocean. By way of contrast, India's strategic relations with the United States are on a steady upward trajectory and, somewhat more hesitantly, so are its security relations with Australia. India simply does not attach equal importance and relevance to the United Kingdom.

As most Indian officials would tell you, the three countries that Prime Minister Modi nowadays refers to as having a "transformational" relationship with India are the United States, Japan, and the United Arab Emirates. Using another metric, the three largest providers of defence equipment to India are Russia, Israel, and the United States.[37] Partly because of its concerns about an uncertain global power structure, India has been experimenting with various groupings, or what are sometimes called "strategic geometries". These include the BRICS formation, a USA–Japan trilateral, the so-called IBSA (with Brazil and South Africa), and, more recently, the "Quad", a collection of "maritime democracies" (with the United States, Japan, and Australia). These formations include a pantheon of countries, including China (through the BRICS). In short, from the perspective of an ambitious and rising country such as India, the world is too complicated and fragmented a place to be captured by the Anglosphere concept, or managed by a grouping in which Britain plays a special and central role.

When it comes to the heart of the bilateral relationship, nostalgia pulls the two countries apart. Indians tend to remember rather well what colonialism meant for their country, and resentment is still high. In the 2017 book *Inglorious Empire*, Shashi Tharoor set out to offer a corrective to the claim that the British Empire served as a benign colonizer.[38] An MP for the Indian National Congress, Tharoor focuses on the British Raj in India to spotlight the greed, depredation, and cruelty at the heart of British imperialism. He reminds readers that in the eighteenth century India was as rich as all of Europe, accounting for around 23 per cent of global GDP at the time. But, by the end of the nineteenth, it had become Britain's single largest source of revenue. When colonial rule ended in 1947, India's backward economy barely represented 3 per cent of global GDP. Meanwhile, 90 per cent of Indians lived in poverty and 84 per cent were illiterate. According to Tharoor, a Commonwealth Free Trade Area would go down in India "like a lead balloon".[39] The positive technological, infrastructural, and educational legacy of the British Empire is not strong enough to over-shadow the humiliation of colonial rule. Even the railways, which many in the United Kingdom consider a colonial gift to India, were actually a symbol of the brutal exploitation of the country. They were primarily intended to transport extracted resources—coal, iron ore, cotton, and so forth—to ports for the British to ship home to use in their factories. Indian passengers were required to sit in squalid, stinking third-class compartments, away from the whites-only coaches.[40] And disillusion-ment was high even among the extremely successful sons of the colo-nial period. Vidiadhar Surajprasad Naipaul, a Trinidad-born British author of Indian origin and Nobel laureate, wrote:

> I lived with the idea of decay. (I had always lived with this idea. It was like my curse: the idea, which I had had even as a child in Trinidad, that I had come into a world past its peak). ... I grew to feel that the gran-deur belonged to the past; that I had come to England at the wrong time; that I had come too late to find the England, the heart of empire, which (like a provincial, from a far corner of the empire) I had created in my fantasy.[41]

Europe and the narrow Channel: linking security

Despite its specificities, the bilateral UK–India relationship reflects many of the dilemmas that Britain faces today. In a changing global scenario of multiple semi-continental "blocs" and shifting alignments, a mid-sized maritime power like the United Kingdom will easily fall victim to either overstretch or marginalization. Even if Britain were able to form new, reliable alliances and nurture or upgrade existing networks, it would probably have to give up the leadership role to other, larger centres of power. In order to leverage extensive networks, one needs to be a large hub, and it is not at all clear what kind of hub the United Kingdom could be. Continental Europe, notwithstanding all its dysfunction, is comparatively a very large hub.

The limitations of both Global Britain and the imperial legacy remind one that power is constantly shifting, but also that it is a relative concept, to be measured against the power of others. It is worth considering that economic-growth differentials are staggering. For instance, today's China is a giant, but a significantly smaller giant than it will be in five or ten years' time, even when making conservative assumptions about its growth rates. In other words, the gap between fast-growing and large, newly emerged economies and any European country is going to widen for the time being. And critical mass is essential if a country wishes to be taken seriously by tomorrow's major economies. Within the European Union, the United Kingdom was certainly a larger member of the family, but on a global scale it is a mid-sized country—despite its glorious past and its continuing role as a permanent member of the United Nations Security Council. The hard truth seems to be that, ultimately, it is the kind of relationship that Britain will forge with traditional partners (the European Union and to some extent the United States) that will make it more or less attractive to others—the Commonwealth and the large Asian economies.

In this context, economics will of course not be the only metric. It is logical for the United Kingdom to also leverage other forms of power and influence, especially in the security and defence sectors. A recurring assumption among Brexiteers—along with non-Brexiteers, who are nonetheless resigned to a post-EU reality and wish to table constructive ideas—is that in the security/defence realm the country enjoys a unique combination of experience, state-of-the-art know-how and capabilities, as well as international connections. This is all largely correct. This has surfaced since the early stages of the tense negotiations with Brussels, as a belief that the European Union will badly need the United Kingdom, now more than ever before, given the increasing turbulence in the international arena.[42]

In parallel, the North Atlantic Treaty Organization (NATO, of which the United Kingdom has always been a key member) continues to be a fundamental pillar of European defence and transatlantic solidarity, despite the many doubts initially sowed by the Trump administration. The Five Eyes network—as we will discuss in Chapter Six—remains the best grouping of its kind on the planet, thanks to its internal cohesion, global outreach, and unsurpassed assets. One therefore might conclude that from a security perspective, Britain will not suffer much due to its departure from the European Union. It retains the capacity to influence events in distant areas of the globe, while relying on NATO to protect its vital interests and the homeland from a number of threats, both old and new. In addition, its security and defence assets will be instrumental to the future development of a special relationship with the European Union.

This is the bright side of the picture. Security is obviously a key element as far as national sovereignty is concerned, which in turn has been at the very heart of Brexit. One reason why security and defence cooperation has come very late in the evolution of the European Union, after the 1954 vote by the French National Assembly to "kill" the initial plan for a defence community, is that for over half a century NATO has been the major security provider and has been guaranteeing, through the United States, an internal balance in Europe. The European Union as such lacked such an undisputed hegemonic power. With Britain out, and with Germany still hesitant to play a consistent role in defence policy, France finds itself in a unique position. The reality, however, is that the French will not be able to sustain a meaningful European security and defence system without a British contribution. This very factor, combined with industrial interests, explains why France has launched the idea of a rapid intervention force (outside the European Union and therefore open to Britain) and has preserved bilateral agreements with Britain in the defence sector (the Lancaster House Treaties of 2010).

At the same time, the future of NATO cannot be taken for granted without a more important contribution from the European Union. For the first time since 1954, pressure on European defence has become increasingly strong, for both political and economic reasons. All over Europe, public opinion supports the idea—as does the United States, with some specific caveats concerning American access to the European defence market. All this makes life somewhat less easy for Britain. In order to keep its pivotal position in Atlantic security, the United Kingdom cannot lose touch with an evolving European defence system. One complication is that the record of UK–EU cooperation is mixed at best, with many on the continent believing that London has in fact acted as a brake on the progress of the so-called Common Security and Defence Policy (CSDP) since its inception. Equally, intelligence sharing between Britain and its European partners remains limited—with Britain giving priority to its Five Eyes network. For this reason, an agreement on information sharing has become a key condition for re-fashioning the relationship between Britain and the EU.[43]

On the whole, the rationale for close UK—EU cooperation in security and defence is stronger than resistance on both sides. Clearly, pragmatic agreements are possible if trust is preserved, something that Britain cannot take for granted. At the same time, Brussels must coherently recognize that security should not be treated on a par with any other elements of the post-Brexit dialogue. While trade deals can be transactional, security is not.

In this context, an agreement on intra-EU security is in the interest of both the United Kingdom and the European Union—which justifies the effort to overcome delicate issues. On external security, after Brexit Britain cannot expect to have a seat at the table in European Union decision-making structures, such as CSDP operations. Brussels will try to protect its decision-making autonomy regarding defence operations and missions. And yet arrangements can be made to maintain regular contact at all levels—probably a more relevant requirement than any formal treaty. Britain could commit to supplying specific types of troops and assets to individual European military operations, provided it is granted close involvement in information sharing and force deployment planning.[44]

A fundamental guiding concept in this unique field is that "security is an interest shared by all European citizens, not only by European Union citizens".[45] In other words, the European continent, rather than the European Union as such, should be seen as the unit of analysis. At the same time, Britain must be involved in the EU's evolving defence infrastructure. With the United Kingdom excluded, the continent will not only lose British assets, it will also potentially undermine the efforts of the European Union itself, given the standing and capabilities of Britain as a security player.

This "inclusive" effort must involve defence industrial cooperation. With the launch of the European Defence Fund (EDF), the European

Union has moved in the direction of Europe-wide projects and commitments, which can clearly be problematic for a non-member state. There will be a general industrial issue of "European preference" to complicate the relationship with Britain. Brussels, however, must bear in mind that the United Kingdom is an integral part of the European defence technological and industrial base. For its part, Britain will have to guarantee a degree of regulatory alignment in this sector.

At a higher strategic level, discussions may also involve the role of British nuclear capability as a component of European security in the broadest sense. This is clearly a delicate matter, and one in which France now enjoys a very significant role as a direct consequence of Brexit. At some point, an overall assessment of pan-European security will require policy choices on the nuclear dimension in which Britain will have to be intimately involved. This is a very strong, additional motivation to consider a unique security partnership between the United Kingdom and the European Union—something that cannot be applied vis-à-vis other third countries. In this field, thinking in terms of British exceptionalism makes sense.

A European nation-state, outside the EU

In February 2018 Boris Johnson tackled head-on the combined practical and spiritual dimensions of the British identity crisis:

> We will continue to be Europeans both practically and psychologically, because our status as one of the great contributors of European culture and civilization—and our status as one of the great guarantors of the security of Europe—is simply not dependent on the Treaty of Rome as amended at Maastricht or Amsterdam or Lisbon.[46]

The "new" Britain wishes to be global and free, but also connected and respectful of the sensitivities of its former European Union partners: a well-behaved former member, one might say, more than the usual awkward partner. It wishes to create new arrangements and be a rule-abiding protagonist of the multilateral system, but not treaty-bound "the EU way". There is a potential, general contradiction in the "go global" attitude of an unchained Britannia: the choice between nationalism and some kind of "post-nationalist" identity. A central problem that Brexiteers (Johnson among them) identified with the European Union was the lack of a "demos" corresponding to the legal order; this is a fair observation about today's Europe, but it is unclear what it means for today's United Kingdom. Once one achieves a perfect match between one's "demos" and the legal order, one is left with a classical nation-state—no more, no less.

Nostalgia is turning out to be ineffective as a way of looking at Britain's identity. As set out in the next chapter, it is extremely unlikely that the UK will be able to launch an Anglosphere of our times, or that it will be happy with a "Singapore plus" status. In fact, it is rediscovering its nature as a mid-sized power in need of stable partners and reliable allies. Given the ubiquitous nature of horizontal connections in today's world, leveraging extensive networks has become a must for contemporary states and societies. By leaving the European Union, Britain will not render this task any easier.

Brexit cannot guarantee a promising return to a post-imperial nation-state partly because the balance of power has shifted (in favour of non-European and non-Western powers), structurally weakening Western democracies in front of authoritarian powers. And yet, a nostalgic view of Britain has been crucial to the Brexit debate, and will not quickly disappear, leaving the United Kingdom more internally divided than in recent history. The dream of a "Global Britain" has a great deal in common with the historical concept of "Greater Britain"—in this sense it is indeed nostalgic and grounded in an idealized past. But it actually rests on the legacy of a "Little England" that is a little too specifically English. It is no coincidence that tensions within the United Kingdom—especially with Scotland and Ireland—quickly surfaced in the context of Brexit. Such a dilemma is not unique to Britain, although each country faces it in its own way. Sovereignty is being eroded and challenged both from within and without, both from above and below the state level. How does one deal with a fragmented world in which power is shifting rapidly, technology is cascading on everyday life at a pace that regulators cannot match, and demographics are inexorably shifting? Clinging to the past can provide a sense of place and identity, but most of these challenges are truly unprecedented. It will take an act of enormous political creativity to build the conditions for prosperity and security in a fragmented and dynamic world. In any case and in any scenario, re-defining the meaning of sovereignty will be a central task.

6

THE ANGLO-SAXON TRIBE

"Only tribes held together by a group feeling can survive in a desert."

Ibn Khaldun

The Anglosphere is a unique political animal.* It exists, even if one cannot see it. There are no secretariats or headquarters. There are few formalized partnerships and a limited number of sectorial working groups. There is no supranational architecture, and of course no founding constitution that clearly identifies it as a distinct political entity. Canada, New Zealand, the United Kingdom, and Australia share the same head of state, the British monarch. But this is also true for twelve other members of the Commonwealth. In its current shape, the Anglosphere can be seen as the sum of all the formal and informal contacts, partnerships, and relationships between Anglo-Saxon governments, corporations, and individuals that are linked by a shared culture and mutual interest.[1] It resembles the Christian Orthodox world more than the Catholic one, with many autocephalous churches bound together by common ideas and traditions rather than a unified institution with a single leader.[2]

---

* This chapter focuses on the core Anglosphere, which includes Australia, Canada, New Zealand, the United Kingdom, and the United States.

When seen with nostalgic eyes, this dense network of relations seems to represent the most positive and virtuous legacy of the former empire. Five countries, including both a "retired" and an active Great Power, defy geographical distance by working together in a variety of fields. The invisibility of this regional grouping implies that its true limits and potential are not fully detectable, thus allowing politicians to easily inflate the opportunities related to it. After all, it is hard to rebut an argument about something that nobody can see. With the slogan "Global Britain", the Leave campaign persuaded its supporters that withdrawal from the European Union did not imply a withdrawal from the world. The Anglosphere, along with a stronger focus on fast-growing emerging economies, was the cornerstone of this global strategy. Equally, the Anglosphere also had something to sell to the Little Englanders. The spontaneous partnerships and alliances that these countries have built over time in the most disparate areas prove that well-established democracies can find common ground, without surrendering their sovereignty to a supranational organization such as the European Union. As summarized by *The Economist*, the Anglosphere "is global where the EU is regional, networked where the EU is bureaucratic, bottom-up where the EU is top-down".[3]

The Anglosphere represents a form of veiled nostalgia; it is implicitly rooted in the past, while being explicitly forward-looking. While addressing the Institute of Chartered Engineers a few months before Brexit, the Eurosceptic MP David Davis stated:

> We must see Brexit as a great opportunity to refocus our economy on global, rather than regional, trade. This is an opportunity to renew our strong relationships with Commonwealth and Anglosphere countries. These parts of the world are growing faster than Europe. We share history, culture and language. We have family ties. We even share similar legal systems. The usual barriers to trade are largely absent.[4]

Similarly, the leading Conservative Boris Johnson stated that when Britain joined the Common Market, it betrayed "our relationships with Commonwealth countries such as Australia and New Zealand".[5] The timing for this kind of statement seemed propitious. Europe was engulfed in a number of overlapping existential crises that were undermining its existence. The other major advanced economies, namely the United States and the United Kingdom, had recovered from the Great Recession faster and more smoothly than the euro-zone, where distrust between North and South had prevented governments from adopting an optimal fiscal and monetary policy mix. Europe looked anything but appealing.

In theory, a more interconnected Anglosphere would reward Brexit: out of the European Union, but with an alternative within the Anglo-Saxon world, the United Kingdom would partly regain its influence in the global arena. At the same time, the United States would move beyond a reliance on European allies, who no longer live under the threat of Soviet military action—although this might be a historic miscalculation given Putin's aggressiveness in Eastern Europe. America could attract countries such as India, Australia, Israel, South Africa, and other former British colonies. With China and Russia being increasingly assertive, and with the European Union deeply embroiled in internal crises, maintaining close ties across the Anglosphere would be appealing both in security and economic terms.

However, like all nostalgic myths, the reality of the Anglosphere is more complex than simplistic electoral slogans are able to acknowledge. The lack of an institutionalized structure represents the main strength, not weakness, of this regional grouping. This is how the Anglosphere has evolved for almost seventy years. It is thanks to its invisibility that English-speaking countries have managed to shape the global liberal order, build a united Western front, and impose their rather homogeneous worldviews—thus never really giving the impression that they were acting in the interest of the Anglo-Saxons alone.

Today, however, power is shifting east and is becoming much more diffused and diluted. At the same time, America is no longer able or willing to bear the burden of the international liberal order—which seems to be under considerable strain. To understand why the Anglosphere is hardly the solution to Britain's existential problems, it is key to dissipate some of the nebulosity that surrounds it and investigate how it functions. We will work at the intersection between myth and reality, remaining as objective as possible. What emerges from this analysis is an indisputable—and in many cases unmatched—affinity between these five countries. And yet, even by making the boldest assumptions about its future, there is little room to consolidate the Anglosphere, or to think of it as the natural end-point of Britain's post-Brexit identity crisis.

The Five Eyes and beyond

The five nations that make up the inner circle of the Anglosphere resemble a global tribe more than a political community. In the jargon of geographer Joel Kotkin, they represent a geographically dispersed group of people who share the quintessential tribal characteristics of common identity and common values, display a great ability to adapt to a changing world, act to benefit their group mates even when they gain nothing, and penalize outsiders seemingly gratuitously.[6] This tribal link annihilates geographical distance and facilitates cooperation in the most disparate fields, even the most sensitive, such as intelligence and security, through ad hoc agreements—sometimes formal, at other times informal. When countries perceive that they belong to a larger family, there is no need for another supranational architecture to sketch out rights and duties. In a way, this is the view of the nineteenth-century anti-federalists, who believed that the bonds between the English-speaking countries were strong enough to make any formal institution redundant.

The Five Eyes partnership, which is probably the most powerful intelligence-gathering alliance in the world, epitomizes the Anglosphere in its purest form.[7] It came to light with the top-secret UKUSA Agreement, which since 1947 has tied America, Britain, Australia, Canada, and New Zealand into a sophisticated spying network, with the US National Security Agency (NSA) as the group's leading intelligence agency, immediately followed by Britain's Government Communications Headquarters (GCHQ). Even without formal institutions governing it, the group is so cohesive that the product of their individual intelligence activities is regularly shared, with operations and facilities covering all time zones and continents, ranging from listening posts in the Australian desert to Asia-based embassies and naval ships to the British countryside and the NSA headquarters in Maryland.[8] Over time, the set of convoluted and overlapping agreements that constitutes the partnership has involved ocean surveillance, covert action, human intelligence collection, and counterintelligence, but also the interception from civilian satellites of communications based on keywords submitted by each of the Five Eyes members.[9]

There is probably no major public figure or large corporation in the world whose actions or words have not, one way or the other, been secretly scrutinized by the Five Eyes. When, in October 2013, whistle-blower Edward Snowden revealed to the world that the NSA used to tap the personal telephone of German Chancellor Angela Merkel, it became apparent that countries who considered themselves close partners on strategic issues are instead targets in the world of electronic intelligence. However, even in the cynical and paranoid world of espionage, there is still a code of conduct that must be honoured. To some extent, spying on friends is tolerable, but not on the members of your own family: the Five Eyes do not snoop on one another. Formally, the United States does not have "no-spy agreements" with any country. But the Review Group on Intelligence and Communication Technologies—convened by President Obama in the wake of Snowden's leaks—revealed that there are exceptions to the rule—typically when America shares with another country "decades of familiarity, transparency, and past performance between the relevant policy and intelligence communities".[10] Reading between the lines of the text of the Review Group, only the Five Eyes meet these requirements.

Perhaps the last time the British spied upon the Americans, and vice versa, was the early 1940s when they started their code-breaking cooperation to defeat the Nazis. In a letter sent in February 1942 to the then American President Franklin Delano Roosevelt, Churchill confessed: "Some time ago our experts claimed to have discovered the system and some code tables used by your Diplomatic Corps. From the moment we became Allies, I gave instruction that this work should cease."[11] The UK–USA agreement, and thus the Five Eyes, originated exactly from this Anglo-American cryptanalysis partnership. Some of the most brilliant American and British minds worked side by side in the rooms of Bletchley Park—the top-secret mansion in Buckinghamshire where the team, led by the mathematician Alan Turing, decrypted the ENIGMA code used by the Axis Powers to secretly exchange information and dispatch military orders. According to Churchill—a hungry consumer of signal intelligence himself—the 10,000 people who worked there were "the geese that laid the gold eggs and never cackled".[12] And an equally fruitful cooperation, this time also including Australian, Canadian, and New Zealand cryptographers, took place in the Far Eastern theatre, when General Douglas MacArthur's Central Bureau cracked the Japanese Army's mainline code.[13]

The successes achieved at Bletchley Park and the Central Bureau contributed to cement the symbiotic relationship between members of the English-speaking world in a way that old Anglo-Saxon loyalties still trump modern Western alliances like NATO. The Five Eyes have no intention of opening the doors of their closed and much-envied snoop club to anyone. Even a request made by an influential outsider such as Germany to join the group was swiftly rejected in October 2013.[14] Michael Hayden, a former NSA director, is openly clear on this: "You can make as many trips to Washington as you want, we don't have the keys to make five [into] six."[15] Equally, the Five Eyes was cited as a good reason for the United Kingdom to leave the European Union. In 2016, the then Justice Secretary Michael Gove argued that Brexit would stop the European Court of Justice from interfering with Britain's security services. In a blog post for the *Huffington Post*, Gove provocatively asked: "How long before the ECJ starts undermining the Five Eyes intelligence sharing agreements that have been a foundation of British security since 1945 and which are the source of jealousy and suspicion in Brussels?"[16]

Intelligence gathering represents only one dimension, albeit probably the most important, of this nebulous regional grouping. In the realm of defence and security, the special relationships between these five countries involve joint programmes aimed at optimizing interoperability and the standardization of training and equipment between their armies (the American, British, Canadian, Australian, and New Zealand Armies' Program, or ABCA), their navies (the Naval Command, Control, Communications and Computers, or AUSCANNZUKUS), their air forces (Air and Space Interoperability Council, or ASIC), and their military scientific communities (the Technical Cooperation Program, or TTCP).[17] Within each programme there are different working groups focused on specific areas. Agile Combat Support; Air Mobility; Aerospace Medicine Group; Intelligence, Surveillance and Reconnaissance; Force Application; Force Protection; and Fuels are the seven standing working groups that comprise the ASIC programme. More recently, these five nations launched the Strategic Alliance Cyber Crime Working Group, which establishes operational partnerships between their law-enforcement communities to fend off cybercrime.[18]

There are then a plethora of bilateral, trilateral, or multilateral agreements that tie these countries together. The United States, New

Zealand, and Australia are part of the collective security agreement ANZUS, whereas the United Kingdom, Australia, and New Zealand have a tripartite force, called ANZUK, to defend the Asia Pacific region. Moreover, Canada and the United States are members of the North American Aerospace Defense Command (NORAD)[19]—a binational organization charged with the mission of aerospace warning and aerospace control for North America—and of the Permanent Joint Board on Defense—a senior advisory body on the continental military defence of North America.[20] The Trans-Tasman Travel Arrangement between Australia and New Zealand allows for the free cross-movement of their citizens. And recent opinion polls show overwhelming support for allowing the Canadians and British to join the deal as well.[21]

A number of educational programmes are aimed at facilitating mutual understanding between the elites of these five countries. The Rhodes Scholarship, which primarily targets talented American, Australian, Canadian, and New Zealand (as well as South African) college students chosen to spend a year at Oxford University, was established more than a century ago with exactly this goal. The imperialistic and greedy Rhodes wanted to train civic-minded leaders, render war impossible among members of the English-speaking kinship, and make Oxford University the educational centre of the Anglo-Saxon world, while preserving the imperial architecture.[22] In his words, "educational relations make the strongest tie".[23] Rhodes scholars notably include one American President (Bill Clinton), three Australian Prime Ministers (Bob Hawke, Tony Abbott, and Malcolm Turnbull), and one Canadian Prime Minister (John Turner). It was only in 2018, as a result of the Rhodes Must Fall campaign that broke out in South Africa in 2015, that the Rhodes Trust decided to open up the scholarship to the rest of the world, although Anglo-Saxon applicants continue to represent the largest group.[24]

Similarly, the Churchill Scholarship, which selects bright American students to study at Cambridge University, honours the former British Prime Minister's commitment to the special relationship with America. And, as living gift to the United States for its post-war efforts, in 1953 the British Parliament created the Marshall Scholarship, which selects intellectually distinguished young Americans to study at any university in the United Kingdom. But also on the other side of the Atlantic there is no shortage of scholarships that almost exclusively target members of the Anglosphere. The Kennedy Fellowship, which was established in 1964, reciprocates the Rhodes Scholarship by allowing British students to study at either Harvard or the Massachusetts Institute of Technology (MIT). Prominent politicians such as David Miliband and Ed Balls, and former Governor of the Bank of England Mervyn King, were recipients of this scholarship. And the Harkness Fellowship pursues similar goals, although it recently opened its doors to a few non-English-speaking nationalities.

This without mentioning the degree of solidarity and complicity in diplomacy that blurs national boundaries in unusual ways. In 1939, Australia declared war on Germany just seventy-two minutes after Britain's entry into the Second World War, and in May 1940, the only fully armed units guarding London from a German invasion during the retreat from Dunkirk were two Canadian divisions.[25] Fast-forward to the present day: in 2012 the United Kingdom and Canada caused great irritation in Brussels when they decided to pool and share embassy facilities abroad, marking the beginning of a "network shift" aimed at boosting relations with Commonwealth states ahead of the Brexit vote.[26] A few years later, diplomacy—the quintessential form of national soft power—was shared in an even more pervasive way within the Anglosphere. When in the immediate aftermath of the Brexit vote, Britain realized that it was short of diplomats to renegotiate its trade relationship with the European Union, New Zealand offered its own diplomats to relieve the understaffed British Civil Service. As Murray McCully, then New Zealand's Foreign Minister, declared: "We as a country that is a long-standing friend ... stand ready to be useful in any way we can be."[27] And in May 2018, the Conservative MP Robert Seely argued (not too credibly) that Britain's seat at the United Nations Security Council should "become an Anglosphere seat", with British, Australian, and Canadian ambassadors rotating.[28]

Thanks to linguistic commonalities, it is not unusual for the assignment of top institutional jobs to transcend simple birthplace arguments.[29] Andrew Bonar Law, who was born and grew up in Canada, became British Prime Minister in 1922.[30] Similarly, Churchill installed Maxwell Aitken (Lord Beaverbrook), who was born in Ontario, as Minister of Aircraft Production in May 1940—a key post in the organization of the war effort against Germany. Julia Eileen Gillard, who was Prime Minister of Australia from 2010 to 2013, was born in Wales and moved with her family to Adelaide when she was four. And she was succeeded by Anthony John Abbott, who was born in London to a British father and an Australian mother, before moving to Sydney when he was three. [31] At the same time, Australian-born Joseph Ward and Michael Joseph Savage became Prime Ministers of New Zealand in the first half of the twentieth century. [32]

For countries that have historically been lands of immigration it is probably not shocking to elect as prime minister, a foreigner who moved there early on in their life. But the closeness between these nations is so profound that it is considered equally acceptable to ask the Head of the Bank of Canada, Mark Carney, to become Governor of the Bank of England. When in 2012, the Chancellor of the Exchequer George Osborne briefed Queen Elizabeth about his intention to appoint Carney, she was unconcerned that the monetary policy of her country was to be handed over to a Canadian central banker. For her, it was simply a sort of intra-company promotion. [33] And when in 2018, discussions about a potential replacement for Carney heated up, the name of the former Governor of the Bank of India and renowned Chicago professor, Raghuram Rajan, immediately popped up in the press—even if he soon denied being interested in the job. [34] Besides his unquestionable professional and academic credentials, his appointment could have helped cement the relationship with India, that in a post-Brexit scenario was seen as a key market in partly offsetting the cost of leaving the European Union. From the perspective of a German, French, or Italian, instead, it would be simply unthinkable to nominate a foreigner as head of the Bundesbank, the Bank of France, or the Bank of Italy—linguistic barriers would certainly matter, but less than the fear of foreign intrusion into delicate domestic issues.

However, what makes the Anglosphere a unique model of transnational community is the process of cross-cultural contamination—which ends up affecting the whole world. International news broadcasters such as CNN and the BBC or global newspapers such as *The New York Times*, *The Economist*, *The Wall Street Journal*, and the *Financial Times* have helped create, develop, and preserve a mutually recognizable linguistic standard. Italians, Germans, and French, instead, have their own newspapers and are unlikely to participate in the same intellectual debate. In addition, the level of shared popular culture within the Anglosphere is such that the bookshops in the airports of London, New York, Ottawa, or Wellington are likely to list the same bestsellers, written by authors such as Ken Follet, John Grisham, or J. K. Rowling, whose birthplaces nobody really cares about.[35] Or think about how the part-Maori New Zealand-born actor Russell Crowe and the Australian actress Nicole Kidman are such dominant figures in the Hollywood film industry as to be perceived as Americans—at least to the eyes of an Anglosphere outsider.

Meme vs. gene

What we have just described, very briefly, is the practical reality of the Anglosphere. But in order to establish a true political community, it is important to have a look at the glue that keeps it together. A common language is the first element necessary for the forging of lasting tribal links. Churchill, after all, wrote the history of the English-speaking peoples, and not of the Anglo-Saxon race. A recent Pew research report has shown that Americans, Canadians, and Australians think that, to be truly "one of us", language matters more than birthplace.[36] A language is not just a systematic means of communicating. It is a sign of identity, culture, and national pride. Linguistic processes shape the way individuals perceive the world, how they live their lives, and, ultimately, their mindset. The same concept expressed with different words in different languages generates different emotions. Linguists call it linguistic relativity, or Whorfianism, in honour of Benjamin Lee Whorf, who elaborated the concept in 1944.[37]

When looking at the long march of Anglo-Saxon history broadly defined, it is precisely this linguistic commonality that has amalgamated the Anglosphere, leading to a striking cultural convergence, despite the dissolution of the empire and the emergence of fierce post-colonial identities. At the turn of the nineteenth century, the American writer Henry James wondered whether the rich English vernacular spoken by even the most educated people in New York would eventually destroy the language and the culture of his forefathers.[38] But he was proven wrong. English is a highly malleable language that tends to include rather than exclude. Over the centuries it has allowed foreigners, immigrants, and refugees to become quickly assimilated when moving to the Anglosphere, without creating a sense of linguistic oppression. As the British commentator Martin Kettle puts it: "We are voluntarily imprisoned in the Anglosphere."[39]

However, speaking the same language is a necessary, but not sufficient condition for being part of the core of the Anglosphere. After all, 700 million people, in twenty-five different countries around the world, speak English as a first language. According to the Anglosphere ideologue James Bennett, only Australia, Canada, New Zealand, the United Kingdom, and the United States share the common historical narrative in which "the Magna Carta, the English and American Bills of Rights, and such Common Law principles as trial by jury, presumption of innocence, 'a man's home is his castle', and 'a man's word is his bond' are taken for granted".[40] As several nineteenth-century intellectuals pointed out at the time of the Imperial Federation debate, this sense of clannishness has a purely civic dimension, with no racial connotations. It is not transferred from one generation to the other through a genetic process, but more through a memetic one—a clearly defined and partly idealized type of society that survives the passage of time.[41] And it could not be otherwise, given the high degree of ethnic heterogeneity that characterizes the Anglosphere.

Talented people from all over the world flock en masse to the Anglosphere, particularly to the United States and the United Kingdom, because of their open, dynamic, and meritocratic socioeconomic systems. According to the 2000 US census, only 8.7 per cent of Americans identify their ancestry as English, which is ranked fourth behind German, Irish, and African-American.[42] England itself emerged as the intermixture of Angles, Saxons, Jutes, Vikings, Celts, and pre-Celtic people in the British Isles.[43] As early as the seventeenth century, the poet Daniel Defoe argued that the English people did not come from racial purity, but from the choice to share certain values and participate in a community shaped by them. So, through a process of civic assimilation even the immigrant could start a new English life:

> "Fate jumbled them together; God knows how;
> Whate'er they were, they're trueborn English now."[44]

The seeds for the emergence of the English-speaking tribe were planted long ago, when the British Empire was on the rise. Over time, the constant flow of communication, migrants, ideas, goods, and other cultural products have knit these countries together firmly. For example, the cultural differences between American regions are overwhelmingly the product of four large waves of migration from Britain. These settlers were all Protestants, spoke distinctive dialects of English, and took pride in enjoying British liberties. But they differed in their religious affiliations, social ranks, loyalties, and regions of birth. The heterogeneity in the socio-cultural backgrounds of the British colonizers helps to explain the open structure of the American social system, which is "stubbornly democratic in its politics, capitalist in its economy, libertarian in its laws and individualist in its society and pluralistic in its culture."[45] And the liberal tradition from the British Empire was further developed by its white-settler colonies. By 1861, all five Australian colonies had secret ballots and universal male suffrage, political rights not fully achieved in Britain until 1918. And New Zealand was the first country in the world to give voting rights to its female population.[46]

As the Australian historian John Adamson put it with reference to his home country: "Australia is a fundamentally British culture, enriched and ornamented by non-British influences into an idiosyncratic synthesis all its own".[47] This cultural homogeneity across the Anglosphere is visible in the so-called Inglehart–Welzel map. The map, based on the World Value Survey, provides an overview of how values and beliefs differ on a global scale, showing distinctive clusters of countries based on similar linguistic and religious traits: Protestant Europe, Catholic Europe, ex-communist Europe, the English-speaking countries, Latin America, South Asia, the Islamic world, and Africa. The world seen through this prism is clearly at odds with the idea of a coherent and homogeneous West. Not only is Europe split within itself, but the Anglosphere narrowly defined is a class of its own.

The values emphasized by different societies usually fall into remarkably coherent patterns that reflect the economic development trajectory and cultural heritage of each society. Interestingly enough, North America, Australasia, and the United Kingdom are the most dispersed group in a geographical map, but also the most culturally homogeneous in the Inglehart–Welzel one. When it comes to religious beliefs, for instance, the English-speaking world tends to be mildly secular.[48] And from the Inglehart–Welzel map it becomes clear how the Anglosphere narrowly defined does not coincide with the Commonwealth of Nations, which excludes a key member such as the United States, while including many countries, particularly in Africa, that in many cases have struggled to fully assimilate into the British tradition.

The British Empire supplied the common culture, language, and civic attitudes at the heart of this sense of clannishness. But it also instilled the mercantile spirit that animates and glues together the English-speaking tribe. As argued by Hannah Arendt, the imperialist Rhodes, who confessed that he would have annexed even the planets if he had had the opportunity, seemed to consider the national flag not as a holy cloth, but as a commercial asset.[49] In the Anglosphere narrowly defined, business is put at the centre, religiously worshipped, and constantly promoted. New Zealand tops the ranking of the Ease of Doing Business Index compiled by the World Bank, and its Anglo-Saxon cousins closely follow suit.[50] Nine of the fifteen largest companies in the world are either American or British, and roughly 50 per cent of global stock value is concentrated in the Anglosphere, as opposed to less than 15 per cent in continental Europe and 33 per cent in Asia (where much of the Hong Kong and Indian stock exchanges play a dominant role, benefiting from their strong English-speaking ties).[51] Moreover, roughly 15 per cent of the working-age population in the United States, Canada, and Australia is involved in some form of entrepreneurial activity, as opposed to around 5 per cent in France, Germany, and Italy.[52]

In addition, all the five members of the Anglosphere promote a form of liberal capitalism that contrasts with that prevailing in continental Europe and in Asia. The Anglo-Saxon assigns a more dominant role to the market over the state than the German, Nordic, Chinese, and Japanese capitalist models.[53] Religious rebels such as the Quakers, Presbyterians, Congregationalists, and Methodists spread the Protestant work ethic, emphasizing the spiritual dimension of capitalism. Work was something good, not just necessary, and worldly success was the harbinger of divine reward in Heaven. Economic success was a sign of God's grace, and the exploitation of one's talent was a way to honour the divine call of the good Christian. In addition, Calvinism helped reject the feudal, anti-commercial ethic of Catholicism and Anglicanism that sought to subordinate individual economic achievement to the moral authority of the Church. These religious attitudes, which promoted self-control, the study of the Bible, and discipline, turned out to be instrumental to Britain's imperial expansion, which was primarily a business endeavour. Greediness, ambition, and adventurism were the driving forces behind it. Unlike the French imperialists, who tried to export their own civilization and honour their *mission civilisatrice*, the British diaspora was primarily interested in opening new trade routes, boosting commercial opportunities, searching for natural resources, and connecting the remote British Isles with the world.[54]

This mercantile spirit has been of paramount importance in breeding the openness to new ideas, willingness to experiment, and thirst for knowledge that ultimately allows a global tribe to survive in a rapidly changing world. Throughout the nineteenth century, the United States and the United Kingdom accounted for half of the world's major inventions. And these two countries have played a leading role in all the four industrial revolutions that the world has experienced so far. In 2016, the United States topped the ranking for the number of patent applications filed worldwide, ahead of Japan and China.[55] The vast majority of the world's leading software, biotechnology, and aerospace firms are still concentrated in English-speaking countries.

Like other successful global diasporas such as the Indians and the Jews, the English-speaking tribe has always placed a premium on the creation and dissemination of knowledge. Thirty-seven of the top fifty universities in the world are in the United States, the United Kingdom, Canada, and Australia.[56] The five English-speaking countries together have been awarded 539 Nobel Prizes, more than twice as many as France, Germany, Italy, and Spain combined.[57] It is true that many of the awards that went to the United States and the United Kingdom were actually granted to foreign-born laureates, but this again speaks to the openness of this political community. The same holds true for the entrepreneurial world. Many of the United States' most innovative entrepreneurs have been immigrants.[58] Nearly half of Fortune 500 companies and one-quarter of all new small businesses were founded by immigrants.[59] Not surprisingly, a recent report published by the INSEAD Business School ranks the United Kingdom, the United States, and Australia in the top six countries worldwide for their ability to produce, attract, and retain talent.[60] Unfortunately, the impact of

Brexit could be the opposite: reducing and not increasing this power of attraction. And were we to add one of Brexit's decisive motivations (reducing immigration) to Trump's "nativist" revolution, the risk is that the Anglosphere might lose some of the key characteristics that determined its primacy during the last century. Paradoxically, the proponents of the Anglosphere as a nostalgic alternative to the European Union might actually weaken their winning model.

Future: the challenge of common action

Since the Victorian era, politicians from across the English-speaking world, and particularly from the United Kingdom, have fiercely discussed the most appropriate institutional arrangements to give shape to what we today call the Anglosphere. But it would take a Herculean effort to transform the Anglosphere from a global tribe into a truly political community. All the rather impressive forms of collaboration in intelligence, diplomacy, education, and security among these countries do not imply the establishment of a more structured political community. What the ideologues of a more integrated Anglosphere seem to ignore is that the trust and affinity among these five countries is not enough to lead to a real political community. As we shall see in the next chapter, even the special relationship between its two key players, the United States and Great Britain, is under pressure. It is also extremely difficult to envisage a future in which the Anglosphere, intelligence sharing aside, could adopt a common foreign policy. Probably, it is precisely the lack of political integration that prevents these countries from clashing on thorny issues, giving the impression of a relatively cohesive grouping—while the European Union appears to be more internally divided when the degree of political integration is higher and for real.

The reality is that each member of the Anglo-Saxon family has its own priorities and interests. Australia and New Zealand are torn between their Asian and Anglo-Saxon identities, whereas many in Canada's French-speaking regions tend to question, or even oppose, the country's support for America's foreign policy. In the United States, a large chunk of the population simply abhors the idea of Anglo-Saxon racial purity promoted by Donald Trump's electoral base. Within the United Kingdom, Scotland and Northern Ireland are more committed to the European project than to the establishment of a modern form of Anglo-Saxon empire. The same holds true for younger generations. As discussed in the previous chapter, the view of the Conservative Party itself often contradicts the whole idea of Global Britain. Sometimes it leans towards a Thatcherite model of unfettered global trade and light government intervention; at other times it seems to reach back to the Chamberlainite tradition of social reforms and industrial intervention. Equally, outside the core of the Anglosphere, no country seems particularly interested in the project. Ireland is deeply attached to the European project; India and South Africa would see any British-led project in this sense as a relic of the empire.

Given the heterogeneity of the national interests of each of its members, each Anglo-Saxon nation will pursue its external goals independently: the Anglosphere will not produce a common international stance. Take, for example, the global trading system. Medium-sized open economies such as the United Kingdom, Australia, or New Zealand have strong incentives to push for increased market access abroad for their goods. All that clashes with Trump's "America First" line—which implies that the Anglosphere will come at least second in his order of choice. When Trump was about to finalize the renegotiation of NAFTA in the summer of 2018, he first reached an agreement with Mexico, temporarily leaving behind Canada.[61] In its attitudes to free trade, Britain is now apparently closer to Brussels than to the United States. Equally, Australia moved on signing the Trans-Pacific Partnership despite America's withdrawal. And the China issue will be divisive. Too often, the United States dangerously walks on the edge of the "Thucydides trap", while the rest of the Anglosphere seeks cooperation with China.[62] China is too big a challenge for its members to act in an uncoordinated manner. In theory, a more "visible" Anglosphere in the international economy would signal the emergence of a new model of globalization, centred on cultural homogeneity in individual regions: regional clusters, more integrated internally and more protected externally. This scenario—however complicated by global value-chains—could gradually become reality; and yet, the Anglosphere as such does not fit into this scheme, especially because of the Asian connections of some of its members. A stronger economic relationship between the

United Kingdom and the United States is a more concrete possibility, but only if and when Britain has completed its withdrawal from the customs union "territory" of the European Union. It will then find itself, in any case, in a position of comparative weakness.

Recently, the much-praised Five Eyes partnership also took a temporary hit. In 2017, classified details of the investigation into the Manchester bombing of 22 May, shared with American security agencies by British police, were leaked to the media. The unauthorized disclosure of shared information violated the cornerstone of the Five Eyes agreement—the control principle. This principle maintains that only the country producing the original intelligence can determine whether it is shared outside the initial arrangement.[63] Ignoring this jeopardizes the trust that underpins these special relationships. As a rather symbolic penalty, the British police temporarily halted sharing information with the United States.[64] This shows how, while trust among these countries is strong, it is not written in the stone.

Besides practical problems in amalgamating geographically diverse countries, any project of increased political cooperation would simply be unrealistic. Robert Conquest's old idea of an Anglo-Oceanic political association that is "weaker than a federation, but stronger than an alliance" clashes with a powerful renationalization trend. The members of the Anglosphere are, by definition, sovereignist: the assumption behind the group is to preserve, not share, national sovereignty. Clearly, an Anglo-Saxon federation is out of the question, but the Anglosphere is equally unlikely to become a traditional alliance. Bilateral or trilateral security relations will combine with NATO—which is likely to remain the alliance of choice for the United States and the United Kingdom.

The Anglosphere will more likely continue to be an informal community of states with preferential relations in a variety of fields. Bilateral deals and partnerships may well expand—and possibly involve all the members of the group. But the truth is that the idea that the English-speaking countries represent a cohesive family is largely a myth. If one looks back at the last fifty years, it's quite impossible to identify a sort of "Anglosphere interest". The Suez Crisis led to a split within the Anglosphere: Australia sided with Britain, Canada with the United States. Eventually, America solved the conflict by imposing a ceasefire through the United Nations and putting an end to the British-led initiative. In 1985, disagreements between America and New Zealand over nuclear tests in the South Pacific induced the United States to suspend its ANZUS obligations to New Zealand, which was downgraded from "ally" to "friend".[65] Only in 2008 did Secretary of State Condoleezza Rice, speaking at the War Memorial Museum in Auckland, describe the host nation as "friend and ally" once more.[66]

Even some of the linguistic differences in terms of pronunciation, accent, and vocabulary across the Anglosphere are often the result of conflictual relations between the members of the Anglo-Saxon world: the English language unites and divides at the same time. Take Canadian English. A skilled philologist would argue that Canadian spelling is a tug-of-war between British and American English. A Vancouverite, like a Londoner, would write "centre" and "colour". But he would also spell "jail" and "analyze" like a New Yorker.[67] This linguistic inconsistency is the result of an ambivalent relationship with both the United Kingdom and the United States that dates back to the time of the American Revolution.[68]

Finally, the celebration of the Anglo-Saxon democratic tradition—as opposed, according to the ideologues of Brexit, to bureaucratic Europe—is starting to clash with reality. In 2016, while compiling its Democracy Index, the Economist Intelligence Unit ranked Norway, Iceland, and Sweden as the top three democracies worldwide, while downgrading the United States to "flawed democracy".[69] This is a questionable assessment; but the point is that a decline of trust in government and elected officials also involves Anglo-Saxon democracies, making them more vulnerable. At the same time, social pressures behind the Brexit vote and the election of Donald Trump prove how the principles of equality of opportunity and social mobility have become a mirage in the English-speaking countries too. Socio-economic roles within these societies are calcified. The odds of being accepted to study for a Bachelor's degree at Oxford or Cambridge increase fourfold if a distant relative attended in 1800.[70] In the United States, class divide still has a racial element. There are no African-Americans on Forbes's list of the 400 wealthiest Americans for 2017. And in all the five Anglo-Saxon countries the income shares of the very richest have risen sharply from the mid-1970s onwards[71]—more than in continental Europe.

All these inconsistencies can hardly make the Anglosphere progress much further from where it stands. The aspirations of the nineteenth-century federalists are unlikely to be vindicated once again. And it is unclear whether this grouping can continue to work as effectively as it has done for decades, thanks to its invisibility. Within a global liberal order reflecting its values and as part of a West confident in its own supremacy, the Anglosphere had a meaningful purpose. Nowadays, however, this whole structure is fragile, while new challengers are emerging. Moreover, the history of the past century shows that the Anglosphere worked at its best when confronted with an external enemy. In the first half of the century the common enemy was Germany. In the second half it was Russia. Today, the United States clearly looks at China as an evolving global rival, but the management of the China risk—as we have just seen—partially divides the Anglosphere. In the meantime, both hardcore Brexiteers and Donald Trump apparently favour a weak Europe. The problem is that a weak Europe might end up weakening Britain too—and vice versa: the end result will be an even more fractured West.

Outside the European Union, and without the backing of a strong West, the United Kingdom would struggle to find a role. The Anglosphere, revived by the politics of nostalgia, will not provide a quick fix.

7

A NOT-SO-SPECIAL RELATIONSHIP

AMERICA AND BRITAIN

"The empires of the future are the empires of the mind."

Winston Churchill

Fifteen weeks is usually a negligible period of time in the long march of history. But the 139 days that separated the Brexit vote from the election of Donald Trump produced a tectonic shift of rare magnitude in world politics, capable of undermining the global liberal order that Britain and America had promoted for the previous seventy years. Troubles that had been stored up for years or even decades suddenly burst through the surface. Trump and the Brexiteers catalyzed similar forms of discontent, but with different purposes in mind. Brexit was about sovereignty; Trumpism was also about re-writing the rules of globalization. Brexit was predicated upon a free-market global paradigm, while pushing for industrial policies and social reforms domestically; Trump endorsed protectionism and unilateralism ("America First"), while upholding a form of ethno-nationalism reminiscent of the Jacksonian movement at the beginning of the 1800s.[1] Despite these differences there was a strong ideological affinity between the Brexiteers and Trump. Both votes represented a challenge to the Western world from within and created the illusion, particularly among hardcore Brexiteers, that the time had come to re-design the global order in purely Anglo-Saxon terms.

The two campaigns and their immediate aftermaths seemed to validate the idea that a renewed US–UK alliance was in the making, and, in an era of nostalgic sentiments, the closeness of Ronald Reagan and Margaret Thatcher was seen as a precedent. In an interview with Fox News in May 2016, Trump declared that Britain would be "better off" outside the European Union—especially because it would finally be able to control its own immigration policy.[2] Trump's pro-Brexit remarks came shortly after he delivered the first major foreign-policy speech of his campaign, in which he sketched out a diplomatic agenda centred on the rejection of the "false song of globalism" and on the idea of putting "America first".[3] In his address, Trump echoed the Brexit campaigners' sovereignist discourse, celebrating the "nation-state" as "the true foundation for happiness and harmony" and criticizing the constraints imposed by international agreements and institutions on the freedom of individual nations. "I am sceptical of international unions that tie us up and bring America down", he declared, adding that as president he would "never enter America into any agreement that reduces our ability to control our own affairs".[4]

During a visit to Scotland on the day following the Brexit referendum, in June 2016, Trump praised Britain's decision to leave the European Union as a "great thing", and attributed it to mounting popular anger at the distant liberal elite and resentment towards mass immigration. Trump stressed that the same sentiments were sweeping the United States, fuelling the success of his campaign and promising him victory in his presidential contest against Hillary Clinton. "I really do see a parallel between what's happening in the United States and what's happening here. People want to see borders," he declared.[5] In a statement released on the same day, the Republican candidate applauded the British people for exercising their "sacred right" by declaring "independence" from the European Union, thus voting to take back control over their "politics, borders, and economy". The statement presented the upcoming presidential election in the United States as an opportunity for the American people to "re-declare their independence", and exhorted them to follow the British example by voting "for trade, immigration and foreign policies that put our citizens first" and to "reject today's rule by the global elite", thus embracing "real change that delivers a government of, by, and for the people".[6]

With the benefit of hindsight, the vote for Brexit probably energized Trump's campaign, allowing him to present his success in the Republican primaries as part of a transnational revolt against the existing political, economic, and social order imposed by globalization. Brexit, together with the rise of populist and nationalist forces in "core" European countries such as Italy and the Netherlands, proved that alternative choices and paradigms—however disruptive, divisive, and seemingly irrational—were possible, despite the experts' scepticism and catastrophic warnings being issued by the establishment, the mainstream media, and international organizations.[7] Nigel Farage, one of Brexit's foremost architects, stressed this point while addressing a crowd of Trump supporters at a rally in August 2016, when the Republican candidate was still struggling in the polls.[8]

In the immediate aftermath of the presidential vote, conservative and "anti-globalist" politicians on both sides of the Atlantic saw the ideological and personal links established during the Brexit debate and the presidential campaign as a potential basis for a revival of the "special" partnership between the United States and Britain. Unlike the decades following the Second World War, however, this would not be based on a shared commitment to multilateral institutions or a liberal world order. On the contrary, its foundation would be the primacy that governments in both America and Britain afforded to their seemingly aligned domestic priorities; national interest first and a revisionist view of international affairs as the real vehicles for a return to the "special relationship"—as articulated by John Bolton before he was brought back on board as Trump's National Security Advisor in 2018.[9]

Trump himself seemed especially eager to encourage the revival of the "special relationship" on a new basis, in particular on the alleged continuity between the domestic political discourse in the United States and Britain. Immediately after moving into the White House, Trump brought Churchill's bust back into the Oval Office (Barack Obama had replaced it with one of Martin Luther King). In politics, after all, symbols matter a lot.[10] As President-elect he broke with diplomatic protocol and resorted to Twitter to publicly call for the appointment of UKIP's Nigel Farage as British Ambassador to the

United States: "Many people would like to see [@Nigel_Farage] represent Great Britain as their Ambassador to the United States, he would do a great job."[11] Despite being little more than diplomatic blunders or purely symbolic gestures, Trump's early expressions of closeness to Britain appealed to pro-Brexit politicians, many of whom also pointed to his Scottish heritage and to his business ties with the United Kingdom as marks of his basic Anglophilia.[12]

During the transition period, and in his first months in office, Trump also displayed an intention of putting Britain at the "front of the queue" in negotiations for a free-trade deal with the United States, in a move clearly designed to contradict Barack Obama's warnings regarding the negative effect that leaving the European Union could have on Britain's economy and trading position.[13] In addition, on 27 January 2017, only a week after Trump's inauguration, Theresa May was the first foreign leader to visit the new president in Washington. On that occasion Trump mentioned the historical significance of the "special relationship", which he described as "one of the great forces in history for justice and for peace", as well as his personal links with Britain, "And by the way, my mother was born in Scotland—Stornoway—which is serious Scotland." For her part, May stressed the "bonds of history, of family, kinship, and common interests" that formed the basis of the Anglo-American alliance and underlined the need to rapidly conclude a bilateral free-trade agreement.[14]

In a speech delivered the day before in Philadelphia, Theresa May had already referred to the ties of "kinship, language, and culture" that linked Britain and the United States, quoting Churchill's statement that the people of the two countries "speak the same language, kneel at the same altars and, to a very large extent, pursue the same ideals".[15] The Prime Minister's words echoed those of Eurosceptic Conservatives in the United Kingdom, who, in the years and months leading up to the Brexit referendum, had resurrected the idea of the Anglosphere as the frame of reference for British foreign, defence, and trade policy. They argued—as we saw in Chapters Four and Five—that the key to ensuring Britain's freedom, influence, and prosperity lay in building stronger ties with English-speaking countries, rather than in pursuing ever-closer cooperation with the rest of Europe.[16] As political scientist Nick Pearce has pointed out, this Anglospheric perspective did not necessarily reflect a concrete or even consistent foreign-policy strategy; instead, it represented an ideological, "imaginary" horizon for post-Brexit Britain, capable of "uniting the United Kingdom with a global trading future as well as a scept'red isle past".[17] In addition to strengthening ties with Commonwealth nations (especially with Canada, Australia, and New Zealand), a revived partnership with the United States was presented by Britain as the cornerstone of its new Anglosphere-centred diplomacy.[18] Without the United States any Anglosphere project would lose meaning, and the future of Britain outside the European Union would be grim.

But this focus on the "special relationship" was based on a delusional national myth. Historically, the specialness, which discounted an enormous gap in terms of power and influence between the two countries, has been more keenly felt in London than in Washington.[19] Since 1945, America's absolute strength and Britain's relative weakness has always determined a highly unbalanced relationship. In the eyes of Dean Acheson—Secretary of State in the Truman Administration—British rhetoric surrounding the "special" connection between the two countries reflected nothing more than the UK's unwillingness to accept its post-imperial status: that of a simple transatlantic intermediary and Anglo-Saxon balancer in European affairs.[20] It has been observed that, from 1945 onwards, the "special relationship" rapidly assumed the character of a "special dependenceship", with Britain very much the junior partner.[21] Currently, the difference in terms of power and influence between the two countries is as great as in the past—if not even greater, given Britain's diminished influence in European affairs. On top of that, bridging the policy inconsistencies between "America First" (based on unilateralism and protectionism) and "Global Britain" (based on multilateralism and free markets) has turned out to be more challenging than initially expected. Nostalgic arguments on both sides of the Atlantic hide a far more complicated political and historical reality.

Pax Americana as "Anglosphere 2.0"

At the end of the Second World War, Winston Churchill was aware that the British Empire was history. Great Britain had saved the honour of the European democracies, at great cost, and with huge sacrifices; but without America's military might—and without Russian resistance on the Eastern Front—the war would have taken a very different turn. While the conflict caused enormous material and economic damage to Britain, the United States emerged from the war vastly stronger and wealthier.[22] With an economy unrivalled in size and industrial capacity, and with superior military forces—characterized by global projection, naval and air primacy, and a nuclear monopoly—the United States now belonged to an entirely different and new category in the international system, that of "superpower".[23] Churchill himself recognized, in his famous "Iron Curtain" speech in March 1946, that the war had finally elevated the United States to the "pinnacle" of world power. The end of the conflict symbolically marked the transition of this influence from the British to the American Anglosphere.

America's strong opposition to British rule in India was one of the reasons why Britain had to give it up in 1947. The Americans had financially supported their British cousins with the implicit condition that new forms of international control and trusteeship would replace colonies. As Christopher Hitchens has rightly observed, "almost from the declaration of war against Nazi Germany, Churchill was engaged in a sort of 'Second Front', to protect the British Empire, against his putative ally".[24] The implications of this power transition within the Anglo-Saxon world became clear to all in 1956 with the Suez Crisis. The United States, without so much as a by-your-leave, blocked the old European colonial powers (including Great Britain) from affecting the new balance of power that was taking shape in the Middle East. In just a decade, the shift from an empire of the past to an empire of the future had been completed.

Cooperation between America and Britain had been unprecedentedly close in all aspects of the war effort, and was epitomized by the extraordinarily friendly and effective (if by no means always harmonious) relationship between US President Franklin Delano Roosevelt and British Prime Minister Winston Churchill.[25] The Anglo-American alliance during the war created the "special relationship", a term popularized by Churchill once again in his "Iron Curtain" speech. Despite persistent differences of perspective and interests, and often sharp disagreement over how to conduct the war or plan the peace, the American and British governments both saw the continuation of their close diplomatic, military, and intelligence partnership as one of the pillars on which to build the post-war world order—the foundation and complement of the broader architecture erected around the newly created United Nations.[26]

According to the "Grand Design" envisaged by Roosevelt during the conflict, Britain was destined to play a role of primary importance within the post-war order, being one of the "Four Policemen" in charge of ensuring world peace and stability, together with the United States, the Soviet Union, and the Republic of China. In particular, Britain was expected to share hegemony over continental Europe with the Soviet Union, allowing the United States to maintain its role as external balancer—similar to the role played by the United Kingdom under the Pax Britannica.[27] The Pax Americana, however, turned out to be something quite different. The rapid deterioration of relations with the Soviet Union, the risk of political and social collapse on a European continent devastated by war, and Britain's inability to autonomously counterbalance Russia induced President Harry Truman to take on a leading role in Western Europe's economic, political, and military reconstruction.[28] The launch of the Marshall Plan in 1947 and the creation of the Atlantic Alliance in 1949 cemented the American presence in Europe and established the United States as the undisputed leader of the West, not a distant balancer or a *primus inter pares* with respect to Britain, but a directly engaged hegemonic power that was "formally invited" to play that role.[29]

Relations within the Anglosphere were thus substantially transformed in the aftermath of the war as a result of the outbreak of the Cold War and of the United States' rise to the status of a global power. While the Cold War ensured that Anglo-American cooperation continued after the conflict, from then on, any illusions of equality between the two prominent members of the Anglo-Saxon community were over, leading to Britain's reluctant if inevitable assumption of a subordinate role with respect to the United States, whatever criteria one cared to use to gauge their respective power.[30]

The relationship between Britain and America retained its "special" connotation throughout the 1950s, and indeed probably until the end of Harold Macmillan's premiership in 1963; and yet it was never again as close as it had been during the war.[31] As NATO's military leader, the

United States was now the dominant power in Western Europe, and even supplanted Britain as the main security partner for the Commonwealth nations—including Canada, which joined the Atlantic Alliance as a founder member in 1949, and even Australia and New Zealand, which signed the ANZUS treaty in 1951.[32] In the meantime the Commonwealth had been formed, with the London Declaration of 1949, to hold the former territories of the British Empire together in a loose organization of "free and equal" member states with the British monarchy at its "head". As a highly imperfect heir to the empire, the Commonwealth was never intended to become a decisive organization in international relations after 1945. It did not even play an especially crucial role in forging British foreign policy. The world's focal point had shifted from the United Kingdom to the United States, and the American Empire was not a simple continuation of the British Empire.

In light of the wide gap in status and responsibilities between the United States and Britain—global for the former, increasingly regional and European for the latter—and given the impact of the Suez Crisis of 1956, the very concept of an Anglosphere began to appear inadequate as an intellectual tool for interpreting international relations. At least throughout the Cold War it lost much of its appeal as a political project, being absorbed and replaced by American hegemony in both diplomatic practice and discourse.

The United States' primacy in the English-speaking world, and in the West as a whole, extended to the realm of culture. Reflecting American military and economic might, and as a result of the ideological competition with the Soviet Union "for the soul of mankind", American cultural products—from Hollywood movies to rock and pop music and literature—"invaded" the Western bloc, where the emergence of mass consumer societies coincided with the adoption of social norms and lifestyles that originated in the United States.[33] In the decade after the fall of the Berlin Wall this phenomenon spread to the rest of the world, as geopolitical "unipolarity" and the emergence of new technologies further accelerated the interconnected processes of economic globalization and cultural Americanization.[34]

Across Western Europe, American cultural penetration was greeted with admiration, but also with resistance, in particular by the older generations.[35] In Britain, fears of cultural "colonization" by the United

States were normally confined to intellectual circles on both sides of the political spectrum—although widespread anti-American sentiment periodically flared up in British grassroots opinion, particularly at times of transatlantic friction.[36] Overall, however, because of its strong preexisting linguistic, historical, and cultural ties with the United States, Britain proved particularly fertile terrain for American cultural exports.[37] Certainly, Anglo-American cultural exchange went in both directions, and Britain was able to exploit elements of American cultural hegemony—most importantly the globalization of the English language—to its own advantage, increasing its ability to project its cultural influence overseas.[38] But even in this respect the "special relationship" was essentially an unequal one. After all, it was the American century, not the Anglo-Saxon century, that dawned after the Second World War.[39]

Transatlantic America for a European Britain

Notwithstanding the cynicism of sceptics such as Dean Acheson regarding the British role, close ties with the United Kingdom in the immediate post-war era—particularly in the fields of military, intelligence and nuclear cooperation—were not simply a British "myth"; they were a diplomatic reality recognized and actively cultivated in Washington.[40] For the Truman Administration, in fact, being able to share the burden of containment of the Soviet Union with Britain was helpful in overcoming congressional objections to new American foreign-policy commitments.[41]

For Britain, the "special relationship" was conceived in the 1950s as an alternative to cooperation with Europe; for America, on the contrary, it made greater sense when also combined with an active British role in Europe. A consensus gradually emerged in the American foreign-policy and defence establishment to the effect that Britain's cooperation with Europe was in the best interests not only of Britain itself, but also of the United States. Only by being involved in European political and security affairs could the United Kingdom effectively play the role of a transatlantic "go-between".[42] This has produced an important corollary; ever since the 1960s, the United States has been looking at its relationship with Britain through a transatlantic rather than an "Anglo-Saxon" lens.

It is true that America's support for a European United Kingdom partly reflected an implicit acknowledgement of the "special" cultural and political affinity colouring the Anglo-American relationship. In America's view, Britain's involvement would ensure that a more united Europe would also be more democratic, open, and—most importantly—loyal to the transatlantic bond.[43] From America's standpoint, Britain's international role was, in any case, post-imperial and regional: a diminished status that the British political establishment and public opinion were far slower to accept, and with which many of them never fully identified—as discussed in Chapter One.

Despite ambiguities and mixed results, the United States thus explicitly encouraged Britain's engagement with the Europeans. American policy towards European cooperation marked a "first" in world history: "It was the first time a major power fostered unity rather than discord among nations in a part of the world where it had significant interests."[44] The dominant view in Washington—especially in the then "Eurocentric" State Department—was that a more integrated Europe within the broader framework of the Atlantic Alliance would serve multiple key American foreign-policy interests, stretching from "dual containment" of the Soviet Union and Germany to the establishment across the Atlantic of a dynamic, integrated market open to American exports and investments.[45]

While bringing different degrees of pressure to bear, both the Truman and Eisenhower administrations advocated British participation in the building up of the European Community—a fact that caused recurrent friction with the United Kingdom. American diplomats complained time and again that their counterparts in London were "dragging their feet" over the issue of European integration, while British officials resented Washington's attempts to dictate the priorities of their country's foreign policy.[46] As one British civil servant put it: "We are being asked to join the Germans, who started two world wars; the French, who had in 1940 collapsed in the face of German aggression; the Italians, who changed sides; and the Low Countries, of whom not much was known but who seemed to have put up little resistance to Germany."[47]

British attitudes started to change in the late 1950s, when the "shock" of the Suez Crisis revealed both the limits of the "special relationship" with America and the decline in Britain's diplomatic freedom and ability to project power globally. By the time Harold Macmillan's Conservative government submitted an application to join the European Economic Community (EEC) in 1961, the United States had been openly encouraging Britain to make Europe the main priority of its foreign policy. "The UK should not be encouraged to oppose or stay apart from that movement [towards European unity] by doubts as to the US attitude or by hopes of a 'special' relation with the US," reads a report submitted by Dean Acheson to President John F. Kennedy in March 1961.[48]

America's explicit advocacy of British membership of the EEC was also partly motivated by a changing economic and political international environment. In particular, America hoped that British membership of the EEC would offset the risk that, under the leadership of French President Charles de Gaulle, an economically resurgent Western Europe would be tempted to adopt both an increasingly protectionist trade policy and greater autonomy in foreign policy, distancing itself from the Atlantic framework.[49]

American pressure encouraged Macmillan to reverse his predecessors' position on the issue, but was not a decisive factor in Britain's decision to finally seek membership of the European club.[50] At the same time, America's explicit support for British membership of the EEC strengthened de Gaulle's fears that Britain would play the role of a "Trojan horse" for the United States, inducing him to veto Britain's first two applications to join the European club and delaying its membership until 1973.[51] With the United Kingdom finally in, successive American administrations sought to prevent British disengagement from the European continent—in 1974–5, for instance, Henry Kissinger informed British Foreign Secretary James Callaghan of America's opposition to Britain's potential withdrawal from the EEC.[52] For the United States, European cooperation, thanks also to Britain's influence, would strengthen rather than weaken the Western world order.

During the 1980s the ideological affinity and close personal bond between Ronald Reagan and Margaret Thatcher renewed the "special relationship".[53] At a personal level, Reagan appeared sympathetic to Thatcher's limited view of Europe—conceived essentially as an area of economic liberalization and intergovernmental cooperation while ruling out political integration.[54] Following the fall of the Berlin Wall,

George H. W. Bush and his Secretary of State James Baker strongly encouraged European cooperation, downplaying the importance of the "special relationship" with the United Kingdom and pressuring a reluctant Thatcher to move closer to Europe.[55] America's support for European integration continued under the Democratic administration of Bill Clinton, who endorsed the steps taken by European governments in the 1990s—including the approval of the Maastricht Treaty, but especially the launching of enlargement to Eastern Europe.[56] American attitudes to the European Union cooled significantly under the presidency of George W. Bush in light of European objections to the war in Iraq.[57] American foreign policy left Europe broadly divided, with the United Kingdom looking once again to its "special relationship" with the United States. In any case, American support for Britain's participation in the European project was not reversed.[58]

In light of this historical record, Barack Obama's support for the United Kingdom's continued membership of the European Union was hardly surprising. It is true that Obama marked a certain amount of distance, in both style and substance, from the "old" transatlantic establishment, presenting himself as the "first Pacific President".[59] Also, as a result of his "pivot to Asia", European expectations that Obama's election would inject new vitality into the transatlantic partnership after the crisis of the Bush years were largely dashed. Relations with the European Union were, and are, no longer at the top of America's list of priorities.[60]

Nevertheless, the United States' fundamental interest in European unity and stability remained unchanged;[61] this explains Barack Obama's open support for Remain, during a visit to London in April 2016, which was probably counterproductive but has to be seen within the context of America's continued stake in Europe.[62] Brexit was opposed by America out of fears that it would destabilize the whole European Union, favouring Russia and shifting intra-European balances even more in Germany's favour. At a joint press conference with David Cameron in London, Barack Obama dismissed the Leave campaigners' claims that, once outside the European Union, Britain could quickly seal a bilateral trade deal with the United States. Instead, the American president stressed that the decision to leave the European Union—America's largest trading partner—would probably relegate Britain to the "back of the queue" in trade relations with Washington.[63]

A NOT-SO-SPECIAL RELATIONSHIP

Small Anglosphere, big world

The first official meeting between May and Trump in January 2017 was greeted by both sides as a crucial first step towards returning the Anglo-American relationship to the intrinsic "specialness" it had enjoyed under Reagan and Thatcher. However, unlike in the 1980s, the initial enthusiasm masked a lack of convergence in terms of national interests and foreign-policy priorities. At a superficial level, ideological affinity prevails—especially on immigration control. Looking a bit deeper, what emerges is a basic inconsistency between Britain and America's sovereignist agendas. The former is about national control in a multilateral environment and about free trade; the latter is about unilateralism and protectionism—or fair trade. In addition, Donald Trump's unpredictability has made it extraordinarily difficult for the British government to consider America a reliable partner in the construction of a successful post-Brexit foreign policy. In March 2017, only a few months after reassuring Theresa May that Britain would be at the "front of the queue" in negotiations for a free-trade agreement with the United States, Trump appeared to suggest that priority would be given to trade relations with the European Union instead[64]—but Trump again mentioned preferential trade relations with Britain during his highly controversial visit to London in July 2018. At a NATO summit in Brussels in May 2018, the American president also appeared to call NATO's usefulness into question, thus undermining the key reference point in Britain's security policy.[65]

On a broader level, Trump's relationship with Britain, and his personal affinity with May in particular, have been far from harmonious. His harsh rhetoric and confrontational policies have made him deeply unpopular with the British public. According to a poll taken in January 2017, only 22 per cent of Britons view him favourably, 50 per cent consider him "dangerous", and 64 per cent deem him a threat to international stability.[66] As a consequence, Trump's planned visit to the United Kingdom was first downgraded from "state" to "official" (after over 2 million people signed a petition demanding its cancellation), and was then postponed to July 2018.[67] For his part, notwithstanding his continuous infatuation with hardcore Brexiteers, the American president hardly indicated any special interest in building a special or strong relationship with Britain, while remarks by Trump himself have caused numerous diplomatic squabbles with the United Kingdom, including on intelligence issues and anti-terrorism, one of the key pillars of the American relationship with Britain.[68]

Friction between America and Britain hit a high point in November 2017, when Trump retweeted three anti-Muslim videos originally posted by the extremist group Britain First, causing outrage across the Atlantic. In responding to criticism by the British Prime Minister's spokesperson, Trump launched a rare personal attack on Theresa May, urging her not to focus on him so much as "on the destructive Radical Islamic Terrorism that is taking place within the United Kingdom".[69] His remarks stirred further controversy, adding to the perception of potential damage to the Anglo-American relationship.[70]

Trump's visit to London, in July 2018, confirmed the volatility of a not-so-special relationship.[71] In the midst of a very serious crisis within the May Cabinet, caused by disagreement about Brexit's management, Trump openly criticized May's soft approach, siding with those hardcore Brexiteers such as Boris Johnson, who were leaving the government. Intervening in Britain's domestic affairs, Trump made the same mistake that Obama had made two years before, even if from opposite positions. And he was then forced to contain the damage by praising May for her "fantastic job".[72]

Alongside Trump's erratic personality and abrasive rhetoric, his support for (a hard) Brexit reveals a deeper inclination for a weakening of the European Union, including Germany, seen more as an unfair economic competitor than as an ally. According to press reports, Trump even offered the mirage of a favourable trade deal to French President Emmanuel Macron in exchange for France quitting the European Union.[73] This is a fundamental shift as compared to the post-war legacy we briefly examined before. And yet this adversarial view of the European Union, shared primarily by hardcore Brexiteers, is an unrealistic basis for a future bilateral relationship.

The existence of major power and policy differences between the United States and the United Kingdom remains a fundamental obstacle to re-launching the "special relationship". For a start, it is first and foremost a relationship between a leading global power and a European power. While the United States can afford an "America First" policy without undermining its global influence (although its soft power may well be impaired), the United Kingdom cannot by definition pursue the same unilateral path without condemning itself to international irrelevance. Only by leveraging the link with the United States can the "Global Britannia" narrative be credible and more than a national myth.

Moreover, the asymmetry between a global power and a mid-sized power is compounded by diverging attitudes towards the world order. Trump's worldview has marked a major departure from the United States' traditional role as guarantor of the liberal international order and is at odds with the "cautious and conventional globalism" of Theresa May.[74] The political class that was propelled to power after the 2016 referendum was committed to preserving the post-war order that Britain had helped to forge. It interpreted the vote as a mandate to engage with the world, as Britain did when it was a maritime power.[75] In essence, Trump is interested in reducing America's financial burden in supporting the old liberal order; whereas post-Brexit Britain is eager to alter the balance of power in Europe without dismantling multilateralism. In addition, from the United States' point of view, a Great Britain less able to influence the dynamics within the European Union will also become a less interesting interlocutor, even if Britain is likely to remain America's most natural European partner of choice in intelligence and security.

The fundamental tension between Trump's inward-looking "America First" strategy and the Brexiteers' outward-looking "world island" narrative has made the relationship far from special and far from harmonious. America and Britain have not been aligned on a number of important policy issues. Trump withdrew from the Paris Climate Agreement, while May's government has continued to subscribe to it, despite refusing to join other G7 members in condemning America's decision.[76] Theresa May described as "unhelpful" for the peace process the decision by the United States to move its embassy in Israel to Jerusalem.[77] Britain has continued to support the Iran nuclear deal even when the Trump administration decided to impose new sanctions on Iran;[78] and Trump's attitudes on trade, combined with his strong aversion to the World Trade Organization (WTO), clash with the free-trade aspirations of a post-Brexit Britain.[79]

In all these instances, the British government adopted positions that largely coincided with those expressed by other European Union countries, which is a powerful indication that Britain's foreign-policy outlook is closer to the continent than to Washington.[80] In reality, an instinctive difference persists between the geopolitical vision of a landbound power such as Germany and that of a former sea empire like Great Britain.[81] Yet there is no doubt that over the past two decades— and after the spectacular failure of its support for the invasion of Iraq in 2003—the United Kingdom has narrowed its gap with the European powers, among other reasons because aligning with America has proven to be costly rather than rewarding on the domestic political front.

Of course, the conflicting agendas of the May Cabinet and the Trump administration have not prevented the two countries from closely cooperating on specific issues—such as the response to the March 2018 poisoning of former Russian spy and British double agent Sergei Skripal and his daughter in Salisbury and, in April 2018, joint airstrikes against three military sites in Syria in the wake of a chemical attack on civilians in Douma.[82] In the former case, the Trump administration joined several Western governments in showing strong solidarity with Britain, and took its boldest action yet against Vladimir Putin's regime by imposing new sanctions and by expelling sixty Russian diplomats—the highest number since the Cold War.[83] In the latter case, the United States, Britain, and France acted in close coordination: according to critics and supporters alike, the determination to display Anglo-American unity played an important role in May's decision over Syria, proving that, in the Middle East at least, Britain remains one of the United States' closest and most useful military partners, alongside France.[84]

If we take a closer look, however, we shall see that both cases can hardly be interpreted as a fresh boost to the "special relationship". In theory, the British position on Russia—which is far tougher than that of either Germany or France (not to mention Italy)—should attract the sympathy and support of America for closer cooperation. In addition, since Russia continues to be a highly divisive issue for European policy when it comes to sanctions, a special relationship with Britain aimed at containing Russia should appeal to America. And yet on a number of important policy issues, Trump's position on Russia is ambiguous, as is his personal relationship with Putin: in fact, the response to the Skripal case is said to have been adopted against Trump's personal inclinations, while Russia is becoming a sensitive issue for domestic rather than foreign policy.[85] As for Syria, May's attempt to highlight Britain's closeness to the United States has largely backfired. Indeed, the intense criticism to which the British Prime Minister was subjected at home for "blindly" joining America's strikes and authorizing a military operation without proper consultation highlighted the fragility of her government's domestic position. In other words, building a "special relationship" with Washington over the Middle East is difficult for domestic political reasons: on a far smaller scale, we can look back to the precedent set by Tony Blair in 2003 at the time of the Iraq invasion.

Despite what many observers believed in 2016, the special relationship is losing shine and is unlikely to generate a new, post-Pax Americana and post-Brexit version of the Anglosphere—even if the leaders of the two countries were to change in the meantime. The United Kingdom, once out of the European Union, cannot realistically aspire to be the United States' interlocutor of choice in Europe, except for intelligence (where the UK-USA agreement underpins the Five Eyes grouping) and hard security (as proved by the fact that the Americans continue to offer the British unparalleled access to their nuclear ballistic missile technology). France is already attempting, but to no avail for the time being, to fill the void left by Brexit, while Germany, given its economic weight, certainly has its cards to play. All that means that the era of "specialness" in US–British relations is probably over: America is likely to follow a path of parallel bilateral links, in different fields, with different European interlocutors.

A genuine new boost to the special relationship between America and Britain could only materialize if the former's relations with Russia degenerate drastically, bringing back the primacy of military and intelligence power, and if Brexit eventually contributes to the breakup of the European Union. However, as long as the European Union continues to exist, Brexit will also reduce Britain's influence over the United States. Paradoxically, the appeal of a tight Anglo-American alliance (tighter than it already is) might diminish for Britain as well. If an "America First" agenda reduces the international credibility of the United States, then the United Kingdom might be less inclined to associate itself with the United States. Similarly, if an increase in tariffs becomes the signature trade policy of the United States going forward, then a post-Brexit United

Kingdom will be forced to distance itself from America in order to preserve its national interest in promoting a more liberalist stance. And there is more: if the United Kingdom remains anchored to the EU through a customs union, a preferential bilateral trade deal with the United States will not be on the cards—as Donald Trump himself pointed out, reiterating, alongside hardcore Brexiteers, his criticism of a "soft" Brexit.

In conclusion, a post-Pax Americana Anglosphere can only emerge over the lifeless body of the European Union. In a breakup scenario, the United States will have a greater incentive to support a preferential relationship with the United Kingdom to counterbalance Europe's potential inclination to gravitate towards Russia. In this case, the Anglosphere and Eurasia could become two rival poles in a continental struggle for power. One might argue that the basic structure of world politics would return to its origins, with the liberal sea powers pitted against the continental land-based powers.[86]

As long as the European Union continues to exist, America's attitude to Europe (both under Trump and afterwards) will be extensively influenced by its (difficult) ties with Germany, and will be centred on trade bargaining with the European Union and on variable bilateral relationships. Leaving aside Trump's volatile rhetoric, the United States will continue to support NATO, while pressing its European members to shoulder more of the financial burden. Like it or not, NATO remains the most efficient solution for the United States to counterbalance Russia in Europe. Equally, from America's point of view, the Anglosphere in any of its possible arrangements is hardly a substitute for the European Union both as trade and foreign-policy partner—while the Five Eyes partnership (along with all the informal types of cooperation mentioned in Chapter Five) already exists, and works rather effectively.

Should the United States ever decide to invest more efforts in strengthening the Anglosphere as a sphere of influence, its plan would probably contradict what the Brexiteers have in mind. In light of its imperial past, Britain still believes itself to be the fulcrum of this regional grouping. But that was the Anglosphere 1.0—something too obsolete and too anachronistic for today's world. Countries that were once the outlying members of the Commonwealth such as Australia and India are potentially becoming leading players in their own right as a result of the ongoing power shift from the West to the East and the growing economic and geopolitical rivalry between America and China.[87] The United Kingdom, outside the European Union, risks losing its influence not only in European affairs but, as a result, within the Anglosphere itself. So, its special relationship with the United States, if it ever was such, will turn out to be rather ordinary. If anything, what is emerging is an Anglosphere 3.0 that crosses the Pacific rather than the Atlantic, based on competition between the United States and China: the old and new "empires of the mind", as Winston Churchill would have put it.

CONCLUSION

NOSTALGIA AND THE FUTURE OF SOVEREIGNTY

"I long therefore I am"
Svetlana Boym

Nostalgia has infected global politics in unexpected ways, becoming a source of comfort for marginalized individuals, but also of chaos for a fragmenting world order. Nostalgia per se would not be a problem. Looking back to the past can virtuously inspire the future. But jingoistic leaders are nourishing this state of mind with negative sentiments such as fear, anger, and resentment displacing optimism as the ruling emotion. In order to deploy nostalgia as an emotional weapon in the political debate, nationalists construct national narratives that produce a desire for restoration, pointing to an idealized temporal destination and creating an artificial sense of historical continuity. They walk on the edge of history and myths, truth and lies, to instil among their citizens a strong—almost unbearable—sense of loss that induces them to make irrational political choices, such as Brexit. Nostalgia freezes time just for a moment, creating the illusion that resetting the world's clock is within reach. But as time goes by and distortions of reality induced by the longing process fade away, it becomes clear how difficult it is for the past, especially a glorious one, to fit an ordinary present. The uncertainty surrounding the future of the United Kingdom outside the European Union epitomizes the gap between restorative aspirations and political reality, up to the point that a future "Breturn" is not completely out of the question.

173

The June 2016 referendum, which grew out of infighting within the Conservative Party, was influenced by nostalgic myths concerning Britain's role in the world. Dreams of a "Global Britain" (unchained from European constraints) or a more "parochial" Anglosphere were thrown into the public debate, also thanks to the continuous but subconscious efforts of the cultural and entertainment industry to revive imperial and patriotic memories. Once again, British exceptionalism was back to the fore at its best. But the twenty-first century looks very different compared to the Edwardian era celebrated by hardcore Brexiteers. Any objective reality check shows that it is highly unlikely for the United Kingdom to act as a power on the world stage without a close relationship with the European Union. In addition, once outside the European Union, Britain will find itself in a highly asymmetric relationship with the United States, which will be tempted to find a new partner to influence the European debate. Since the British Empire no longer exists and the Commonwealth is a more than imperfect substitute, the ideal of "Greater Britain" appears not just too ambitious, but simply unrealistic, and even anachronistic. As hard as it may sound to the ears of a proud Leaver, Britain is no longer in a position to become the political hub of a network of geographically dispersed and independent countries. At the other end of the spectrum, the idealized "Little England", which would turn the United Kingdom inward, is simply too small and too divided even to keep its constituents united. After the nostalgic hangover following the vote, a process of rational adjustment to the consequences of Brexit has started to take place in Britain. But, as *The Economist* wrote in December 2018, it will be difficult to return to normality any time soon: "The political system is all but paralysed, the country is divided into warring ideological tribes, the civil service is overwhelmed and, in the event of no deal, Britain would be staring into the abyss."[1]

Britain is the first country to have experienced a true form of nostalgic nationalism that has resulted in a temporally regressive decision—divorce from the European Union. When a country falls victim to this nostalgic malaise, it projects itself into a different era and perceives itself as something "temporally" different from the rest of the world. The United Kingdom initially entered Brexit negotiations with the perceived strength of a global status that had actually vanished many decades earlier. To say the least, the Brexit vote was supposed to take Britain back to 1973—actually, not a really bright political, economic, or historical moment. But hardcore Brexiteers probably believed that they were travelling back to a more glorious past. They used nostalgia defensively to restore full sovereignty, offensively to re-establish Britain as a dominant power, and cooperatively to envisage a future of tight relations with their Anglo-Saxon cousins. Nowhere else is nostalgia so multifaceted.

Although it is difficult to identify another place where national consciousness and dissatisfaction with its current global role are as intertwined as in Britain, similar forms of nostalgic nationalism might affect other countries in the future. Nostalgia, after all, has penetrated the foundations of the socio-political fabric of several nations, and structural forces such as ageing populations, mass immigration, and technological disruptions will reinforce attitudes of longing. This is why it is important to start a serious discussion about the "nostalgic politics" that is likely to become a distinctive feature of this part of the twenty-first century and a threat to the liberal international order. As we have discussed throughout this book, the problem with nostalgia is that it induces individuals to shift their political attitudes in favour of a nationalist agenda. In the end, the politics of nostalgia can be seen as part of the battle for sovereignty to regain control over the fate of a nation and its identity.

The consequences of this emotional political swing are huge, as sovereignty, with all its facets, is at the heart of global politics. States interact with one another, aggressively or cooperatively, on the basis of their right to exercise certain powers or certain degrees of power. At a global level, this propensity to reclaim sovereignty and draw exclusionary group boundaries on the basis of nostalgic narratives risks creating a Hobbesian scenario, fuelling Great Power competition at its best. Within the Anglosphere, restorative arguments might not be enough to build a more cohesive network of Anglo-Saxon countries. After all, Britain yearns for a time that its cousins actually prefer to forget—a time at which they were subservient to the Mother Country. But it is the idea of an integrated West that is most threatened by the nostalgic rhetoric of bygone times when countries were (supposedly) in full control of their sovereignty.

Two competing forms of sovereignty run through the Western world: the Anglo-Saxon view of pure national sovereignty; and the European concept of hybrid sovereignty. The former is embodied in the NATO alliance; the latter is exemplified by the European Union. From its start NATO was designed as a political–military alliance of sovereign nations, centred on an American guarantee and based upon pooling resources—not sharing sovereignty. It has functioned on the basis of a specific power relationship, in which the United States' status as "superpower" and its readiness to protect Europe were taken for granted. Sovereignty was never lost in foreign policy, security, and defence. Throughout its evolution, instead, the entire European project has challenged traditional views of the nation-state, resting on the adoption of a flexible idea of sovereignty: surrendering part of it was in fact necessary to create a multi-layered institutional structure. Shared sovereignty—more than an alliance, less than a super-state— was the European answer to many twentieth-century challenges: a response made possible by America's security umbrella, i.e. by a tangible manifestation of an adapted (American-led) Anglosphere.

The NATO+EU configuration has never been a well-oiled mechanism, but it has proved to work pretty well most of the time. Each organization developed its distinct way of doing things, and even different "strategic cultures" (NATO being, inevitably, much more Anglo-Saxon than continental European). Yet, certain differences turned out to be strengths, not weaknesses. The two groupings specialized in largely complementary tasks, while growing in membership at their own pace. As long as Britain safely belonged to both overlapping circles of close partners and allies, it was also able to exploit its unique position at the confluence of the European and Anglo-Saxon worlds. As we have seen with respect to the Five Eyes network, in the field of intelligence gathering and sharing, Britain maintained a double-track policy approach by relying on the Anglosphere, even while cautiously exploring the possibility of European arrangements in areas related to internal and external security. It has positively contributed to this "hybrid" experiment in distinctive ways, not only as an active member of NATO, but also, of course, as a member (albeit reluctant) of the European Union. Nostalgia is thus consistent with NATO, but less so with the European experiment—despite the many opt-outs granted to the United Kingdom over the years.

CONCLUSION

Britain is now leaning towards an Anglo-Saxon form of pure sovereignty, while rejecting the European hybrid. In doing so, it is leveraging memories of its imperial past, or at least of its full pre-1973 sovereignty. By filtering out all the negative aspects of the British Empire, nostalgia exalts the prestige, power, and influence that came with the imperial endeavour. In the United Kingdom's case, a return to a more traditional form of nation-state does not include the negative connotations of authoritarian governance, lost wars, and foreign occupation. It is more a form of patriotism than nationalism. This is in sharp contrast to the experience of continental Europe, where nationalism was one of its trademarks and turned the first half of the twentieth century into a violent nightmare. The solution developed by Western Europe was exactly an Anglo/European combination to its sovereignty conundrum; just as NATO provided the hard edge to counter the Soviets, the European Community/European Union relied on "soft power" and evolved into an elaborate structure enabling its members to pursue their key national interests without thwarting those of their partners. The wider NATO framework thus made it easier for Europeans to focus on their shared goals rather than on their competing interests—those, obviously, never disappeared.

However, having a less troublesome "nationalistic" past does not imply that the British can really re-establish a full form of national sovereignty based on a rational analysis of today's global realities. In other words, the issue is whether a bright option for Britain outside Europe does exist, especially at a time when the global role of the United States is at best uncertain. One of the illusions sparked by Brexit is that the United Kingdom can provide a solid link between North America and Europe, fulfilling the connecting role originally envisaged by Winston Churchill after the Second World War. The signals from across the pond are not encouraging, as we have analyzed in this book. Sovereignty as embodied by the Trump presidency ("America First") is hardly compatible with such a British role, but the same can be said of many of the social and political forces behind Brexit. Indeed, nationalism—especially when coloured by nativist sentiments—is not conducive to any long-term alliance, as it ultimately relies on the primacy of the national interest in a way that makes compromises very difficult to sell domestically. Of course, traditional "realism" is also rooted in the primacy of national interests, but the pragmatic and flex-ible nature of realpolitik allows for many tactical adjustments that often prove intolerable to hard-line nationalists of the twenty-first-century type—also because of their constant appeal to emotional factors.

Britain's nostalgia risks compromising the future not just of the United Kingdom, but also of the European Union. Even if the British have often prevented Brussels from pursuing further integration, they have always been a fundamental counterweight to Franco-German pre-dominance: with Brexit, the internal balance of power within the EU will be fundamentally altered. Should Brexit remain a one-off event, Brussels can still absorb it. However, should nostalgic aspirations aimed at regaining full sovereignty become viral across the continent, then the whole European integration process would be endangered. This would mean returning to where European countries have come from, rather than moving towards what they desired to achieve when they launched the European project. Nostalgia reinforces traditional sovereignty as a response to globalization's challenges, but also to some of the problems generated by European integration itself in terms of accountability and effectiveness—hence the aspiration to "take back control". Hardcore Eurosceptics, after all, believe that the nation-state remains the only political space in which freedom and democracy thrive.

Brexit could reinforce centrifugal trends in many European Union members, encouraging nationalists of various stripes to take their chances and raise the stakes. Whatever one thinks of Brexit, the picture concerning the European project that the Leave campaign depicted was troubling, with weak common institutions that fail to deliver on most of the issues that citizens really care about, a fragmented union (East–West, North–South) in an even more fragmented European continent, with immigration as a perceived threat that voters want to see con-tained by "sovereignist" governments and a growing Atlantic divide. The contest between "sovereignist" parties, taking advantage of the debate on immigration and border control, and pro-European ones is already on full display across the continent. This phenomenon now clearly involves core countries such as Italy, and will probably create the con-ditions for other coalition governments willing to openly challenge the status quo. More than a contagion, this seems to be a knock-on effect, because populism produces political movements that feed on each other and could—at least theoretically—cause inter-state competition to spiral out of control. It is fair to say, however, that the Italian case also offers some reassurance that economic constraints have a powerful moderating influence on new "sovereignist" leaders. In other words, some of the costs of challenging or just renegotiating the status quo must be met up front, well before the "Exit stage".

The lesson of Brexit, in the end, could play in favour of the "Remainers", rather than the "Leavers" who are active across the continent. The Brexit negotiations have proved that, when confronted with an existential risk, the European Union can react in a cohesive way. Despite Europe's internal weaknesses, Brexit shows the costs of the divorce option based on nostalgic claims that are completely detached from reality—and possibly the resilience of the European "core", which is now forced to deliver on its basic promises just in order to survive.

A partly integrated Europe can accommodate various degrees of "inter-governmentalism", and with it a certain degree of traditional sovereignty, but not "sovereignism" as the normal rule of the game. Its leaders and citizens need to understand that they cannot have both hard borders and freely-flowing goods, or an assertive zero–sum competition among governments as well as the win–win benefits of institutionalized cooperation. Brussels may probably withstand a mild form of nostalgic identity politics. For a large number of European citizens, nostalgia does not require a return to the past, but more likely a rejection of further change. The European Union must prove—with deeds, not words—the benefits of continental cooperation so as to address the global destabilizing forces that are knocking on Europe's door. A form of European resilience may manifest itself, and saving some sort of European "union" (at least with a small "u")—or, at a minimum, a functioning network of European states—may well become an imperative in the twenty-first century. While "Global Britannia" is proving to be an unrealistic fantasy, Britain itself is struggling to find its own post-Brexit path. For the reasons analysed in this book, Britain will be better off staying anchored to the European Union even once it divorces Brussels. It is in its interest that the European project should not fall apart. Equally, although the Trump administration tries to capitalize on Europe's internal weaknesses, America needs to avoid a sort of eastward drift of continental Europe towards Eurasia and away from the Atlantic.

Ending today's epidemic of nostalgia will not be easy. When the malaise was first studied in the seventeenth century, it was regarded as a disease that could be cured with leeches, warm hypnotic emulsions, opium and purging. If the conventional remedies of the time failed to produce a good result, a patient's symptoms could usually be alleviated by a physical return to the beloved motherland. Yet, at a time when experts and the traditional media are so distrusted, countering the false restorative nostalgia of nationalist and jingoistic leaders is not so straightforward. The resurgence of nostalgic politics and the nation-state as the locus of identity and sovereignty points to an important trend— re-nationalization that might end up triggering the disintegration of the West. Unless nationalist and protectionist pressures are kept in check, the Atlantic world and the West in its twentieth-century configuration may just turn out to be short-lived accidents of history. To succeed in the game of today's emotional politics, mainstream parties need to play by its rules. They should themselves leverage the past, which offers ample evidence that progress in the future is always still possible. They can counter restorative nostalgia with reflective nostalgia, fighting homesickness by making their citizens somewhat sick of home.

NOTES

INTRODUCTION

1. Pew Research Center, "Worldwide, People Divided on Whether Life Today is Better than in the Past", December 2017, http://www.pewglobal.org/2017/12/05/worldwide-people-divided-on-whether-life-today-is-better-than-in-the-past/, last accessed 2 June 2018.
2. Jamil Anderlini, "The Return of Mao: A New Threat to China's Politics", *Financial Times*, 29 September 2016, https://www.ft.com/content/63a5a9b2-85cd-11e6-8897-2359a58ac7a5, last accessed 10 June 2018.
3. Gideon Rachman, "Trump, Putin, Xi and the Rise of Nostalgic Nationalism", *Financial Times*, 2 January 2017, https://www.ft.com/content/198efe76-ce8b-11e6-b8ce-b9c03770f8b1, last accessed 20 June 2018.
4. Albert Weale, "Nostalgic Democracy Triumphs over Democratic Internationalism", *Political Quarterly* 87 (3), 2016, pp. 352–4.
5. Stuart Tannock, "Nostalgia Critique", *Cultural Studies* 9 (3), 1995, pp. 453–64.
6. David Cannadine, *Victorious Century: The United Kingdom 1800–1906*, New York: Viking, 2017, p. 476.
7. See Daron Acemoglu and James Robinson, *Why Nations Fail: The Origins of Power, Prosperity, and Poverty*, New York: Crown Business, 2012.
8. Tony Barber, "The Battle for Europe", *Financial Times*, 25 May 2016, https://www.ft.com/content/a326be86–20f7–11e6–9d4d-c11776a5124d, last accessed 20 April 2018.
9. Rafal Kierzenkowski, Nigel Pain, Elena Rusticelli, and Sanne Zwart, "The Economic Consequences of Brexit: A Taxing Decision", *OECD Economic Policy Papers*, No. 16, Paris: OECD Publishing, 2016, https://doi.org/10.1787/5jm0lsvdkf6k-en.

10. Thomas M. Nichols, *The Death of Expertise: The Campaign against Established Knowledge and Why it Matters*, Oxford: Oxford University Press, 2017.

11. Peter Walker, "Vince Cable Denies Calling Brexit Supporters Racist", *The Guardian*, 12 March 2018, https://www.theguardian.com/politics/2018/mar/12/vince-cable-denies-calling-brexit-supporters-racist, last accessed 26 June 2018.

12. For a thorough discussion about the distinction between national and imperial identities see Krishan Kumar, *The Idea of Englishness: English Culture, National Identity and Social Thought*, London: Routledge, 2016, pp. 31–46.

13. In the literature there is controversy over whether the United Kingdom built an imperial society on top of an imperial nation. The historians Bernard Porter and John MacKenzie originated the debate. Porter argued that the expansion of the empire had little effect on ordinary people in Britain, while MacKenzie stated that colonialism dominated British popular culture for much of the period. Both historians, however, agree that the United Kingdom was an imperial nation at the beginning of the nineteenth century. See Bernard Porter, *The Absent-Minded Imperialists: Empire, Society, and Culture in Britain*, Oxford: Oxford University Press, 2004, and John M. MacKenzie, "'Comfort' and 'Conviction': A Response to Bernard Porter", *Journal of Imperial and Commonwealth History* 36 (4), 2008, pp. 659–68.

14. Michael Kenny and Nick Pearce, *Shadows of Empire: The Anglosphere in British Politics*, London: Polity Press, 2018, pp. 156–7.

15. Anthony Barnet, "It's England's Brexit", *Open Democracy*, 4 June 2016, https://www.opendemocracy.net/uk/anthony-barnett/it-s-england-s-brexit, last accessed 10 June 2018.

16. See David Goodhart, *The Road to Somewhere: The Populist Revolt and the Future of Politics*, London: Hurst, 2017.

17. Andrew Roberts, *History of the English-Speaking Peoples Since 1990*, London: Weidenfeld & Nicolson, 2006, p. 1.

18. Andrea Bosco, *The Round Table Movement and the Fall of the "Second" British Empire (1909–1919)*, Cambridge: Cambridge Scholars Publishing, 2017, p. 98.

19. Lord Ashcroft, "How the United Kingdom Voted on Thursday … and Why", Lord Ashcroft Polls, 24 June 2016, https://lordashcroftpolls.com/2016/06/how-the-united-kingdom-voted-and-why/, last accessed 28 June 2018.

20. Ibid.

21. David Gowland, *Britain and the European Union*, London: Routledge, 2016, p. 28.

22. Menno Spiering, *A Cultural History of British Euroscepticism*, London: Routledge, 2015.
23. Christine Berberich, "This Green and Pleasant Land: Cultural Constructions of Englishness", in Robert Burden and Stephan Kohl (eds), *Landscape and Englishness*, Amsterdam: Rodopi, 2006, p. 207.
24. Kate Fox, *Watching the English: The Hidden Rules of English Behaviour*, London: Hodder, 2005, p. 210.
25. As discussed above, it is conceptually important to make a distinction between British and English identity, and this is an issue that has gained prominence in recent years in academic literature. Throughout the book, however, we will be less careful in taking this difference into account, and will often use the terms English and British ignoring the subtleties behind them in terms of sub-national identities and all their implications.
26. David Edgerton, *The Rise and Fall of the British Nation: A Twentieth-Century History*, London: Allen Lane, 2018, p. xxx.
27. Ibid., pp. xix–xxx.
28. Oliver Wright, "EU Referendum: Clegg Warns Brexit Will Leave Britain with 'no Empire, no Union and no Special Relationship' with US", *The Independent*, 20 April 2016, https://www.independent.co.uk/news/uk/politics/eu-referendum-nick-clegg-warns-brexitwill-leave-britain-with-no-empire-no-union-and-no-special-a6993371.html, last accessed 20 April 2018.
29. A very important contribution to the analysis of the politics of emotion in global affairs was offered by Dominique Moisi, *The Geopolitics of Emotion: How Cultures of Fear, Humiliation, and Hope are Reshaping the World*, London: Anchor, 2010. Moisi's book is not focused on nostalgia.

1. A GLOBAL EPIDEMIC

1. Richard Evans, *The Pursuit of Power: Europe, 1815–1914*, London: Penguin, 2016, pp. 334–5.
2. Stephen Constantine, "Migrants and Settlers", in William Roger Louis (ed.), *The Oxford History of the British Empire*, vol. IV: *The Twentieth Century*, ed. Judith M. Brown, Oxford: Oxford University Press, 2004, chapter 7.
3. Piers Brendon, *The Decline and Fall of the British Empire: 1781–1997*, London: Jonathan Cape, 2008, p. 640.
4. Will Dahlgreen, "The British Empire is Something to be Proud Of", *YouGov Report*, 26 July 2014, https://yougov.co.uk/topics/lifestyle/articles-reports/2014/07/26/britain-proud-its-empire, last accessed 26 June 2018.

5. Jeffrey M. Richards, "Imperial Heroes for a Post-Imperial Age: Films and the End of Empire", in Stuart Ward (ed.), *British Culture and the Empire*, Manchester: Manchester University Press, 2001, p. 143.

6. Niall Ferguson, *Empire: How Britain Made the Modern World*, London: Penguin, 2004, pp. xiv–xvii.

7. Krishan Kumar, *Visions of Empire: How Five Imperial Regimes Shaped the World*, Princeton: Princeton University Press, 2017, pp. 465–75.

8. Peter Pomerantsev, "The New British Exceptionalism", *The American Interest*, 27 August 2018, https://www.the-american-interest.com/2018/08/27/the-new-british-exceptionalism/, last accessed 31 December 2018.

9. Peter Dominiczack and Ben Riley-Smith, "Theresa May Opens Door to Re-Commissioning of Royal Yacht *Britannia*", *Daily Telegraph*, 20 September 2016, https://www.telegraph.co.uk/news/2016/09/19/theresa-may-opens-door-to-recommissioning-of-royal-yacht-britann/, last accessed 26 June 2018.

10. Martin Belam, "Liam Fox, Here is the UK History our Readers Want to Remind You Of", *The Guardian*, 7 March 2016, https://www.the-guardian.com/politics/2016/mar/07/liam-fox-here-is-the-uk-history-our-readers-want-to-remind-you-of, last accessed 26 June 2018.

11. Warren F. Kimball, *The Juggler: Franklin Roosevelt as Wartime Statesman*, Princeton: Princeton University Press, 1991, p. 66.

12. Ronald Brownstein, "Trump's Rhetoric of White Nostalgia", *The Atlantic*, 2 June 2016, https://www.theatlantic.com/politics/archive/2016/06/trumps-rhetoric-of-white-nostalgia/485192/, last accessed 28 July 2018.

13. Elizabeth C. Economy, *The Third Revolution: Xi Jinping and the New Chinese State*, New York: Oxford University Press, 2018, pp. 3–5 and 191–6.

14. Hirakawa Sukehiro, "Japan's Turn to the West", in Bob Tadashi Wakabayashi (ed.), *Modern Japanese Thought*, Cambridge: Cambridge University Press, 1998, p. 65.

15. Shinzo Abe, "New Year's Reflection by Prime Minister Shinzo Abe", speech, 1 January 2018, https://japan.kantei.go.jp/98_abe/statement/201801/_00001.html, last accessed 28 June 2018.

16. Gideon Rachman, "Trump, Putin, Xi and the Rise of Nostalgic Nationalism", *Financial Times*, 2 January 2017, https://www.ft.com/content/198efe76-ce8b-11e6-b8ce-b9c03770f8b1, last accessed 20 June 2018.

17. Rupam Jain and Tom Lasseter, "By Rewriting History, Hindu Nationalists Aim to Assert their Dominance over India", Reuters, 6 March 2018, https://www.reuters.com/investigates/special-report/india-modi-culture/, last accessed 18 June 2018.

18. Nick Danforth, "Turkey's New Maps are Reclaiming the Ottoman Empire", *Foreign Policy*, 23 October 2016, https://foreignpolicy.com/2016/10/23/turkeys-religious-nationalists-want-ottoman-borders-iraq-erdogan/, last accessed 28 June 2018.

19. Joseph V. Micallef, "Erdogan the Magnificent, Turkey's Neo-Ottoman Revival", Military.com, 13 March 2018, https://www.military.com/daily-news/2018/03/13/op-ed-erdogan-magnificent-turkeys-neo-ottoman-revival.html, last accessed 28 June 2018.

20. Vladimir Kara-Murza, "Putin's Russia is Becoming More Soviet by the Day", *The Washington Post*, 26 February 2018, https://www.washingtonpost.com/news/democracy-post/wp/2018/02/26/putins-russia-is-becoming-more-soviet-by-the-day/?utm_term=.8e7e525bcb9c, last accessed 28 June 2018.

21. "Transcript: Putin Says Russia Will Protect the Rights of Russians Abroad", *The Washington Post*, 18 March 2014, https://www.washingtonpost.com/world/transcript-putin-says-russia-will-protect-the-rights-of-russians-abroad/2014/03/18/432a1e60-ae99-11e3-a49e-76adc9210f19_story.html?utm_term=.f9b5cc5b4370, last accessed 28 June 2018.

22. Chase Jefferson, "AfD Co-Chair Petry Wants to Rehabilitate Controversial Term", *Deutche Welle*, https://www.dw.com/en/afd-co-chair-petry-wants-to-rehabilitate-controversial-term/a-19543222, last accessed 28 April 2018.

23. Andrew Roberts, "France and the Benefits of a Little Dictatorship", *The New York Times*, 28 April 2017, https://www.nytimes.com/2017/04/28/opinion/sunday/france-and-the-benefits-of-a-little-dictatorship.html, last accessed 26 June 2018.

24. In what follows, unless specified differently, the main reference for the cultural and medical dimension of nostalgia is Svetlana Boym, *The Future of Nostalgia*, New York: Basic Books, 2002, chapters 1–4.

25. Marcos Piason Natali, "History and the Politics of Nostalgia", *Iowa Journal of Cultural Studies*, Fall 2004, pp. 11–25.

26. Michael S. Roth, *Memory, Trauma, and History: Essays on Living with the Past*, New York: Columbia University Press, 2012, p. 29.

27. Zygmunt Bauman, *Retrotopia*, London: Polity Press, 2017, p. 61.

28. X. Zhou, C. Sedikides, T. Wildschut, and D. G. Gao, "Counteracting Loneliness: On the Restorative Function of Nostalgia", *Psychological Science* 19 (10), 2008, pp. 1023–9.

29. Betsy Cooper, Daniel Cox, Rachel Lienesch, and Robert P. Jones, *The Divide over America's Future: 1950 or 2050? Findings from the 2016 American Values Survey*, Washington, DC: Public Religion Research Institute, 25 October 2016.

30. Pew Research Center, "Worldwide, People Divided on Whether Life

Today is Better than in the Past", December 2017, http://www.pew-global.org/2017/12/05/worldwide-people-divided-on-whether-life-today-is-better-than-in-the-past/, last accessed 20 June 2018.

31. YouGov, "Sunday Times Survey Results", 2–3 February 2012, http://cdn.yougov.com/cumulus_uploads/document/1or1j1cocr/YG-Archives-Pol-ST-results-03–050212.pdf, last accessed 31 December 2018.

32. Thomas Sherlock, "The Real Reasons Russians Still Have Soviet Nostalgia", *The National Interest*, 25 December 2016, https://nationalinterest.org/feature/the-real-reason-russians-still-have-soviet-nostalgia-18851, last accessed 29 April 2018.

33. "Getting Back Together is so Hard", *The Economist*, 18 September 2014, https://www.economist.com/europe/2004/09/16/getting-back-together-is-so-hard, last accessed 28 April 2018.

34. Christopher de Bellaigue, "Turkey: The Return of the Sultan", *New York Review of Books*, 9 March 2017, http://www.nybooks.com/daily/2017/03/09/turkey-the-return-of-the-sultan/, last accessed 28 June 2018.

35. Pew Research Center, "Religious Belief and National Belonging in Central and Eastern Europe", 10 May 2017, http://www.pewforum.org/2017/05/10/religious-belief-and-national-belonging-in-central-and-eastern-europe/, last accessed 15 June 2018.

36. Daniel Kahneman, *Thinking Fast and Slow*, New York: Penguin, 2011, p. 324.

37. Hulsey Cason, "The Learning and Retention of Pleasant and Unpleasant Activities", *Archives of Psychology* 134, 1932, pp. 1–96.

38. Nancy Martha West, *Kodak and the Lens of Nostalgia*, Charlottesville: University of Virginia Press, 2000, p. 1.

39. Alberto Alesina and Nicola Fuchs-Schündeln, "Goodbye Lenin (or Not?): The Effect of Communism on People's Preferences", *American Economic Review* 97 (4), 2007, pp. 1507–28.

40. Sophie Gaston and Sacha Hilhorst, *At Home in One's Past: Nostalgia as a Cultural and Political Force in Britain, France and Germany*, London: Demos Report, 2018, p. 207.

41. Neil MacGregor, *Germany: Memories of a Nation*, London: Penguin Random House, 2014, p. xxxii.

42. Will Dahlgreen, "The British Empire is Something to be Proud of", YouGov Report, 26 July 2014, https://yougov.co.uk/topics/lifestyle/articles-reports/2014/07/26/britain-proud-its-empire, last accessed 26 June 2018.

43. This sentence is commonly attributed to Shaw, but there are no official texts documenting it.

44. See Acemoğlu and Robinson, *Why Nations Fail*.
45. Piers Brendon, "A Moral Audit of the British Empire", *History Today* 57 (10), October 2007, pp. 44–7.
46. Rowena Mason, "Jamaica Calls for Britain to Pay Billions of Pounds in Reparations for Slavery", *The Guardian*, 29 September 2015, https://www.theguardian.com/world/2015/sep/29/jamaica-calls-britain-pay-billions-pounds-reparations-slavery, last accessed 26 June 2018.
47. Alesina and Fuchs-Schündeln, "Goodbye Lenin (or Not?)", *American Economic Review* 97 (4), 2007, pp. 1507–28.
48. Dan Bilefsky, "As if the Ottoman Empire Never Ended", *The New York Times*, 29 October 2012, https://www.nytimes.com/2012/10/30/movies/in-turkey-ottoman-nostalgia-returns.html, last accessed 28 June 2018.
49. Gideon Rachman, "How Wars can be Started by History Textbooks", *Financial Times*, 17 March 2014, https://www.ft.com/content/d3f9 eeb6-ab7e-11e3-aad9-00144feab7de, last accessed 28 April 2018.
50. Arthur R. Kroeber, *China's Economy*, New York: Oxford University Press, 2016, pp. 43–4.
51. Ian Cobain, Owen Bowcott, and Richard Norton-Taylor, "Britain Destroyed Records of Colonial Crimes", *The Guardian*, 18 April 2012, https://www.theguardian.com/uk/2012/apr/18/britain-destroyed-records-colonial-crimes, last accessed 25 June 2018. For a more nuanced description of the historical relevance of these documents see Philip Murphy, "It Makes a Good Story—but the Cover-up of Britain's Savage Treatment of the Mau Mau was Exaggerated", *The Conversation*, https://theconversation.com/it-makes-a-good-story-but-the-cover-up-of-britains-savage-treatment-of-the-mau-mau-was-exaggerated-65583, last accessed 5 October 2018.
52. Richard Haass, "The Age of Nonpolarity: What Will Follow US Dominance", *Foreign Affairs* 87 (3), May/June 2008, pp. 44–56.
53. Adam Taylor, "Putin Says he Wishes the Soviet Union had not Collapsed: Many Russians Agree", *The Washington Post*, 3 March 2018, https://www.washingtonpost.com/news/worldviews/wp/2018/03/03/putin-says-he-wishes-he-could-change-the-collapse-of-the-soviet-union-many-russians-agree/?noredirect=on&utm_term=.b412d412 f5e4, last accessed 30 June 2018.
54. Alana Abramson, "'I Can be More Presidential than any President': Read Trump's Ohio Rally Speech", *Time*, 26 July 2017, http://time.com/4874161/donald-trump-transcript-youngstown-ohio/, last accessed 26 June 2018.
55. Elizabeth C. Economy, "Beijing is no Champion of Globalization", *Foreign Affairs*, 22 January 2011, https://www.foreignaffairs.com/arti-

cles/china/2017–01–22/beijing-no-champion-globalization,   last accessed 28 June 2018.

56. The data comes from Eurostat Database: http://ec.europa.eu/eurostat/web/population-demography-migration-projections/population-data/database.

57. Ashok Jansari and Alan Parkin, "Things that go Bump in your Life: Explaining the Reminiscence Bump in Autobiographical Memory", *Psychology and Aging* 11, March 1996, pp. 85–91.

58. Simon Shuster, "The UK's Old Decided for the Young in the Brexit Vote", *Time*, 24 June 2016, http://time.com/4381878/brexit-generation-gap-older-younger-voters/, last accessed 20 June 2018.

59. Thomas Sherlock, "The Real Reasons Russians Still Have Soviet Nostalgia", *The National Interest*, 25 December 2016, https://nationalinterest.org/feature/the-real-reason-russians-still-have-soviet-nostalgia-18851, last accessed 29 April 2018.

60. Catherine E. de Vries and Isabell Hoffmann, "The Power of the Past: How Nostalgia Shapes European Public Opinion", EUOpinions, Bertelsmann Stiftung, 5 November 2018, https://eupinions.eu/de/text/the-power-of-the-past/, last accessed 10 December 2018.

61. Trevor Thrall and Erik Goepner, "Millennials and US Foreign Policy: The Next Generation's Attitudes toward Foreign Policy and War (and Why they Matter)", *Cato Institute Report*, Washington, 2011, https://object.cato.org/sites/cato.org/files/pubs/pdf/20150616_thrallgoepner_millennialswp.pdf, last accessed 28 July 2018.

62. Raj Chetty, David Grusky, Maximilian Hell, Nathaniel Hendren, Robert Manduca, and Jimmy Narang, "The Fading American Dream: Trends in Absolute Income Mobility since 1940", *NBER Working Paper* No. 22910, December 2016.

63. Pew Charitable Trusts, *Pursuing the American Dream: Economic Mobility Across Generations*, Washington, DC: Pew Charitable Trusts, 2012, p. 2.

64. Andy Beckett, "From Trump to Brexit Power has Leaked from Cities to the Countryside", *The Guardian*, 12 December 2016, https://www.theguardian.com/commentisfree/2016/dec/12/trump-brexit-cities-countryside-rural-voters, last accessed 20 June 2018.

65. Conrad Hackett, "By 2050, India to Have World's Largest Populations of Hindus and Muslims", Pew Research Center, 21 April 2015, http://www.pewresearch.org/fact-tank/2015/04/21/by-2050-india-to-have-worlds-largest-populations-of-hindus-and-muslims/, last accessed 28 June 2018. The issue of an American identity crisis under threat was analysed by Samuel Huntington in *Who Are We? The Challenges to America's National Identity*, New York: Simon & Schuster, 2005.

66. Richard Alba, "The Myth of a White Minority", *The New York Times*, 11

June 2015, https://www.nytimes.com/2015/06/11/opinion/the-myth-of-a-white-minority.html, last accessed 28 June 2018.

67. Carol Graham, "Unhappiness in America", Brookings Institution, Opinions, 27 May 2016, https://www.brookings.edu/opinions/unhap-piness-in-america/, last accessed 28 June 2018.

68. Amy Chua, "Tribal World: Group Identity is All", *Foreign Affairs*, July/August 2018, pp. 25–33.

69. Rich Morin, "The Most (and Least) Culturally Diverse Countries in the World", Pew Research Center, 18 July 2013, http://www.pewre-search.org/fact-tank/2013/07/18/the-most-and-least-culturally-diverse-countries-in-the-world/, last accessed 28 April 2018.

70. See Ivan Krastev, *After Europe*, Philadelphia: University of Pennsylvania Press, 2017.

71. Tony Barber, "Europe Risks Failure on Migration", *Financial Times*, 20 August 2018, https://www.ft.com/content/e45c4b5e-9fcc-11e8–85da-eeb7a9ce36e4, last accessed 25 August 2018.

72. Gaston and Hilhorst, *At Home in One's Past*, p. 15.

73. Ibid., p. 80.

74. Scott-Ross Baker, Nicholas Bloom, and David Steven, "Immigration Fears and Policy Uncertainty", Voxeu.org, 15 December 2015, https://voxeu.org/article/immigration-fears-and-policy-uncertainty, last accessed 28 April 2018.

75. Heather Stewart and Rowena Mason, "Nigel Farage's Anti-Migrant Poster Reported to Police", *The Guardian*, 16 June 2016, https://www.theguardian.com/politics/2016/jun/16/nigel-farage-defends-ukip-breaking-point-poster-queue-of-migrants, last accessed 28 April 2018.

76. Edoardo Campanella, "No Small Change: How to Manage the Costs of Innovation", *Foreign Affairs*, 15 May 2017, https://www.foreignaf-fairs.com/reviews/review-essay/2017–05–15/no-small-change, last accessed 25 June 2018.

77. Carl Benedikt Frey and Michael Osborne, "The Future of Employment: How Susceptible are Jobs to Computerisation?", *Oxford Martin Working Paper*, March 2013.

78. International Monetary Fund, *World Economic Outlook, April 2017: Gaining Momentum?*, Washington, DC, 2017, https://www.imf.org/en/Publications/WEO/Issues/2017/04/04/world-economic-outlook-april-2017, last accessed 13 December 2018.

79. Fred Davis, *Yearning for Yesterday: A Sociology of Nostalgia*, New York: Free Press, 1979, p. 35.

80. Ben Rowen, "The End of Forgetting: Technology Delivers Nostalgia on Demand", *The Atlantic*, June 2017, https://www.theatlantic.com/

magazine/archive/2017/06/the-end-of-forgetting/524523/, last accessed 29 April 2018.

2. NOSTALGIA AS AN EMOTIONAL WEAPON

1. Simon Heffer, *The Age of Decadence: Britain 1880 to 1914*, London: Penguin Random House, 2017, pp. 442–70.
2. Gaston and Hilhorst, *At Home in One's Past*, p. 31.
3. William Cunningham Bissell, "Engaging Colonial Nostalgia", *Cultural Anthropology* 20 (2), 2005, pp. 215–48.
4. See, for instance, Michael Kenny, "Back to the Populist Future? Understanding Nostalgia in Contemporary Ideological Discourse", *Journal of Political Ideologies* 22 (3), 2017, pp. 256–73.
5. Kathleen Stewart, "Nostalgia: A Polemic", *Cultural Anthropology* 3 (3), 1988, pp. 227–41.
6. Tony Barber, "Nostalgia and the Promise of Brexit", *Financial Times*, 19 July 2018, https://www.ft.com/content/bf70b80e-8b39-11e8-bf9e-8771d5404543, last accessed 28 July 2018.
7. Michael Gove, "Why I'm Backing Brexit", *The Spectator*, 20 February 2016, https://blogs.spectator.co.uk/2016/02/michael-gove-why-im-backing-leave/, last accessed 28 June 2018.
8. Oliver Wright, "EU Referendum: Clegg Warns Brexit Will Leave Britain with 'no Empire, no Union and no Special Relationship' with US", *The Independent*, 20 April 2016, https://www.independent.co.uk/news/uk/politics/eu-referendum-nick-clegg-warns-brexit-will-leave-britain-with-no-empire-no-union-and-no-special-a6993371.html, last accessed 28 June 2018.
9. Linda Colley, "Brexiters are Nostalgics in Search of a Lost Empire", *Financial Times*, 22 April 2016, https://www.ft.com/content/63de3610-07b0-11e6-9b51-0fb5e65703ce, last accessed 28 June 2018; Kevin Andrews, "Colonial Nostalgia is Back in Fashion, Blinding us to the Horrors of Empire", *The Guardian*, 24 August 2016, https://www.theguardian.com/commentisfree/2016/aug/24/colonial-nostalgia-horrors-of-empire-britain-olympic, last accessed 28 June 2018.
10. Andrew Sparrow, "Brexit Minister Apologises to Peers for Saying Article 50 Cannot be Revoked", *The Guardian*, 20 November 2017, https://www.theguardian.com/politics/blog/live/2017/nov/20/brexit-bill-voters-will-go-bananas-if-uk-offers-40bn-to-eu-former-tory-minister-warns-may-ahead-of-key-meeting-politics-live?page=with%3Ablock-5a12da9e930f310725ecdd9c, last accessed 18 June 2018.
11. David Runciman, *Politics: Ideas in Profile*, New York: Profile Books, 2014, p. 52.

12. Boym, *The Future of Nostalgia*, p. 41.
13. Ibid., p. 354.
14. Stuart Tannock, "Nostalgia Critique", *Cultural Studies* 9 (3), 1995, pp. 453–64.
15. Gaston and Hilhorst, *At Home in One's Past*, pp. 145–8.
16. Adam Taylor, "The Subtle Messages in Emmanuel Macron's Official Portrait", *The Washington Post*, 29 June 2017, https://www.washingtonpost.com/news/worldviews/wp/2017/06/29/the-subtle-messages-in-emmanuel-macrons-official-portrait/?utm_term=.b5ff36769b04, last accessed 28 June 2018.
17. Huntington, *Who Are We?*, p. 21.
18. Michael Freeden, "After the Brexit Referendum: Revisiting Populism as an Ideology", *Journal of Political Ideologies* 22 (1), 2017, pp. 1–11.
19. Jan Willem Duyvendak, *The Politics of Home: Belonging and Nostalgia in Western Europe and the United States*, London: Palgrave, 2016, p. 117.
20. Gabriella Elgenius and Jens Rydgren, "Frames of Nostalgia and Belonging: The Resurgence of Ethno-Nationalism in Sweden", *European Societies*, 2018, pp. 1–21.
21. Nichols, *The Death of Expertise*, pp. 209–10.
22. Nick Gass, "Trump: The Experts are Terrible", Politico, 4 April 2016, https://www.politico.com/blogs/2016-gop-primary-live-updates-and-results/2016/04/donald-trump-foreign-policy-experts-221528, last accessed 28 June 2018.
23. Alan Jay Levinovitz, "It Never Was Golden", Aeon, 17 August 2016, https://aeon.co/essays/nostalgia-exerts-a-strong-allure-and-extracts-a-steep-price, last accessed 29 June 2018.
24. George Orwell, "Notes on Nationalism", Polemic, May 1945, http://www.orwell.ru/library/essays/nationalism/english/e_nat, last accessed 28 June 2018.
25. Michael Ignatieff, *Blood and Belonging: Journeys into the New Nationalism*, London: Vintage, 1995, p. 3.
26. Ibid., pp. 4–5.
27. Michael Keating, *Nations against the State*, London: Macmillan, 1996, pp. 7–8; "League of Nationalists", *The Economist*, 19 November 2016, https://www.economist.com/international/2016/11/19/league-of-nationalists, last accessed 18 June 2018.
28. Patrick J. Geary, *The Myth of Nations*, Princeton: Princeton University Press, 2002, p. 15.
29. Benedict Anderson, *Imagined Communities: Reflections on the Origin and Spread of Nationalism*, London: Verso, 1983.
30. Boym, *The Future of Nostalgia*, p. xvi.

31. Anthony D. Smith, *Ethno-Symbolism and Nationalism: A Cultural Approach*, Abingdon: Routledge, 2009, p. 36.
32. See Edgerton, *The Rise and Fall of the British Nation*.

3. CONSTRUCTING A NOSTALGIC NARRATIVE

1. Sarah E. Chinn, *Spectacular Men: Race, Gender, and Nation on the Early American Stage*, Oxford: Oxford University Press, 2017, p. 84.
2. H. E. Marshall, *Our Island Story: A Child's History of England*, New York: Wilder Publications, 2009, pp. 5–6.
3. Patrick Wintour, "David Cameron Sets out 'Emotional, Patriotic' Case to Keep Scotland in UK", *The Guardian*, 7 February 2014, https://www.theguardian.com/politics/2014/feb/07/david-cameron-scottish-independence-referendum-olympic-park, last accessed 28 June 2018.
4. Michael Gove, "All Pupils Will Learn our Island Story", speech, 5 October 2010, https://conservative-speeches.sayit.mysociety.org/speech/601441, last accessed 28 June 2018.
5. Niall Ferguson, "On the Teaching of History, Michael Gove is Right", *The Guardian*, 15 February 2013, https://www.theguardian.com/commentisfree/2013/feb/15/history-teaching-curriculum-gove-right, last accessed 28 June 2018.
6. Jonathan Scott, *When the Waves Ruled Britannia: Geography and Political Identities, 1500–1800*, Cambridge: Cambridge University Press, 2011, pp. 6–8.
7. Timothy Garton Ash, *Free World: America, Europe, and the Surprising Future of the West*, London: Vintage, 2014, pp. 16–18.
8. Krishan Kumar, "1066 and All That: Myths of the English", in Gérard Bouchard (ed.), *National Myths: Constructed Pasts, Contested Presents*, London and New York: Routledge, 2013, pp. 94–100.
9. Kumar, *The Idea of Englishness*, p. 202.
10. Jeremy Black, *A History of the British Isles*, London: Palgrave Macmillan, 2012, p. 335.
11. Quoted in Gaston and Hilhorst, *At Home in One's Past*, p. 43.
12. Walter Russell Mead, *God and Gold: Britain, America and the Making of the Modern World*, New York: Vintage, 2007, pp. 80–1.
13. See, for instance, David Gress, *From Plato to NATO: The Idea of the West and its Opponents*, New York: Free Press, 2004.
14. Margaret Thatcher, "The Bruges Speech", speech to the College of Europe, 20 September 1988, https://www.margaretthatcher.org/document/107332, last accessed 20 June 2018.
15. See Brendan Simms, *Britain's Europe: A Thousand Years of Conflict and Cooperation*, London: Penguin, 2016.

16. Ernest Renan, "What is a Nation?", lecture delivered at the Sorbonne on 11 March 1882, http://ucparis.fr/files/9313/6549/9943/What_is_a_Nation.pdf, last accessed 28 July 2018.
17. Georges Sorel, *Reflections on Violence*, Glencoe, IL: Free Press, 1950, p. 58.
18. Kumar, *The Idea of Englishness*, p. 202.
19. Jon Stone, "EU Referendum: Full Transcript of David Cameron's Last-Ditch Plea for Britain to Remain", *The Independent*, 21 June 2016, https://www.independent.co.uk/news/uk/politics/eu-referendum-brexit-latest-live-david-cameron-full-speech-remain-leave-a7093426.html, last accessed 28 June 2018.
20. Marco Giannngeli, "EUROPEAN EMPIRE: Powerless Britain to Become Mere COLONY if we Don't Quit Brussels", *Daily Express*, 24 April 2016, https://www.express.co.uk/news/uk/663846/EU-referendum-David-Cameron-Europe-UK-power-Roman-Governor-Brexit, last accessed 28 June 2018.
21. Daniel Hannan, "The Magna Carta: The Text that Makes us who we Are", *National Post*, 15 June 2015, http://nationalpost.com/opinion/daniel-hannan-the-magna-carta-the-text-that-makes-us-who-we-are, last accessed 30 April 2018.
22. Gaston and Hilhorst, *At Home in One's Past*, p. 47.
23. Ibid., p. 81.
24. Steve Buckledee, *The Language of Brexit: How Britain Talked its Way Out of the European Union*, London: Bloomsbury, 2018, p. 203.
25. "We Urge our Readers to BeLEAVE in Britain and Vote to Quit the EU on June 23", *The Sun*, 13 June 2016, https://www.thesun.co.uk/news/1277920/we-urge-our-readers-to-believe-in-britain-and-vote-to-leave-the-eu-in-referendum-on-june-23/, last accessed 28 June 2018.
26. Otto English, "The Poppy has Lost its Original Meaning—Time to Ditch it", *The Independent*, 1 November 2018, https://www.independent.co.uk/voices/poppy-wear-why-not-remembrance-wars-soldiers-veterans-poppies-moeen-ali-a8031746.html, last accessed 20 April 2018.
27. Heather Stewart and Mark Brown, "Benedict Cumberbatch and Paloma Faith among 250 stars Backing EU", *The Guardian*, 20 May 2016, https://www.theguardian.com/politics/2016/may/19/british-cultural-heavyweights-sign-250-letter-backing-eu-benedict-cumberbatch-paloma-faith, last accessed 14 April 2018.
28. British Election Study Team, "Brexit Britain: British Election Study Insights from the Post-EU Referendum Wave of the BES Internet Panel", press release, 6 October 2016, http://www.britishelectionstudy.com/bes-resources/brexit-britain-british-election-study-insights-

from-the-post-eu-referendum-wave-of-the-bes-internet-panel/, last accessed 20 April 2018.

29. John M. MacKenzie, *Propaganda and Empire: The Manipulation of British Public Opinion 1880–1960*, Manchester: Manchester University Press, 1986, pp. 2–10.

30. Thomas Hajkowski, *The BBC and National Identity in Britain, 1922–53*, Manchester: Manchester University Press, 2017, pp. 26–32.

31. Keynote of Empire, 1928, BBC WAC, Scripts, School Broadcasting Scripts, Reel 1/2.

32. Alex von Tunzelmann, "Winston Churchill's Black Dog: Portraying the 'Greatest Briton' on Screen", *The Guardian*, 9 June 2017, https:// www.theguardian.com/film/2017/jun/09/winston-churchill-black-dog-films-gary-oldman-brian-cox, last accessed 18 April 2018.

33. Gaston and Hilhorst, *At Home in One's Past*, p. 56.

34. "We Must Vote Leave to Create a Britain Fit for the Future", *Sunday Telegraph*, 18 June 2016, https://www.telegraph.co.uk/opinion/2016/06/18/we-must-vote-leave-to-create-a-britain-fit-for-the-future/, last accessed 31 December 2018.

35. Peter Pomerantsev, "The Idealistic Pull of the 'Anglosphere'", Politico, 13 July 2016, https://www.politico.eu/article/the-idealistic-pull-ofthe-anglosphere-leave-brexit-emotions/, last accessed 28 June 2018.

36. Steve Hawkes, Lynn Davidson, and Harry Cole, "Boris Johnson Urges *Sun* Readers 'With History in their Hands' to Back Brexit", *The Sun*, 23 June 2016, https://www.thesun.co.uk/news/1326774/boris-johnson-urges-sun-readers-with-history-in-their-hands-to-back-brexit/, last accessed 28 June 2018.

37. Stan Neal, "Is Brexit Britain Suffering from an Imperial Hangover?", Aljazeera, 29 March 2017, https://www.aljazeera.com/indepth/opinion/2017/03/brexit-britain-suffering-imperial-hangover-1703291414 20962.html, last accessed 28 June 2018.

38. Christopher Hope, "Millionaire Funds 10,000 Union Flags for Last Night of the Proms to Combat Pro-EU Protest Plans", *The Daily Telegraph*, 9 September 2016, https://www.telegraph.co.uk/news/2016/09/09/millionaire-funds-10000-union-flags-for-last-night-of-the-proms/, last accessed 20 April 2018.

39. Nick Groom, *The Union Jack: The Story of the British Flag*, London: Atlantic Books, 2017.

40. Ferguson, *Empire*.

41. Benedict Brogan, "It's Time to Celebrate the Empire, Says Brown", *Daily Mail*, 15 January 2015, http://www.dailymail.co.uk/news/article-334208/Its-time-celebrate-Empire-says-Brown.html, last accessed 28 June 2018.

42. Derrick Wirtz, Justin Kruger, Christie Napa Scollon, and Ed Diener,

"What to Do on Spring Break? The Role of Predicted, On-Line, and Remembered Experience in Future Choice", *Psychological Science* 14 (5), 2003, pp. 520–4.

43. Martin Fletcher, "The Polite Extremist: Jacob Rees-Mogg's Seemingly Unstoppable Rise", *New Statesman*, 20 February 2018, https://www. newstatesman.com/politics/uk/2018/02/polite-extremist-jacob-rees-mogg-s-seemingly-unstoppable-rise, last accessed 20 June 2018.

44. "Jacob Rees-Mogg, Pinstriped Populist", *The Economist*, 1 February 2018, https://www.economist.com/britain/2018/02/01/jacob-rees-mogg-pinstriped-populist, last accessed 28 June 2018.

45. John Crace, "BoGo's Freedom of Conscience Trumps Anything the EU Offers", *The Guardian*, 22 February 2018, https://www.theguardian. com/politics/2016/feb/22/bogos-freedom-of-conscience-trumps-any-thing-the-eu-has-to-offer, last accessed 28 June 2018.

46. Gaston and Hilhorst, *At Home in One's Past*, p. 83.

47. Trevor Owen Lloyd, *Empire, Welfare State, Europe: English History 1906–1992*, London: Oxford University Press, 1993, p. 2.

48. David Powell, *The Edwardian Crisis*, Basingstoke: Palgrave Macmillan, 1996, p. vii.

49. Katherine Byrne, *Edwardians on Screen: From* Downton Abbey *to* Parade's End, London: Palgrave Macmillan, 2015, pp. 1–2.

50. Ibid., p. 159; Jeremy Egner, "A Bit of Britain Where the Sun Never Sets", *The New York Times*, 6 January 2013, https://www.nytimes. com/2013/01/06/arts/television/downton-abbey-reaches-around-the-world.html?_r=0, last accessed 20 April 2018.

51. Chris Hastings, "'I'm Downton and OUT!': TV Writer Julian Fellowes Claims EU is Like Austro-Hungarian Empire (and Look How That Ended)", *Daily Mail*, 6 March 2016, http://www.dailymail.co.uk/debate/article-3478563/I-m-Downton-TV-writer-Julian-Fellowes-claims-EU-like-Austro-Hungarian-empire-look-ended.html, last accessed 20 March 2018.

52. David Miliband, "Keir Hardie Memorial Lecture", Mountain Ash, Cynon Valley, 9 July 2010, https://labourlist.org/2010/07/david-milibands-keir-hardie-lecture-full-speech/, last accessed 28 July 2018.

53. Jacky Hyams, *The Real Life* Downton Abbey: *How Life Was Really Lived in Stately Homes a Century Ago*, London: John Blake, 2012, p. 7.

54. Byrne, *Edwardians on Screen*, p. 18.

55. Siobhan Fenton, "EU Referendum: David Cameron is Called a 'Twenty-First Century Chamberlain' in Heated Question Time Debate", *The Independent*, 19 June 2016, https://www.independent.co.uk/news/uk/politics/eu-referendum-david-cameron-is-called-a-twenty-first-cen-tury-chamberlain-in-heated-question-time-a7090696.html, last accessed 28 June 2018.

56. Simon Walters, "Withering Verdict by Tory MP … Calm Down Boris, You're no Winston in our Darkest Hour—You're More Like the Two Dodgy Randolphs!", *Daily Mail*, 27 January 2018, http://www.dailymail.co.uk/news/article-5320719/Calm-Boris-youre-no-Winston-Churchill-Tory-MP-says.html, last accessed 28 June 2018.

57. Vinoo Alluri, Petri Toiviainen, Liro P. Jääskeläinen, Enrico Glerean, Mikko Sams, and Elvira Brattico, "Large-Scale Brain Networks Emerge from Dynamic Processing of Musical Timbre, Key and Rhythm", *NeuroImage*, 2011, https://www.ncbi.nlm.nih.gov/pubmed/22116038, last accessed 28 June 2018.

58. Vanessa Thorpe, "UKIP's Use of *Great Escape* Theme Tune Grates with Composer's Sons", *The Guardian*, 28 May 2016, https://www.theguardian.com/politics/2016/may/28/great-escape-theme-tune-ukip-composer, last accessed 18 April 2018.

59. Penny Mordaunt, "The Spirit of Dunkirk will see us Thrive Outside the EU", *Daily Telegraph*, 25 February 2016, https://www.telegraph.co.uk/news/newstopics/eureferendum/12173650/The-spirit-of-Dunkirk-will-see-us-thrive-outside-the-EU.html, last accessed 28 June 2018.

60. Steve Rose, "The Dunkirk Spirit: How Cinema is Shaping Britain's Identity in the Brexit Era", *The Guardian*, 20 July 2017, https://www.theguardian.com/film/2017/jul/20/dunkirk-spirit-british-film-brexit-national-identity-christopher-nolan, last accessed 28 June 2018.

61. Tom Flack, "One in Five Doubt they will Wear a Poppy", *Consumer Intelligence Press Release*, 1 November 2017, https://www.consumerintelligence.com/articles/one-in-five-doubt-they-will-wear-a-poppy-this-year, last accessed 28 June 2018.

62. Jonathan Jones, "The Tower of London Poppies are Fake, Trite and Inward-Looking—a UKIP-Style Memorial", *The Guardian*, 28 October 2014, https://www.theguardian.com/artanddesign/jonathanjones-blog/2014/oct/28/tower-of-london-poppies-ukip-remembrance-day, last accessed 28 June 2018.

63. Matt Chorley, "Disgusting! Leave.EU Campaign Slammed for Claiming that Staying in the EU Threatens the Freedoms Won by the War Dead", *Daily Mail*, 8 November 2015, http://www.dailymail.co.uk/news/article-3309180/Disgusting-Leave-EU-campaign-slammed-claiming-staying-EU-threatens-freedoms-won-war-dead.html, last accessed 28 June 2018.

64. Chris Johnston, "Second World War Veterans Say Brexit Risks Stability they Fought for", *The Guardian*, 9 May 2016, https://www.theguardian.com/politics/2016/may/09/war-veterans-brexit-risk-stability, last accessed 28 June 2018.

65. See the New Narrative project of the European Commission, https://
ec.europa.eu/culture/policy/new-narrative_en.

66. Steven Swinford, "David Cameron: Brexit Could Lead to Europe
Descending into War", *Daily Telegraph*, 8 May 2016, https://www.tele-
graph.co.uk/news/2016/05/08/cameron-brexit-will-increase-risk-of-
europe-descending-into-war/, last accessed 28 June 2018.

67. "Victory for Churchill as he Wins the Battle of the Britons", BBC press
release, 25 November 2002, http://www.bbc.co.uk/pressoffice/press-
releases/stories/2002/11_november/25/greatbritons_final.shtml, last
accessed 18 April 2018.

68. Andrew Roberts, "Andrew Roberts' Guide to Churchill on Screen",
The Spectator, 13 January 2018, https://www.spectator.co.uk/2018/
01/andrew-robertss-guide-to-churchill-on-screen/, last accessed 18
April 2018.

69. Ian Jack, "*Dunkirk* and *Darkest Hour* Fuel Brexit Fantasies—Even if they
Weren't Meant to", *The Guardian*, 27 January 2018, https://www.the-
guardian.com/commentisfree/2018/jan/27/brexit-britain-myths-war-
time-darkest-hour-dunkirk-nationalist-fantasies, last accessed 18 April
2018.

70. Rowena Mason, Anushka Asthana, and Peter Walker, "David Cameron
Says he Must do More to Make Case for Remaining in EU", *The
Guardian*, 19 June 2016, https://www.theguardian.com/politics/
2016/jun/19/david-cameron-case-remain-eu-referendum-bbc-question-
time-special, last accessed 28 June 2018.

71. John Kampfner, "*The Churchill Factor* Review: Boris Johnson's Flawed
but Fascinating Take on his Hero", *The Guardian*, 3 November 2014,
https://www.theguardian.com/books/2014/nov/03/churchill-factor-
review-boris-johnson-winston, last accessed 28 June 2018.

72. Boris Johnson, "UK and America can be Better Friends than Ever Mr
Obama … if we LEAVE the EU", *The Sun*, 22 April 2016, https://
www.thesun.co.uk/archives/politics/1139354/boris-johnson-uk-and-
america-can-be-better-friends-than-ever-mr-obama-if-we-leave-the-eu/,
last accessed 28 June 2018.

73. David Ramiro Troitiño, Tanel Kerikmäe, Archil Chochiap, and Andrea
Hrebickova, "Cooperation or Integration? Chuchill's Attitude towards
the Organization of Europe", in David Ramiro Troitiño, Tanel
Kerikmäe, and Archil Chochiap (eds.), *Brexit: History, Reasoning and
Perspectives*, Cham: Springer, 2018, p. 42.

74. Adam Kirsch, "The Bard of his Own Backyard", *Foreign Policy*, 5
September 2016, http://foreignpolicy.com/2016/09/05/man-of-the-
world-shakespeare-anniversary-england-legacy-globalization-coloniza-
tion/, last accessed 28 June 2018.

75. Harry Cole, "Boris Johnson Demands Plotters against him Reveal

Themselves as he Compares Bitter Brexit Battles to Shakespeare's Tragedies", *The Sun*, 23 October 2017, https://www.thesun.co.uk/news/4750480/boris-johnson-demands-plotters-against-him-reveal-themselves-as-he-compares-bitter-brexit-battles-to-shakespeares-trage-dies/, last accessed 28 June 2018.

76. Alan Cowell, "A British Divorce from Europe? Henry VIII Blazed the Trail", *The New York Times*, 21 June 2016, https://www.nytimes.com/2016/06/21/world/europe/a-british-divorce-from-europe-henry-viii-blazed-the-trail.html, last accessed 28 June 2018.

77. Emma Kentish, "Rule Britannia? Colonial Language in the Brexit Debate", *Cafébabel*, 3 May 2016, https://cafebabel.com/en/article/rule-britannia-colonial-language-in-the-brexit-debate-5ae00afcf-723b35a145e700b/, last accessed 28 June 2018.

78. Kimiko De Freytas-Tamura, "In Brexit Debate, English Fishermen Eye Waters Free of EU", *The New York Times*, 15 April 2016, https://www.nytimes.com/2016/04/15/business/international/many-in-british-fishing-port-want-eu-out-of-their-waters.html, last accessed 18 April 2018.

79. Samuel Earle, "The Toxic Nostalgia of Brexit", *The Atlantic*, 5 October 2017, https://www.theatlantic.com/international/archive/2017/10/brexit-britain-may-johnson-eu/542079/, last accessed 28 June 2018.

80. Owen Bennett, *The Brexit Club: The Inside Story of the Leave Campaign's Shock Victory*, London: Biteback Publishing, 2016.

81. Nigel Farage, "Farage on Friday: EU Referendum is our Modern Day Battle of Britain", *Daily Express*, 10 July 2010, https://www.express.co.uk/news/politics/590396/Nigel-Farage-European-Union-EU-referendum-Battle-of-Britain, last accessed 28 June 2018.

82. Peter Walker, "Brexiteers Seek Campaign Memorabilia for 'Museum of Sovereignty'", *The Guardian*, 10 April 2018, https://www.theguardian.com/politics/2018/apr/10/brexit-museum-of-sovereignty-leave-campaign-memorabilia, last accessed 14 April 2018.

83. Tim Ross, "Boris Johnson Interview: We can be the 'Heroes of Europe' by Voting to Leave", *The Daily Telegraph*, 14 May 2016, http://www.telegraph.co.uk/news/2016/05/14/boris-johnson-interview-we-can-be-the-heroes-of-europe-by-voting/, last accessed 28 June 2018.

84. Roy Greenslade, "The *Sun* Dares to Use the Queen again in Brexit Front Page", *The Guardian*, 22 June 2016, https://www.theguardian.com/media/2016/jun/22/the-sun-queen-brexit-front-page,   last accessed 28 June 2018.

85. Buckledee, *The Language of Brexit*.

86. Jon Kelly, "Brexit: How Much of a Generation Gap is there?", BBC.com, 24 June 2016, https://www.bbc.com/news/magazine-36619342, last accessed 28 June 2018.

87. Drew Westen, *The Political Brain: The Role of Emotion in Deciding the Fate of the Nation*, New York: PublicAffairs, 2005, p. 5.

88. Marshall, *Our Island Story*, pp. 3–4.

4. BIRTH OF AN IDEA

1. Eran Shalev, *Rome Reborn on Western Shores: Historical Imagination and the Creation of the American Republic*, Charlottesville: University of Virginia Press, 2009, pp. 28–32.

2. Boris Johnson, *The Churchill Factor: How One Man Made History*, London: Riverhead Books, 2014, p. 314.

3. Winston Churchill, *A History of the English-Speaking Peoples*, vols. I–IV, London: Bloomsbury, 2015; Anderson, *Imagined Communities*.

4. Martin Gilbert, *Churchill and America*, New York: Simon & Schuster, 2005, p. 2.

5. Winston S. Churchill, "The Gift of a Common Tongue", speech at Harvard University, 6 September 1943, https://www.winstonchurchill.org/resources/speeches/1941-1945-war-leader/the-price-of-greatness-is-responsibility/, last accessed 19 December 2018.

6. Candice Millard, *Hero of the Empire: The Boer War, a Daring Escape, and the Making of Winston Churchill*, New York: Random House, 2016.

7. Gilbert, *Churchill and America*, p. 421; Warren Dockter (ed.), *Winston Churchill at* The Telegraph, London: Aurum Press, 2015, p. 128.

8. Gilbert, *Churchill and America*, p. 150.

9. Douglas Jay, president of the Board of Trade in the British Labour government of 1964–7, suggested the establishment of a "North Atlantic Free Trade Area", comprising the United States, the United Kingdom, Canada, and the European Free Trade Area. See Robert Conquest, "Toward an English-Speaking Union", *The National Interest* 57, 1999, pp. 64–70.

10. Probably, the most influential proposal was sketched out by the *New York Times* journalist Clarence Streit in the book *Union Now*, published in 1939. Streit proposed a "nucleus" of fifteen nations that he regarded as relatively mature democracies: the United States, the United Kingdom, Canada, Australia, New Zealand, South Africa, Ireland, France, Belgium, the Netherlands, Switzerland, Denmark, Norway, Sweden, and Finland. This union was to be organized roughly along the lines of the federal system of the United States, after holding a federal convention similar to the one that in 1787 led to the birth of the American Constitution in Philadelphia. Countries that the federation deemed worthy of membership would subsequently be added on

the basis of their commitment to democracy, with the hope that the union would eventually come to encompass the entire globe.

11. Christopher Hill, *The Future of British Foreign Policy*, London: Polity, 2018, p. 11.

12. The term Anglosphere is a neologism that made its appearance in the mid-1990s in Neal Stephenson's science-fiction novel *The Diamond Age*. Around a core group made up of the United States, Britain, Canada, New Zealand, and Australia, there is an outer rim of countries that includes the Republic of South Africa, Singapore, India, Ireland, and a few other members of the Commonwealth of Nations.

13. For a thorough analysis of this topic see Hannah Arendt, *The Origins of Totalitarianism*, New York: Harcourt Brace Jovanovich, 1968, chapter 5.

14. Lucian Oldershaw, *England: A Nation. Being the Papers of the Patriots' Club*, London: R. Brimley Johnson, 1904, p. 14.

15. Quoted in Robert J. Mayhew, *Enlightenment Geography: The Political Languages of British Geography, 1650–1850*, London: Palgrave Macmillan, 2000, p. 243.

16. John Robert Seeley, *The Expansion of England: Two Courses of Lectures*, Cambridge: Cambridge University Press, 2010 [1880], p. 63.

17. Duncan Bell, *Reordering the World: Essays on Liberalism and Empire*, Princeton: Princeton University Press, 2016, pp. 167–8.

18. On Anglo-German relations see the classic work by Paul M. Kennedy, *The Rise of the Anglo-German Antagonism, 1860–1914*, Dublin: Ashfield Press, 1980. For a panoramic view of British foreign policy during the reign of Queen Victoria see Kenneth Bourne, *The Foreign Policy of Victorian England, 1830–1902*, Oxford: Clarendon Press, 1970.

19. Srdjan Vucetic, *The Anglosphere: A Genealogy of a Racialized Identity in International Relations*, Stanford: Stanford University Press, 2011, pp. 30–1.

20. John Kendle, *Federal Britain: A History*, London: Routledge, 1997, p. 123.

21. W. H. Forster, "Our Colonial Empire", *The Times*, 6 November 1875, p. 9.

22. For an overview of the transport revolution see Philip Bagwell, *The Transport Revolution 1770–1985*, London: Routledge, 2002, pp. 76–181. Data on wheat prices are from Kevin H. O'Rourke, "The European Grain Invasion, 1870–1913", *Journal of Economic History* 57, 1997, p. 782.

23. Thomas Misa, *Leonardo to the Internet: Technology and Culture from the Renaissance to the Present*, Baltimore: Johns Hopkins University Press, 2011, pp. 306–7.

24. Quoted in Tony Ballantyne and Antoinette Burton, *Empires and the Reach of the Global: 1870–1945*, Cambridge, MA: Harvard University Press, 2012, p. 97.
25. For a discussion of what follows see Kenny and Pearce, *Shadows of Empire*, pp. 135–7.
26. Manmohan Singh, Address in Acceptance of an Honorary Degree of Doctor of Civil Law from the University of Oxford, 8 July 2005, https://www.thehindu.com/2005/07/10/stories/2005071002301000.htm, last accessed 27 April 2018.
27. Quoted in John Lloyd, "The Anglosphere Project", *The New Statesman*, 13 March 2000, https://www.newstatesman.com/node/193400, last accessed 16 February 2018.
28. Jeffrey A. Frankel, "Assessing the Efficiency Gains from Further Liberalization", John F. Kennedy School of Government, Harvard University, Faculty Research Working Papers Series, 2000, RWP01–030.
29. Charles Wentworth Dilke, *Greater Britain: A Record of Travel in English-Speaking Countries During 1866 and 1867*, New York: Cosimo, Inc., 2005 [1867].
30. Ibid., p. 398.
31. Duncan Bell, *The Idea of Greater Britain*, Princeton and Oxford: Princeton University Press, 2007, p. 55.
32. Ibid., p. 14.
33. John E. Flint, *Cecil Rhodes*, Boston: Little, Brown, 1974, pp. 248–52.
34. Ferguson, *Empire*, p. 227.
35. Alejandro Mejías-López, *The Inverted Conquest: the Myth of Modernity and the Transatlantic Onset of Modernism*, Nashville: Vanderbilt University Press, 2009, p. 47.
36. Bell, *Reordering the World*, p. 175.
37. Quoted in William Roger Louis, "Introduction", in William Roger Louis (ed.), *The Oxford History of the British Empire*, vol. V: *Historiography*, ed. Robin W. Winks, Oxford: Oxford University Press, 2007, p. 9.
38. Kenny and Pearce, *Shadows of Empire*, p. 17.
39. Robert Stout, "Imperial Federation League: Nature and Objects of the League", in *The Pamphlet Collection of Sir Robert Stout: Volume 57*, http://nzetc.victoria.ac.nz/tm/scholarly/tei-Stout57-t3-body-d1.html, last accessed 22 December 2018.
40. Paul Johnson, "Why Britain Should Join America", *Forbes Magazine*, 5 April 1999, http://www.forbes.com/forbes/1999/0405/6307082a_print.html, last accessed 16 February 2018.
41. Conquest, "Toward an English-Speaking Union".
42. Robert Conquest, *The Dragons of Expectation: Reality and Delusion in the Course of History*, London: Duckworth, 2006, pp. 221–31.

43. James C. Bennett, *The Anglosphere Challenge: Why the English-Speaking Nations will Lead the Way in the Twenty-First Century*, Lanham: Rowman & Littlefield, 2004, p. 41.

44. Ibid., pp. 80–1.

45. Daniel Hannan, "Time for an Anglosphere Free Trade Area", *Sunday Telegraph*, 1 July 2018, https://www.pressreader.com/uk/the-sunday-telegraph/20180701/282003263168652, last accessed 28 July 2018.

46. Andrew Lilico, "Why CANZUK is Britain's Best Hope after Brexit", *CapX*, 23 January 2017, https://capx.co/why-canzuk-is-britains-best-hope-after-brexit/, last accessed 28 June 2018.

47. See the pamphlet written by James Bennett, *A Time for Audacity: How Brexit has Created the CANZUK Option*, London: Pole to Pole Publishing, 2016.

48. Andrew Roberts, "CANZUK: After Brexit, Canada, Australia, New Zealand and Britain can Unite as a Pillar of Western Civilization", *Daily Telegraph*, 13 September 2016, https://www.telegraph.co.uk/news/2016/09/13/canzuk-after-brexit-canada-australia-new-zealand-and-britain-can/, last accessed 28 June 2018.

49. Peter Pomerantsev, "The Idealistic Pull of the 'Anglosphere'", *Politico*, 13 July 2016, https://www.politico.eu/article/the-idealistic-pull-of-the-anglosphere-leave-brexit-emotions/, last accessed 28 June 2018.

50. Quoted in Olivier Beaud, "Federation and Empire: About a Conceptual Distinction of Political Forms", in Amnon Lev (ed.), *The Federal Idea: Public Law between Governance and Political Life*, London: Bloomsbury, 2017, p. 59.

51. Bosco, *The Round Table Movement*, p. 79.

52. Bell, *The Idea of Greater Britain*, p. 16.

53. Ibid., pp. 155–6.

54. Donald Read, *The Age of Urban Democracy: England 1868–1914*, London: Routledge, 1979, p. 353.

55. A team of bright Oxford graduates who worked with Alfred Milner—the High Commissioner for Southern Africa and Governor of the Cape Colony—and contributed to the formation of the Union of South Africa in 1910 with the status of Dominion. Milner was a sort of spiritual leader for the group, and his imperialist ideas, which originated from his South African experience, became a sort of religious faith—the *religio Milneriana*. See Shula Marks, "Southern Africa", in Louis (ed.), *The Oxford History of the British Empire*, vol. IV: *The Twentieth Century*, pp. 544–5.

56. The Round Table was the most influential and enduring organization created during the Edwardian era to promote the unity of the British Empire. A full list of such organizations, in chronological order, would include the Victoria League and the League of the Empire (1901), the

Empire Day Movement and the Tariff Reform League (1903), the Royal Colonial Institute and the Empire Press Union (1909), the Over-Seas Club (1910) and the Empire Parliamentary Association (1911). But unlike them, the Round Table has played a key role in the global political debate of the twentieth century, has survived the passage of time, and still exists as a Commonwealth ginger group. See, for instance, William Roger Louis, "Preface", in Alexander May (ed.), *The Commonwealth and International Affairs: The Round Table Centennial Selection*, London: Routledge, 2010, p. vii.

57. Andrea Bosco, *June 1940, Great Britain and the First Attempt to Build a European Union*, Cambridge: Cambridge Scholars Publishing, 2016, pp. 7–9.

58. Alexander May, "The Round Table: 1910–66", D.Phil. thesis, University of Oxford, 1995, p. 71, https://ora.ox.ac.uk/objects/uuid:ee7ebd01-f085-44e9-917b-98d21a0f4206, last accessed 22 December 2018.

59. Kendle, *Federal Britain*, p. 85.

60. Duncan Hall, *The British Commonwealth of Nations: A Study of its Past and Future Development*, London: Methuen, 1920.

61. Herbert Vere Evatt, *The King and his Dominion Governors, 1936*, New York and London: Routledge, 2013, p. 271; B.H. Fletcher, "Hall, Hessel Duncan (1891–1976)", *Australian Dictionary of Biography*, National Centre of Biography, Australian National University, Melbourne: Melbourne University Publishing, 1996, http://adb.anu.edu.au/biography/hall-hessel-duncan-10394/text18417, last accessed 9 November 2017.

62. Robert MacGregor Dawson, *The Development of Dominion Status, 1900–1936*, London: Frank Cass & Co. Ltd., 1965, p. 106.

63. Vucetic, *The Anglosphere*, p. 22.

64. Ibid., p. 29.

65. Jean-François Drolet and James Dunkerley, (eds), *American Foreign Policy: Studies in Intellectual History*, Manchester: Manchester University Press, 2017, p. 47.

66. Bell, *Reordering the World*, p. 195.

67. John Dumbrell, *A Special Relationship: Anglo-American Relations from the Cold War to Iraq*, London: Palgrave Macmillan, 2006, p. 17.

68. Roberts, *History of the English-Speaking Peoples since 1990*, p. 1.

69. Menno Spiering, "British Euroscepticism", *European Studies* 20, 2004, pp. 127–49.

5. THE FOREIGN POLICY OF NOSTALGIA

1. Sam Morgan, "EU Parliament Trolls UK's Blue Passports for April Fool's Day", Euractiv, 3 April 2018, https://www.euractiv.com/section/

United Kingdom-europe/news/eu-parliament-trolls-United Kingdoms-blue-passports-for-april-fools-day/, last accessed 2 June 2018.

2. B. Kentish and P. Walker, "Half of Leave Voters Want to Bring Back the Death Penalty after Brexit", *The Independent*, 29 March 2016, https://www.independent.co.United Kingdom/news/United Kingdom/politics/brexit-poll-leave-voters-death-penalty-yougov-results-light-bulbs-a7656791.htm, last accessed 2 June 2018.

3. Boris Johnson, "Uniting for a Great Brexit: Foreign Secretary's Speech", speech, 14 February 2018, https://www.gov.uk/government/speeches/foreign-secretary-speech-uniting-for-a-great-brexit, last accessed 28 June 2018.

4. Boris Johnson, "UK Will Prosper after Brexit by 'Going Global'", speech, 14 February 2018, http://www.aparchive.com/metadata/youtube/cab182b889169a584141fe664da4e678, last accessed 28 June 2018.

5. Boris Johnson, "Foreign Secretary's Mansion House Speech at the Lord Mayor's Easter Banquet 2018", speech, 28 March 2018, https://www.gov.United Kingdom/government/speeches/foreign-secretarys-lord-mayors-easter-banquet-speech-at-mansion-house-wednesday-28-march, last accessed 28 June 2018.

6. Michael Kenny and Nick Pearce trace the origins of this divergence and the complex story of its protagonists in *Shadows of Empire*. Part of the book focuses on the role played in this debate by Enoch Powell, an unorthodox conservative and anti-establishment figure, since the 1950s. See pp. 157–8.

7. Gabriela Baczynska, "Still Too Many Questions, Few Answers in Brexit Talks—EU's Barnier", Reuters, 6 July 2018, https://www.reuters.com/article/uk-britain-eu-barnier/still-too-many-questions-few-answers-in-brexit-talks-eus-barnier-idUSKBN1JW1M4, last accessed 28 July 2018.

8. George Parker, Alex Barker, Jim Brunsden, and Mehreen Khan, "Theresa May's Focus Shifts to Hard Sell after Sealing Brexit Deal", *Financial Times*, 25 November 2018, https://www.ft.com/content/7a4c015e-f08b-11e8-9623-d7f9881e729f, last accessed 25 November 2018.

9. Boris Johnson, "The Rest of the World Believes in Britain. It's Time That we do", *Sunday Telegraph*, 15 July 2018, https://www.telegraph.co.United Kingdom/politics/2018/07/15/rest-world-believes-britain-time-did/, last accessed 20 July 2018.

10. For an interesting discussion of Europe's evolving role in British foreign policy, see Hill, *The Future of British Foreign Policy*.

11. Theresa May, "Prime Minister's Letter to Donald Tusk", 19 March

2018, https://www.gov.uk/government/publications/prime-ministers-letter-to-donald-tusk-19-march-2018, last accessed 20 July 2018.

12. Theresa May, "PM Speech on our Future Economic Partnership with the European Union", 2 March 2018, https://www.gov.uk/government/speeches/pm-speech-on-our-future-economic-partnership-with-the-european-union, last accessed 28 June 2018.

13. Ibid.

14. Ibid.

15. Ibid.

16. Ibid.

17. It is interesting that in the Conservative Manifesto of 2018, Chamberlain is cited as the party's "forgotten hero". May's intention to sign trade deals with "old friends and new partners" and her interventionist industrial strategy echoes Chamberlain's push for free trade within the empire. But when nostalgia drives politics, picking the right political heroes matters. Few Tories would look at Chamberlain with admiration, and most would agree with John Maynard Keynes, who described him as a "fanatical charlatan". See Nicholas Macpherson, "Joseph Chamberlain Sets the Tories a Bad Example", *Financial Times*, 24 May 2017, https://www.ft.com/content/00a5c60c-3f0a-11e7–82b6–896b95f30f58, last accessed 28 November 2018.

18. Sir Simon Fraser, "The World is our Oyster? Britain's Future Trade Relationships", The Tacitus Lecture 2017, http://www.world-traders.org/2017/02/23/tacitus-lecture-2017–2/, last accessed 29 December 2018.

19. OECD, *Looking Beyond Tariffs: The Role of Non-Tariff Barriers in World Trade*, Paris: OECD Trade Policy Studies, 2005.

20. Ying Staton, "Singapore of the North Atlantic: A Viable Option for Post-Brexit Britain?", *Global Counsel*, 28 October 2016, https://www.global-counsel.co.United Kingdom/blog/singapore-north-atlantic-viable-option-post-brexit-britain, last accessed 28 April 2018.

21. Paul Nuttall, "Forget Brussels—the UK Should be Doing Business with the Commonwealth", *Sunday Express*, 22 June 2016, https://www.express.co.United Kingdom/comment/expresscomment/682269/Brussels-UK-business-Commonwealth-PAUL-NUTTALL-United Kingdomip-trade, last accessed 28 April 2018.

22. Eva Namousoke, "A Divided Family: Race, the Commonwealth and Brexit", *The Round Table* 105 (5), (2016), pp. 463–76.

23. Philip Murphy, *Empire's New Clothes: The Myth of the Commonwealth*, London: Hurst, 2018, p. 206.

24. Commonwealth Secretariat, "The Commonwealth in the Unfolding Global Trade Landscape: Commonwealth Trade Review 2015", *The*

Commonwealth, pp. xxi–xxiii, http://thecommonwealth.org/common-wealth-unfolding-global-trade-landscape, last accessed 23 December 2018.

25. Ronald Sanders, "World View—the Commonwealth: What's in it for the Small States?", Tribune 242, 16 April 2018, http://www.tribune242.com/news/2018/apr/16/world-view-commonwealth-whats-it-small-states/, last accessed 28 April 2018.
26. Edgerton, *The Rise and Fall of the British Nation*, pp. 1–5.
27. Stephan Richter, "Britain's Confused Soul in the Age of Brexit", The Globalist, 27 April 2018, https://www.theglobalist.com/united-kingdom-brexit-germany-commonwealth/, last accessed 28 June 2018.
28. Simon Fraser, "Bracing ourselves for Brexit", *The World Today*, April/May 2017, pp. 38–40, https://www.chathamhouse.org/system/files/publications/twt/Bracing%20ourselves%20for%20Brexit%20Fraser.pdf, last accessed 28 June 2018.
29. Ibid.
30. Joel Kotkin, "The New World Order", Legatum Institute, November 2011, https://www.li.com/docs/default-source/surveys-of-entrepreneurs/new-world-order-2011_final.pdf, last accessed 28 April 2018.
31. Amy Chua, *Day of Empire: How Hyperpowers Rise to Global Dominance—and Why they Fall*, New York: Anchor, 2007, p. 229.
32. This section draws from the article by Pramit Pal Chaudhuri, "Perchè l'India ama poco l'Anglosfera?", *Aspenia* 81, 2018, pp. 169–82.
33. See the World Value Survey at http://www.worldvaluessurvey.org/WVSContents.jsp
34. See for instance, Harsha Vardhana Singh, "Trade Policy Reform in India since 1991", Brookings Working Paper, March 2018, https://www.brookings.edu/research/working-paper-trade-policy-reform-in-india-since-1991/, last accessed 28 July 2018.
35. Pramit Pal Chaudhuri, "Perchè l'India ama poco l'Anglosfera?", *Aspenia* 81, 2018, pp. 169–82.
36. Caroline Mortimer, "Two Countries Have Already Told the UK they Must Relax Immigration Rules if they Want Free Trade", *The Independent*, 22 January 2017, https://www.independent.co.uk/news/uk/politics/brexit-latest-australia-india-tell-uk-relax-immigration-rules-free-trade-deal-eu-visa-restrictions-a7540036.html, last accessed 22 April 2018.
37. See http://armstrade.sipri.org/armstrade/html/export_values.php
38. Shashi Tharoor, *Inglorious Empire: What the British Did to India*, London: Penguin, 2017, pp. 175–85.
39. David Olusoga, "Empire 2.0 is Dangerous Nostalgia for Something that Never Existed", *The Guardian*, 19 March 2017, https://www.the-

guardian.com/commentisfree/2017/mar/19/empire-20-is-dangerous-nostalgia-for-something-that-never-existed, last accessed 28 April 2018.

40. Tharoor, *Inglorious Empire*, pp. 176–82.
41. Vidiadhar Surajprasad (V.S.) Naipaul, *The Enigma of Arrival: A Novel in Five Sections*, London: Picador, 2011, p. 139.
42. As examples of official policy: "Foreign Policy, Defence and Development: A Future Partnership Paper", Department for Exiting the European Union, September 2017, https://www.gov.uk/government/publications/foreign-policy-defence-and-development-a-future-partnership-paper, last accessed 31 December 2018; "PM Speech at Munich Security Conference: 17 February 2018", Prime Minister's Office, February 2018, https://www.gov.uk/government/speeches/pm-speech-at-munich-security-conference-17-february-2018, last accessed 31 December 2018.
43. Sophia Besch, *Plugging in the British: EU Defense Policy*, Center for European Reform, April 2018, https://www.cer.eu/publications/archive/policy-brief/2018/plugging-british-eu-defence-policy, last accessed 24 December 2018.
44. Ibid.
45. Marta Dassù, Wolfgang Ischinger, Pierre Vimont, and Robert Cooper, "Keeping Europe Safe after Brexit", Policy Brief, European Council on Foreign Relations, March 2018, p. 3, https://www.ecfr.eu/page/-/keeping_europe_safe_after_brexit.pdf, last accessed 28 June 2018.
46. Boris Johnson, "Brexit Speech", *The Spectator*, 14 February 2018, https://blogs.spectator.co.uk/2018/02/full-text-boris-johnsons-brexit-speech/, last accessed 28 June 2018.

6. THE ANGLO-SAXON TRIBE

1. Kenny and Pearce, *Shadows of Empire*.
2. We thank Walter Russell Mead for crystallizing the structure of the Anglosphere with this religious comparison.
3. "Global Britain or Globaloney", *The Economist*, 15 March 2018, https://www.economist.com/britain/2018/03/15/global-britain-or-globaloney, last accessed 28 June 2018.
4. David Davis, "Brexit: What Would it Look Like?", speech at the Institute of Chartered Engineers, 4 February 2016, http://www.daviddavismp.com/david-davis-speech-on-brexit-at-the-institute-of-chartered-engineers/, last accessed 25 June 2018.
5. Boris Johnson, "The Aussies are Just Like us, so Let's Stop Kicking them Out", *Sunday Telegraph*, 25 August 2013, https://www.telegraph.co.uk/news/politics/10265619/The-Aussies-are-just-like-us-so-lets-stop-kicking-them-out.html, last accessed 25 June 2018.

6. Joel Kotkin, *Tribes: How Race, Religion, and Identity Determine Success in the New Global Economy*, New York: Random House, 1993, p. 4.

7. Richard J. Aldrich, *GCHQ: The Uncensored Story of Britain's Most Secret Intelligence Agency*, London: Harper, 2010, p. 89.

8. Richard McGregor, "Intelligence: The All-Seeing Eyes", *Financial Times*, 13 December 2013, https://www.ft.com/content/719f86bc-63ea-11e3–98e2–00144feabdc0?mhq5j=e5, last accessed 1 January 2018.

9. This symbiotic collaboration contrasts quite starkly with what happens in continental Europe. For decades, conflicting national interests and asymmetries in intelligence capabilities have prevented a stronger cooperation from developing, particularly between Eastern and Western European countries. As Bernard Squarcini, France's spy chief under former President Nicolas Sarkozy, put it: "With eastern European countries as EU members, no one wants to share details on sensitive operations. It's a question of trust. Europol is useful to arrest Serbian criminals. But no one wants to disclose details on covert operations, the sources you have infiltrated or taken out of judicial procedures, you want to protect your sources." This unwillingness to cooperate became clear with the Bataclan terror attacks that shocked Paris and the world in 2015. At that time, only half of the EU's twenty-eight members had registered foreign fighters on the Europol Information System, its main database on crime. Even if after the attacks more countries joined the system, many continued not to use it because of the lack of synchronization between Europol's regional crime database and the data available to police at the external borders of the EU's passport-free area in the Schengen Information System, which alerts border guards to whether a traveller has a criminal record or is wanted. For more details see Björn Fägersten, "For EU Eyes Only? Intelligence and European Security", European Union Institute for Security Studies, March 2016 https://www.iss.europa.eu/sites/default/files/EUISSFiles/Brief_8_EU_Intelligence_Cooperation.pdf, last accessed 1 January 2018; and Jim Brunsden, Anne-Sylvaine Chassany, and Sam Jones, "Europe's Failure to Share Intelligence Hampers Terror Fight", *Financial Times*, 4 April 2016, https://www.ft.com/content/f9baf7e8-f975-11e5-b3f6-11d5706b613b?mhq5j=e5, last accessed 1 January 2018.

10. The President's Review Group on Intelligence and Communications Technologies: Richard A. Clarke, Michael J. Morell, Geoffrey R. Stone, Cass R. Sunstein, and Peter Swire, "The NSA Report: Liberty and Security in a Changing World", 12 December 2013, p. 175, https://obamawhitehouse.archives.gov/sites/default/files/docs/2013–12–12_rg_final_report.pdf, last accessed 28 June 2018.

11. Joseph E. Persico, *Roosevelt's Secret War: FDR and World War II Espionage*, New York: Random House, 2002, pp. 159–60.

12. Patrick Delaforce, *The Battle of the Bulge: Hitler's Final Gamble*, London: Pearson Longman, 2006, p. 81.

13. Roberts, *History of the English-Speaking Peoples since 1990*, pp. 331–2.

14. Richard McGregor, "Intelligence: The All-Seeing Eyes", *Financial Times*, 13 December 2013, https://www.ft.com/content/719f86bc-63ea-11e3–98e2–00144feabdc0?mhq5j=e5, last accessed 1 January 2018.

15. Alan Yuhas, "Former NSA Director: *Charlie Hebdo* Attack was 'Kind of Inevitable'", *The Guardian*, 10 March 2015, https://www.theguardian.com/us-news/2015/mar/10/former-nsa-director-michael-hayden-charlie-hebdo, last accessed 1 January 2018.

16. Michael Gove, "The Facts of Life Say Leave: Why Britain and Europe Will be Better off after we Vote Leave", *Huffington Post*, 19 April 2016, https://www.huffingtonpost.co.uk/michael-gove/michael-gove-vote-leave_b_9728548.html, last accessed 28 June 2018.

17. Enrico Fels, *Shifting Power in Asia Pacific? The Rise of China, Sino-US Competition and Regional Middle Power Allegiance*, Cham: Springer, 2016, pp. 381–2.

18. See the FBI's website: https://archives.fbi.gov/archives/news/stories/2008/march/cybergroup_031708, last accessed 28 June 2018.

19. See NORAD's official website: http://www.norad.mil/About-NORAD/, last accessed 1 January 2018.

20. Stanley W. Dziuban, *Military Relations between the United States and Canada, 1939–1945*, Washington, DC: Center of Military History, United States Army, pp. 26–7.

21. Elle Hunt, "Reciprocal Living and Working Rights Backed in UK, Australia, NZ and Canada", *The Guardian*, 14 March 2016, https://www.theguardian.com/world/2016/mar/14/reciprocal-living-and-working-rights-backed-in-uk-australia-nz-and-canada, last accessed 1 January 2018.

22. Dr Donald Markwell (Warden of Rhodes House, Oxford), "To 'Render War Impossible': The Rhodes Scholarships, Educational Relations between Countries, and Peace", speech delivered at the Sailing Dinner of the Canadian Association of Rhodes Scholars, Ottawa, Saturday 24 September 2011, https://www.rhodeshouse.ox.ac.uk/media/2926/ottawa_september_2011_to_render_war_impossible.pdf, last accessed 5 February 2019.

23. Philip Ziegler, *Legacy: Cecil Rhodes, the Rhodes Trust and the Rhodes Scholarships*, New Haven: Yale University Press, 2008, Appendix 1.

24. Richard Adams, "Rhodes Scholarships Opened Up to Students from UK and Rest of World", *The Guardian*, 19 February 2018, https://www.theguardian.com/education/2018/feb/19/rhodes-scholarships-

opened-up-to-students-from-uk-and-rest-of-world, last accessed 7 March 2018.

25. Robert Menzies, *Afternoon Light: Some Memories of Men and Events*, London: Cassell, 1967, p. 6.

26. James Blitz and Hannah Kuchler, "UK and Canada to Share Embassies", *Financial Times*, 24 September 2012, https://www.ft.com/content/4a31dcac-0625-11e2-a28a-00144feabdc0, last accessed 3 January 2018.

27. Peter Spence, "New Zealand Offers UK its Top Trade Negotiators for Post-Brexit Deals", *Daily Telegraph*, 29 June 2016, http://www.telegraph.co.uk/business/2016/06/29/new-zealand-offers-uk-its-top-trade-negotiators-for-post-brexit/, last accessed 3 January 2018.

28. Greg Sheridan, "British Push to Share UN Security Council Seat with Canberra", *The Australian*, 2 May 2018, https://www.theaustralian.com.au/national-affairs/foreign-affairs/british-push-to-share-un-security-council-seat-with-canberra/news-story/7c09cd537ee4ef5d601c163b65038b52, last accessed 28 June 2018.

29. Karl W. Deutsch, *Political Community and the North Atlantic Area: International Organization in the Light of Historical Experience*, Princeton: Princeton University Press, 1957, p. 66.

30. Andrew Roberts, "Canada Comes to the Rescue of Great Britain Again", *Daily Beast*, 28 November 2012, https://www.thedailybeast.com/canada-comes-to-the-rescue-of-great-britain-again, last accessed 3 January 2018.

31. See https://www.britannica.com/biography/Tony-Abbott, last accessed 28 June 2018.

32. See https://nzhistory.govt.nz/politics/premiers-and-prime-ministers, last accessed 28 June 2018.

33. A member of the Cameron Cabinet recounted this anecdote to us during a meeting of the Trilateral Commission.

34. Chris Giles, "Rajan Says he Won't Apply to be BoE Governor", *Financial Times*, 16 May 2018, https://www.ft.com/content/75c0692c-5941-11e8-bdb7-f6677d2e1ce8, last accessed 20 May 2018.

35. House of Commons, *Global Security: UK–US Relations*, Foreign Affairs Committee, London: HM Stationery Office Limited, 28 March 2010.

36. Bruce Stokes and Rhonda Stewart, "What it Takes to Truly be 'One of Us'", Pew Research Center, February 2017, http://assets.pewresearch.org/wp-content/uploads/sites/2/2017/04/14094140/Pew-Research-Center-National-Identity-Report-FINAL-February-1-2017.pdf, last accessed 1 January 2018.

37. Benjamin Whorf, "Science and Linguistics", *Technology Review* 42 (6), 1940, pp. 229–31, 247–8.

38. Randolph Quirk, *The English Language and Images of Matter*, Oxford: Oxford University Press, 1972, pp. 32–3.

39. Martin Kettle, "Trapped in the Anglosphere, we've Lost Sight of Next Door", *The Guardian*, 19 August 2010, https://www.theguardian.com/commentisfree/2010/aug/19/the-anglosphere-is-interesting-enough, last accessed 1 January 2018.

40. James C. Bennett, "An Anglosphere Primer", Explorers Foundation, 2002, http://explorersfoundation.org/archive/anglosphere_primer.pdf, last accessed 3 January 2018.

41. In 1976 the evolutionary anthropologist Richard Dawkins used the term meme to describe a unit of cultural transmission analogous to the gene, arguing that replication also happens in culture. The concept of memetic applied to the Anglosphere was used by James C. Bennett in *The Anglosphere Challenge*, pp. 93–7.

42. See the official website of the census: https://www.census.gov/prod/2004pubs/c2kbr-35.pdf.

43. Bennett, *The Anglosphere Challenge*, p. 94.

44. Daniel Defoe, *The True-Born Englishman: A Satire*, Leeds: Alice Mann, 1836, p. 18.

45. David Hackett Fischer, *Albion's Seed: Four British Folkways in America*, Oxford: Oxford University Press, 1989, p. 4.

46. Roberts, *History of the English-Speaking Peoples since 1990*, p. 15.

47. John Adamson, "Down Under Comes out on Top", *Daily Telegraph*, 27 July 2004, http://www.telegraph.co.uk/culture/books/3621288/Down-under-comes-out-on-top.html, last accessed 1 January 2018.

48. Ronald Inglehart and Christian Welzel, "How Development Leads to Democracy", *Foreign Affairs* 88 (2), 2009, pp. 33–48.

49. Arendt, *The Origins of Totalitarianism*, chapter 5.

50. The World Bank ranking can be found at http://www.doingbusiness.org/rankings.

51. For detailed data see http://money.visualcapitalist.com/all-of-the-worlds-stock-exchanges-by-size/.

52. For detailed data see the website of the Global Entrepreneurship Monitor: http://www.gemconsortium.org/data/key-aps.

53. Peter Hall and David Soskice, *Varieties of Capitalism: The Institutional Foundations of Comparative Advantage*, Oxford: Oxford University Press, 2003, pp. 1–64.

54. For a thorough analysis about this topic see Arendt, *The Origins of Totalitarianism*.

55. See the factsheet provided by the World Intellectual Property Organization: http://www.wipo.int/export/sites/www/ipstats/en/docs/infographic_pct_2016.pdf.

56. See QS World Universities Ranking: https://www.topuniversities.com/university-rankings/world-university-rankings/2018.

57. For a full list see https://en.wikipedia.org/wiki/List_of_Nobel_lau-reates_by_country.

58. Vivek Wadhwa, *The Immigrant Exodus: Why America is Losing the Global Race to Capture Entrepreneurial Talent*, Philadelphia: Wharton Digital Press, 2012, p. 22.

59. Ibid.

60. The INSEAD report on global talent competitiveness can be found at https://www.insead.edu/news/2017-global-talent-competitiveness-index-davos.

61. Jacob M. Schlesinger and Robbie Whelan, "Trump Hails US–Mexico Trade Pact, Says 'We'll See' With Canada", *The Wall Street Journal*, 28 August 2018, https://www.wsj.com/articles/mexico-u-s-nafta-nego-tiators-signal-confidence-after-marathon-sunday-session-1535372909, last accessed 28 August 2018.

62. The Thucydides Trap refers to the fear caused by a rising power in an established power, which escalates towards war. See Graham Allison, *Destined for War: Can America and China Escape Thucydides' Trap?*, New York: Scribe Publications, 2017.

63. Henry Overton, "The Five Eyes in the Trump Era: Dominant or Diminished?", Foreign Brief, 7 July 2017, https://www.foreignbrief.com/united-states/five-eyes-trump-era-dominant-diminished/, last accessed 28 June 2018.

64. Elizabeth Piper and Estelle Shirbon, "Trump Condemns Leaks after UK Police Briefly Halt Information Sharing", Reuters, 25 May 2017, https://www.reuters.com/article/us-britain-security-manchester/trump-condemns-leaks-after-uk-police-briefly-halt-information-sharing-idUSKBN18L0QU, last accessed 28 June 2018.

65. Vucetic, *The Anglosphere*, p. 123.

66. Ibid., p. 73.

67. James Harbeck, "Why is Canadian English Unique?", BBC News, 20 August 2015, http://www.bbc.com/culture/story/20150820-why-is-canadian-english-unique, last accessed 1 January 2018.

68. The English-speaking people who founded Canada were the United Empire Loyalists. Originally British settlers living in America, they sided with the Crown during the War of Independence and were forced to leave when America broke away from Britain. In compen-sation, the Queen offered them land in Canada, where they set the social standards, including language. The outcome is this hybrid English that reflects their loyalty to the Queen and their love for the United States, which they left because they did not want to ditch the empire. See Mark M. Orkin, *Speaking Canadian English: An Informal Account of the English Language in Canada*, London: Routledge, 2015, p. 49.

69. See the official website of the Economist Intelligence Unit: https://infographics.economist.com/2017/DemocracyIndex/.

70. Gregory Clark, *The Son Also Rises: Surnames and the History of Social Mobility*, Princeton: Princeton University Press, 2014, pp. 99–105.

71. Antony Atkinson and Andrew Leigh, "The Distribution of Top Incomes in Five Anglo-Saxon Countries Over the Long Run", *Economic Record* 89, 2013, pp. 31–47.

7. A NOT-SO-SPECIAL RELATIONSHIP: AMERICA AND BRITAIN

1. Walter Russell Mead, "The Jacksonian Revolt: American Populism and the Liberal Order", *Foreign Affairs* 96 (2), March/April 2017.

2. Sam Levin, "Donald Trump Backs Brexit, Saying UK Would be 'Better off' Without EU", *The Guardian*, 5 May 2016, https://www.theguardian.com/us-news/2016/may/05/donald-trump-brexit-uk-leaving-european-union, last accessed 28 June 2018.

3. "Transcript: Donald Trump's Foreign Policy Speech", *The New York Times*, 28 April 2016, https://www.nytimes.com/2016/04/28/us/politics/transcript-trump-foreign-policy.html, last accessed 2 April 2018.

4. Ishaan Tharoor, "Donald Trump's Real Foreign Policy: A Clash of Civilizations", *The Washington Post*, 28 April 2016, https://www.washingtonpost.com/news/worldviews/wp/2016/04/28/donald-trumps-real-foreign-policy-a-clash-of-civilizations/?utm_term=.5a5fdeaea4ed, last accessed 2 April 2018.

5. Chris Cillizza, "Donald Trump's Brexit Press Conference Was Beyond Bizarre", *The Washington Post*, 24 June 2016, https://www.washingtonpost.com/news/the-fix/wp/2016/06/24/donald-trumps-brexit-press-conference-was-beyond-bizarre/?utm_term=.7078760af7e2,   last accessed 3 April 2018.

6. James Hohmann, "Brexit Vote Shows Why Trump Can Win", *Boston Globe*, 24 June 2016, https://www.bostonglobe.com/news/world/2016/06/24/brexit-vote-shows-why-trump-can-win/EH18rp22m6Dxez6jQzw2xK/story.html, last accessed 5 April 2018.

7. Anne Applebaum, "Britain's Decision to Leave the EU is a Warning to America", *The Washington Post*, 24 June 2016, https://www.washingtonpost.com/opinions/global-opinions/after-brexit-what-will-and-wont-happen/2016/06/24/c9f7a2f6–39f1–11e6–8f7c-d4c723a2becb_story.html?utm_term=.39dc4bbe911c, last accessed 25 April 2018.

8. Donald J. Trump, "Remarks at the Mississippi Coliseum in Jackson, Mississippi", 24 August 2016, http://www.presidency.ucsb.edu/ws/index.php?pid=123198, last accessed 3 April 2018.

9. John R. Bolton, "The Return of the 'Special Relationship' Between the

US and UK", *Boston Globe*, 30 January 2017, https://www.boston-globe.com/opinion/2017/01/30/the-return-special-relationship-between-and/F5QXTfmrdu8skebEpfON8L/story.html, last accessed April 2018.

10. Press Association, "Churchill Bust in Oval Office Again as Donald Trump Settles in", *The Guardian*, 21 January 2017, https://www.the-guardian.com/world/2017/jan/21/churchill-bust-returns-to-oval-office-as-donald-trump-settles-in, last accessed 28 June 2018.

11. Donald J. Trump, Twitter post, 21 November 2016, 6.22 p.m., https://twitter.com/realDonaldTrump/status/800887087780294656, last accessed 3 April 2018.

12. Elizabeth Anderson, "Why President Trump Could be Good for the UK", inews.co.uk, 9 November 2016, https://inews.co.uk/news/business/donald-trumps-victory-good-uk/, last accessed 25 April 2018.

13. Ben Riley-Smith, "Britain Will be Front of the Queue for Trade Deal with US under Donald Trump's New Commerce Secretary", *The Daily Telegraph*, 17 December 2016, https://www.telegraph.co.uk/news/2016/12/17/exclusive-britain-will-front-queue-trade-deal-us-donald-trumps/, last accessed 4 April 2018.

14. "The President's News Conference with Prime Minister Theresa May of the United Kingdom", American Presidency Project, 27 January 2017, http://www.presidency.ucsb.edu/ws/index.php?pid=122543, last accessed 28 April 2018.

15. David Wilkinson, "Transcript of Theresa May's Speech to US Republicans", CNN, 26 January 2017, https://www.cnn.com/2017/01/26/politics/theresa-may-us-speech-transcript/index.html, last accessed 8 April 2018.

16. Ben Wellings, "The Anglosphere in the Brexit Referendum", *Revue Française de Civilisation Britannique* 22 (2), May 2017, http://journals.openedition.org/rfcb/1354, last accessed 28 April 2018.

17. Nick Pearce, "After Brexit: The Eurosceptic Vision of an Anglosphere Future", Open Democracy, 3 February 2016, https://www.opendemocracy.net/uk/nick-pearce/after-brexit-eurosceptic-vision-of-anglosphere-future, last accessed 28 April 2018.

18. Andrew Mycock and Ben Wellings, "Beyond Brexit: 'Global Britain' Looks to the Emerging Anglosphere for New Opportunities", The Conversation, 17 May 2017, https://theconversation.com/beyond-brexit-global-britain-looks-to-the-emerging-anglosphere-for-new-opportunities-77562, last accessed 28 April 2018.

19. Matthew Grant, "'Leading the World? The Historical Fantasy of May's Vision for Post-Brexit Britain", History and Policy, 28 January 2017, http://www.historyandpolicy.org/opinion-articles/articles/leading-

the-world-the-historical-fantasy-of-mays-vision-for-post-brexit, last accessed 28 April 2018; Eleanor Newbigin, "Brexit, Nostalgia and the Great British Fantasy", Open Democracy, 15 February 2017, https://www.opendemocracy.net/eleanor-newbigin/brexit-britain-and-nostalgia-for-fantasy-past, last accessed 28 April 2018.

20. David Reynolds, "Rethinking US–British Relations", *International Affairs* 65 (1), Winter 1988–9, pp. 89–111.

21. Julian Lindley-French, "US–UK: Special Relationship or Special Dependenceship?", paper for Aspen Institute Italia, November 2018.

22. George C. Herring, *From Colony to Superpower: US Foreign Relations since 1776*, Oxford: Oxford University Press, 2008, pp. 595–7.

23. Paul M. Kennedy, *The Rise and Fall of the Great Powers: Economic Change and Military Conflict from 1500 to 2000*, London: Vintage, 1988, pp. 357–8.

24. Christopher Hitchens, *Blood, Class and Nostalgia: Anglo-American Ironies*, London: Vintage, 1991, pp. 203–4.

25. Warren F. Kimball, *Forged in War: Churchill, Roosevelt and the Second World War*, London: Ivan R. Dee, 1998, pp. 1–34.

26. E.J. Hughes, "Winston Churchill and the Formation of the United Nations Organization", *Journal of Contemporary History* 9 (4), 1974, pp. 179–80.

27. John Lamberton Harper, *American Visions of Europe: Franklin D. Roosevelt, George F. Kennan, and Dean G. Acheson*, Cambridge: Cambridge University Press, 1996, pp. 107–8.

28. Tony Judt, *Postwar: A History of Europe since 1945*, London: Penguin, 2005, pp. 13–40.

29. Geir Lundestad, *The United States and Western Europe since 1945: From "Empire" by Invitation to Transatlantic Drift*, Oxford and New York: Oxford University Press, 2003; Benn Steil, *The Marshall Plan: Dawn of the Cold War*, New York: Simon & Schuster, 2018, pp. 1–13.

30. John Kent and John Young, "British Policy Overseas: The 'Third Force' and the Origins of NATO—in Search of a New Perspective", in Beatrice Heuser and Robert O'Neill (eds.), *Securing Peace in Europe, 1945–62: Thoughts for the Post-Cold War Era*, London: Palgrave, 2016, pp. 41–64.

31. David Reynolds, "A 'Special Relationship'? America, Britain and the International Order since the Second World War", *International Affairs* 62 (1), December 1985, p. 4.

32. David Reynolds, *Britannia Overruled: British Policy and World Power in the Twentieth Century*, London: Routledge, 2000, p. 176.

33. Melvyn P. Leffler, *For the Soul of Mankind: The United States, the Soviet Union, and the Cold War*, New York: Hill & Wang, 2009, pp. 3–10.

34. Stephan Alexander, "Cold War Alliances and the Emergence of Transatlantic Competition: An Introduction", in Stephan Alexander (ed.), *The Americanization of Europe: Culture, Diplomacy, and Anti-Americanism after 1945*, Oxford: Berghahn, 2007, pp. 1–20.

35. Jessica Gienow-Hecht, "Culture and the Cold War in Europe", in Melvyn P. Leffler and Odd Arne Westad (eds.), *The Cambridge History of the Cold War*, Cambridge: Cambridge University Press, 2010, vol. I: *Origins*, ed. Melvyn P. Leffler and Odd Arne Westad, pp. 411–16.

36. Brendon O'Connor and Martin Griffiths (eds.), *Anti-Americanism: History, Causes, and Themes*, Oxford: Greenwood World Publishing, 2007, pp. 254–5.

37. David W. Ellwood, "American Myth, American Model, and the Quest for a British Modernity", in Laurence R. Moore and Maurizio Vaudagna (eds.), *The American Century in Europe*, Ithaca: Cornell University Press, 2003, pp. 138–40.

38. Dumbrell, *A Special Relationship*, pp. 34–6.

39. Alan Brinkley, "The Concept of an American Century", in Moore and Vaudagna (eds.), *The American Century in Europe*, pp. 7–24.

40. Ibid., pp. 7–10.

41. David Reynolds, "A 'Special Relationship'? America, Britain and the International Order since the Second World War", *International Affairs* 62 (1), December 1985, p. 8.

42. David Gowland and Arthur Turner, *Reluctant Europeans: Britain and European Integration 1945–1998*, London: Routledge, 2014, pp. 69–82.

43. Wilson D. Miscamble, *George F. Kennan and the Making of American Foreign Policy, 1947–1950*, Princeton: Princeton University Press, 1992, pp. 289–90.

44. Armin Rappaport, "The United States and European Integration: The First Phase", *Diplomatic History* 5 (2), April 1981, pp. 121–50.

45. Terrence R. Guay, *The United States and the European Union: The Political Economy of a Relationship*, London: Sheffield Academic Press, 2000, pp. 24–5.

46. David Gowland and Arthur Turner, *Britain and European Integration: A Documentary History*, London: Routledge, 2000, p. 38 and pp. 45–6.

47. Greg Behrman, *The Most Noble Adventure: The Marshall Plan and the Time When America Helped Save Europe*, New York: Simon & Schuster, 2007, pp. 270–1.

48. Alan Dobson, "The Special Relationship and European Integration", *Diplomacy and Statecraft* 2 (1), March 1991, pp. 79–102.

49. Sebastian Reyn, *Atlantis Lost: The American Experience with de Gaulle, 1958–1969*, Amsterdam: Amsterdam University Press, 2010, p. 97.

50. Lundestad, *The United States and Western Europe*, pp. 120–1; Alan S.

Milward, *The Rise and Fall of a National Strategy: The UK and the European Community*, London: Routledge, 2002, pp. 310–51.

51. Stanley Hoffmann, "De Gaulle, Europe, and the Atlantic Alliance", *International Organization* 18 (1), 1964, pp. 1–28.

52. Robin Renwick, *Fighting with Allies: America and Britain in Peace and War*, London: Palgrave Macmillan, 1996, p. 279.

53. Gowland and Turner, *Reluctant Europeans*, pp. 249–50. For a recent critical assessment of the Reagan–Thatcher relationship see Richard Aldous, *Reagan and Thatcher: The Difficult Relationship*, London: W. W. Norton, 2012.

54. John Redwood, *Superpower Struggles: Mighty America, Faltering Europe, Rising Asia*, London: Palgrave Macmillan, 2005, p. 149.

55. Ibid., pp. 149–50; Dumbrell, *A Special Relationship*, p. 229.

56. Geir Lundestad, *East, West, North, South: International Relations since 1945*, London: Sage, 2014, pp. 193–200.

57. Lundestad, *The United States and Western Europe*, pp. 269–93.

58. Mark A. Pollack, "Unilateral America, Multilateral Europe?", in John Peterson and Mark A. Pollack (eds.), *Europe, America, Bush: Transatlantic Relations in the Twenty-First Century*, London: Routledge, 2004, pp. 115–27.

59. Barack Obama, "Remarks at Suntory Hall, Tokyo", 14 November 2009.

60. Michelle Egan and Neill Nugent, "The Changing Context and Nature of the Transatlantic Relationship", in Laurie Buonanno, Natalia Cuglesan, and Keith Henderson (eds.), *The New and Changing Transatlanticism: Politics and Policy Perspectives*, Abingdon and New York: Routledge, 2015, pp. 23–42.

61. "What's Obama's European Legacy?", Politico, 21 April 2016, https://www.politico.eu/article/what-will-define-barack-obamas-european-legacy-eu-us/, last accessed 3 March 2018.

62. Andrew Moran, "Barack Obama and the Return of 'Declinism': Rebalancing American Foreign Policy in an Era of Multipolarity", in Edward Ashbee and John Dumbrell (eds.), *The Obama Presidency and the Politics of Change*, London: Palgrave Macmillan, 2017, pp. 265–87.

63. "Remarks by President Obama and Prime Minister Cameron in Joint Press Conference", 22 April 2016, https://obamawhitehouse.archives.gov/the-press-office/2016/04/22/remarks-president-obama-and-prime-minister-cameron-joint-press, last accessed April 2018.

64. James Dean, Bruno Waterfield, and Oliver Wright, "Trump Puts EU Ahead of Britain in Trade Queue", *The Times*, 22 April 2017, https://www.thetimes.co.uk/article/trump-puts-eu-ahead-of-britain-in-trade-queue-l7t8zwn7k, last accessed 29 April 2018.

65. Michael Shear, Mark Landler, and James Kanter, "Trump's Message to

NATO is Pay Up, Not 'All for One'", *The New York Times*, 26 May 2017, http://www.nytimes.com/images/2017/05/26/nytfrontpage/scannat.pdf, last accessed 18 April 2018.

66. "US Image Suffers as Publics around World Question Trump's Leadership", Pew Research Center, Washington, DC, 26 June 2017, http://www.pewglobal.org/2017/06/26/u-s-image-suffers-as-publics-around-world-question-trumps-leadership/#, last accessed 28 April 2018; Adam Drummond, "Half of the British Public Think Trump is 'Dangerous'", *The Guardian*, 5 February 2017, https://www.theguardian.com/commentisfree/2017/feb/05/donald-trump-dangerous-opinium-poll-uk-voters, last accessed 28 April 2018.

67. Freddy Gray, "The 'Special Relationship' is in Trouble", *The National Interest*, 16 January 2018, https://nationalinterest.org/feature/the-special-relationship-trouble-24084, last accessed 31 December 2018.

68. Nicola Slawson, "In Trump Era, US–UK 'Special Relationship' Faces— and Causes—New Trials", *Christian Science Monitor*, 7 December 2017, https://www.csmonitor.com/World/Europe/2017/1207/In-Trump-era-US-UK-special-relationship-faces-and-causes-new-trials, last accessed 28 April 2018.

69. Donald J. Trump, Twitter post, 29 November 2017, 5.02 p.m., https://twitter.com/realDonaldTrump/status/936037588372283392, last accessed 24 April 2018.

70. Zakheim Dov, "Donald Trump is Single-Handedly Wrecking the Special Relationship", Foreign Policy, 30 November 2017, http://foreignpolicy.com/2017/11/30/donald-trump-is-singlehandedly-wrecking-the-special-relationship-with-britain/, last accessed 29 April 2018.

71. Philip Stephens, "Brexit and a Not-So-Special Relationship", *Financial Times*, 12 July 2018, https://www.ft.com/content/f699f272–84eb-11e8-a29d-73e3d454535d, last accessed 28 June 2018.

72. "Trump, in Britain, Tells May Ties are at Highest Level of Special", *The New York Times*, 13 July 2018, https://www.nytimes.com/2018/07/13/world/europe/donald-trump-uk-london-visit.html, last accessed 28 June 2018.

73. Andrew Gray, "Macron on Trump Suggestion to Leave EU: 'You can Imagine my Response'", Politico, 29 June 2018, https://www.politico.eu/article/macron-on-trump-suggestion-to-leave-eu-you-can-imagine-my-response/, last accessed 22 November 2018.

74. Gideon Rachman, "Donald Trump and Brexit are no Longer Identical Twins", *Financial Times*, 8 January 2018, https://www.ft.com/content/214ca7da-f455–11e7–88f7–5465a6ce1a00, last accessed 2 April 2018.

75. Tim Oliver and Mark Williams, "Making the 'Special Relationship' Great Again?", LSE IDEAS Strategic Update, January 2017, http://

www.lse.ac.uk/ideas/research/updates/special-relationship-great, last accessed 29 April 2018.

76. Arthur Beesley, "G7 Allies Lead Anger at Trump's Exit from Paris Climate Agreement", *Financial Times*, 2 June 2017, https://www.ft.com/content/eb1b25d6–4768–11e7–8519–9f94ee97d996, last accessed 29 April 2018.

77. "PM Statement on US Decision to Move Embassy to Jerusalem", Prime Minister's Office, 6 December 2017, https://www.gov.uk/government/news/pm-statement-on-us-decision-to-move-embassy-to-jerusalem-6-december-2017, last accessed 28 April 2018.

78. Ben Riley-Smith, "British Ministers Fear Further Rift with US over Iran Deal after Donald Trump Appoints Hardline Advisers", *Daily Telegraph*, 25 March 2018, https://www.telegraph.co.uk/news/2018/03/25/british-ministers-fear-rift-us-iran-deal-donald-trump-appoints/, last accessed 28 April 2018.

79. Noah Gordon, "Trump is no Ally on Trade for Post-Brexit Britain", Euractiv.com, 9 March 2018, https://www.euractiv.com/section/economy-jobs/opinion/trump-is-no-ally-on-trade-for-post-brexit-britain/, last accessed 2 April 2018.

80. Gideon Rachman, "Donald Trump and Brexit are no Longer Identical Twins", *Financial Times*, 8 January 2018, https://www.ft.com/content/214ca7da-f455–11e7–88f7–5465a6ce1a00, last accessed 2 April 2018.

81. Mead, *God and Gold*, pp. 296–7. Mead quotes the words of Admiral A. T. Mahan, who described the rise of British power as the "power of the sea".

82. Helene Cooper and Ben Hubbard, "US Says Strikes Took out 'Heart' of Assad Threat", *The New York Times*, 15 April 2018, http://www.nytimes.com/images/2018/04/15/nytfrontpage/scannat.pdf, last accessed 28 April 2018.

83. Katie Rogers and Eileen Sullivan, "Trump and Western Allies Expel Scores of Russians in Sweeping Rebuke over UK Poisoning", *The New York Times*, 26 March 2018, https://nyti.ms/2pFW9Mh, last accessed 2 April 2018.

84. Alissa J. Rubin and Stephen Castle, "For France and Britain, Distinct Political Reasons to Back Trump on Strikes", *The New York Times*, 14 April 2018, https://www.nytimes.com/2018/04/14/world/europe/france-britain-syria-strikes.html, last accessed 28 April 2018.

85. Greg Jaffe, John Hudson, and Philip Rucker, "Trump, a Reluctant Hawk, has Battled his Top Aides on Russia and Lost", *The Washington Post*, 15 April 2018, https://www.washingtonpost.com/world/national-security/trump-a-reluctant-hawk-has-battled-his-top-aides-on-russia-and-lost/2018/04/15/a91e850a-3f1b-11e8–974f-aacd97698cef_story.html, last accessed 29 April 2018.

86. Mead, *God and Gold*, p. 291.

87. It must be recalled that Australia is the only country in the world that sent military forces to fight with the Americans in the Korean and Vietnam wars, before joining the United States in the two interventions against Iraq. See ibid., p. 400.

CONCLUSION: NOSTALGIA AND THE FUTURE OF SOVEREIGNTY

1. "Crisis? What Crisis?", *The Economist*, 24 November 2018, print edition.

SELECT BIBLIOGRAPHY

Here we list the books that we have consulted. Academic papers and newspaper articles are referenced in the endnotes only.

Acemoğlu, Daron, and Robinson, James A., *Why Nations Fail: The Origins of Power, Prosperity, and Poverty*, New York: Crown Business, 2012.

Aldous, Richard, *Reagan and Thatcher: The Difficult Relationship*, London: W. W. Norton, 2012.

Aldrich, Richard J., *GCHQ: The Uncensored Story of Britain's Most Secret Intelligence Agency*, London: Harper, 2010.

Alexander, Stephan (ed.), *The Americanization of Europe: Culture, Diplomacy, and Anti-Americanism after 1945*, Oxford: Berghahn, 2007.

Allison, Graham, *Destined for War: Can America and China Escape Thucydides' Trap?* New York: Scribe Publications, 2017.

Anderson, Benedict, *Imagined Communities: Reflections on the Origin and Spread of Nationalism*, London: Verso, 1983.

Angé, Olivia, and Berliner, David, *Anthropology and Nostalgia*, Oxford: Berghahn, 2015.

Arendt, Hannah, *The Origins of Totalitarianism*, New York: Harcourt Brace Jovanovich, 1968.

Ash, Timothy Garton, *Free World: America, Europe, and the Surprising Future of the West*, London: Vintage, 2014.

Bagwell, Philip, *The Transport Revolution 1770–1985*, London: Routledge, 2002.

Ballantyne, Tony, and Burton, Antoinette, *Empires and the Reach of the Global: 1870–1945*, Cambridge, MA: Harvard University Press, 2012.

Bauman, Zygmunt, *Retrotopia*, London: Polity, 2017.

Behrman, Greg, *The Most Noble Adventure: The Marshall Plan and the Time When America Helped Save Europe*, New York: Simon & Schuster, 2007.

Bell, Duncan, *The Idea of Greater Britain*, Princeton and Oxford: Princeton University Press, 2007.

SELECT BIBLIOGRAPHY

Bell, Duncan, *Reordering the World: Essays on Liberalism and Empire*, Princeton: Princeton University Press, 2016.

Bennett, James C., *The Anglosphere Challenge: Why the English-Speaking Nations will Lead the Way in the Twenty-First Century*, Lanham: Rowman & Littlefield, 2004.

Bennett, James C., *A Time for Audacity: How Brexit has Created the CANZUK Option*, London: Pole to Pole Publishing, 2016.

Bennett, Owen, *The Brexit Club: The Inside Story of the Leave Campaign's Shock Victory*, London: Biteback Publishing, 2016.

Black, Jeremy, *A History of the British Isles*, London: Palgrave Macmillan, 2012.

Bosco, Andrea, *June 1940, Great Britain and the First Attempt to Build a European Union*, Cambridge: Cambridge Scholars Publishing, 2016.

Bosco, Andrea, *The Round Table Movement and the Fall of the "Second" British Empire (1909–1919)*, Cambridge: Cambridge Scholars Publishing, 2017.

Bouchard, Gérard (ed.), *National Myths: Constructed Pasts, Contested Presents*, London and New York: Routledge, 2013.

Bourne, Kenneth, *The Foreign Policy of Victorian England, 1830–1902*, Oxford: Clarendon Press, 1970.

Boym, Svetlana, *The Future of Nostalgia*, New York: Basic Books, 2002.

Brendon, Piers, *The Decline and Fall of the British Empire: 1781–1997*, London: Jonathan Cape, 2008.

Buckledee, Steve, *The Language of Brexit: How Britain Talked its Way out of the European Union*, London: Bloomsbury, 2018.

Buonanno, Laurie, Cuglesan, Natalia, and Henderson, Keith (eds.), *The New and Changing Transatlanticism: Politics and Policy Perspectives*, Abingdon and New York: Routledge, 2015.

Burden, Robert, and Kohl, Stephan (eds.), *Landscape and Englishness*, Amsterdam: Rodopi, 2006.

Burgess, Michael, *The British Tradition of Federalism*, London: Leicester University Press, 1995.

Byrne, Katherine, *Edwardians on Screen: From* Downton Abbey *to* Parade's End, London: Palgrave Macmillan, 2015.

Cannadine, David, *Victorious Century: The United Kingdom 1800–1906*, New York: Viking, 2017.

Chinn, Sarah E., *Spectacular Men: Race, Gender, and Nation on the Early American Stage*, Oxford: Oxford University Press, 2017.

Chua, Amy, *Day of Empire: How Hyperpowers Rise to Global Dominance—and Why they Fall*, New York: Anchor Books, 2007.

Churchill, Winston, *A History of the English-Speaking Peoples*, Volumes I–IV, London: Bloomsbury, 2015.

Clark, Gregory, *The Son Also Rises: Surnames and the History of Social Mobility*, Princeton: Princeton University Press, 2014.

SELECT BIBLIOGRAPHY

Conquest, Robert, *The Dragons of Expectation: Reality and Delusion in the Course of History*, London: Duckworth, 2006.

Davis, Fred, *Yearning for Yesterday: A Sociology of Nostalgia*, New York: Free Press, 1979.

Dawson, Robert MacGregor, *The Development of Dominion Status, 1900–1936*, London: Frank Cass & Co. Ltd., 1965.

Defoe, Daniel, *The True-Born Englishman: A Satire*, Leeds: Alice Mann, 1836.

Delaforce, Patrick, *The Battle of the Bulge: Hitler's Final Gamble*, London: Pearson Longman, 2006.

Deutsch, Karl W., *Political Community and the North Atlantic Area: International Organization in the Light of Historical Experience*, Princeton: Princeton University Press, 1957.

Dilke, Charles Wentworth, *Greater Britain: A Record of Travel in English-Speaking Countries during 1866 and 1867*, New York: Cosimo, Inc., 2005 [1867].

Dockter, Warren (ed.), *Winston Churchill at* The Telegraph, London: Aurum Press, 2015.

Drolet, Jean-Francois, and Dunkerley, James (eds.), *American Foreign Policy: Studies in Intellectual History*, Manchester: Manchester University Press, 2017.

Dumbrell, John, *A Special Relationship: Anglo-American Relations from the Cold War to Iraq*, London: Palgrave Macmillan, 2006.

Duyvendak, Jan Willem, *The Politics of Home: Belonging and Nostalgia in Western Europe and the United States*, London: Palgrave, 2016.

Economy, Elizabeth C., *The Third Revolution: Xi Jinping and the New Chinese State*, New York: Oxford University Press, 2018.

Edgerton, David, *The Rise and Fall of the British Nation*, London: Allen Lane, 2018.

Elgenius, Gabriella, *Symbols of Nations and Nationalism: Celebrating Nationhood*, Basingstoke: Palgrave, 2011.

Evans, Richard, *The Pursuit of Power: Europe, 1815–1914*, London: Penguin, 2016.

Evatt, Herbert Vere, *The King and his Dominion Governors, 1936*, New York and London: Routledge, 2013.

Fels, Enrico, *Shifting Power in Asia Pacific? The Rise of China, Sino-US Competition and Regional Middle Power Allegiance*, Cham: Springer, 2016.

Ferguson, Niall, *Empire: How Britain Made the Modern World*, London: Penguin, 2004.

Fischer, David Hackett, *Albion's Seed: Four British Folkways in America*, Oxford: Oxford University Press, 1989.

Flint, John E., *Cecil Rhodes*, Boston: Little Brown, 1974.

Fox, Kate, *Watching the English: The Hidden Rules of English Behaviour*, London: Hodder, 2005.

SELECT BIBLIOGRAPHY

Fukuyama, Francis, *Trust: The Social Virtues and the Creation of Prosperity*, New York: Free Press, 1996.

Gaston, Sophie, and Hilhorst, Sacha, *At Home in One's Past: Nostalgia as a Cultural and Political Force in Britain, France and Germany*, London: Demos Report, 2018.

Geary, Patrick J., *The Myth of Nations*, Princeton: Princeton University Press, 2002.

Gilbert, Martin, *Churchill and America*, New York: Simon & Schuster, 2005.

Goodhart, David, *The Road to Somewhere: The Populist Revolt and the Future of Politics*, London: Hurst, 2017.

Gowland, David, *Britain and the European Union*, London: Routledge, 2016.

Gowland, David, and Turner, Arthur, *Britain and European Integration: A Documentary History*, London: Routledge, 2000.

Gowland, David, and Turner, Arthur, *Reluctant Europeans: Britain and European Integration 1945–1998*, London: Routledge, 2014.

Gress, David, *From Plato to NATO: The Idea of the West and its Opponents*, New York: Free Press, 2004.

Groom, Nick, *The Union Jack: The Story of the British Flag*, London: Atlantic Books, 2017.

Guay, Terrence R., *The United States and the European Union: The Political Economy of a Relationship*, London: Sheffield Academic Press, 2000.

Hajkowski, Thomas, *The BBC and National Identity in Britain, 1922–53*, Manchester: Manchester University Press, 2017.

Hall, Duncan, *The British Commonwealth of Nations: A Study of its Past and Future Development*, London: Methuen, 1920.

Hall, Peter, and Soskice, David, *Varieties of Capitalism: The Institutional Foundations of Comparative Advantage*, Oxford: Oxford University Press, 2003.

Harper, John Lamberton, *American Visions of Europe: Franklin D. Roosevelt, George F. Kennan, and Dean G. Acheson*, Cambridge: Cambridge University Press, 1996.

Heffer, Simon, *The Age of Decadence: Britain 1880 to 1914*, London: Penguin Random House, 2017.

Herring, George C., *From Colony to Superpower: US Foreign Relations since 1776*, Oxford: Oxford University Press, 2008.

Heuser, Beatrice, and O'Neill, Robert (eds.), *Securing Peace in Europe, 1945–62: Thoughts for the Post-Cold War Era*, London: Palgrave, 2016.

Hill, Christopher, *The Future of British Foreign Policy*, London: Polity, 2018.

Hitchens, Christopher, *Blood, Class and Nostalgia: Anglo-American Ironies*, London: Vintage, 1991.

Huntington, Samuel, *Who Are We? The Challenges to America's National Identity*, New York: Simon & Schuster, 2005.

SELECT BIBLIOGRAPHY

Hyams, Jacky, *The Real Life Downton Abbey: How Life Was Really Lived in Stately Homes a Century Ago*, London: John Blake, 2012.

Ignatieff, Michael, *Blood and Belonging: Journeys into the New Nationalism*, London: Vintage, 1995.

Johnson, Boris, *The Churchill Factor: How One Man Made History*, London: Riverhead Books, 2014.

Judt, Tony, *Postwar: A History of Europe since 1945*, London: Penguin, 2005.

Kahneman, Daniel, *Thinking Fast and Slow*, New York: Penguin, 2011.

Keating, Michael, *Nations against the State*, London: Macmillan, 1996.

Kendle, John, *Federal Britain: A History*, London: Routledge, 1997.

Kennedy, Paul M., *The Rise of the Anglo-German Antagonism, 1860–1914*, Dublin: Ashfield Press, 1980.

Kennedy, Paul M., *The Rise and Fall of the Great Powers: Economic Change and Military Conflict from 1500 to 2000*, London: Vintage, 1988.

Kenny, Michael, and Pearce, Nick, *Shadows of Empire: The Anglosphere in British Politics*, London: Polity, 2018.

Kimball, Warren F., *The Juggler: Franklin Roosevelt as Wartime Statesman*, Princeton: Princeton University Press, 1991.

Kimball, Warren F., *Forged in War: Churchill, Roosevelt and the Second World War*, London: Ivan R. Dee, 1998.

Kotkin, Joel, *Tribes: How Race, Religion, and Identity Determine Success in the New Global Economy*, New York: Random House, 1993.

Krastev, Ivan, *After Europe*, Philadelphia: University of Pennsylvania Press, 2017.

Kroeber, Arthur R., *China's Economy*, New York: Oxford University Press, 2016.

Kumar, Krishan, *The Idea of Englishness: English Culture, National Identity and Social Thought*, London: Routledge, 2016.

Kumar, Krishan, *Visions of Empire: How Five Imperial Regimes Shaped the World*, Princeton: Princeton University Press, 2017.

Leffler, Melvyn P., *For the Soul of Mankind: The United States, the Soviet Union, and the Cold War*, New York: Hill & Wang, 2009.

Leffler, Melvyn P., and Westad, Odd Arne (eds.), *The Cambridge History of the Cold War*, Cambridge: Cambridge University Press, 2010.

Lev, Amnon, (ed.), *The Federal Idea: Public Law between Governance and Political Life*, London: Bloomsbury, 2017.

Lloyd, Trevor Owen, *Empire, Welfare State, Europe: English History 1906–1992*, London: Oxford University Press, 1993.

Louis, William Roger (ed.), *The Oxford History of the British Empire*, volume IV: *The Twentieth Century*, ed. Judith M. Brown, Oxford: Oxford University Press, 2004.

Louis, William Roger (ed.), *The Oxford History of the British Empire*, volume V:

Historiography, ed. Robin W. Winks, Oxford: Oxford University Press, 2007.

Lundestad, Geir, *"Empire" by Integration: The United States and European Integration, 1945–1997*, Oxford and New York: Oxford University Press, 1998.

Lundestad, Geir, *The United States and Western Europe since 1945: From "Empire" by Invitation to Transatlantic Drift*, Oxford and New York: Oxford University Press, 2003.

Lundestad, Geir, *East, West, North, South: International Relations since 1945*, London: Sage, 2014.

MacGregor, Neil, *Germany: Memories of a Nation*, London: Penguin Random House, 2014.

MacKenzie, John M., *Propaganda and Empire: The Manipulation of British Public Opinion 1880–1960*, Manchester: Manchester University Press, 1986.

Marshall, H. E., *Our Island Story: A Child's History of England*, New York: Wilder Publications, 2009 [1905].

May, Alexander (ed.), *The Commonwealth and International Affairs: The Round Table Centennial Selection*, London: Routledge, 2010.

May, Alexander, "The Round Table: 1910–66", D.Phil. thesis, University of Oxford, 1995, https://ora.ox.ac.uk/objects/uuid:ee7ebd01-f085-44e9-917b-98d21a0f4206.

Mayhew, Robert J., *Enlightenment Geography: The Political Languages of British Geography, 1650–1850*, London: Palgrave Macmillan, 2000.

Mead, Walter Russell, *God and Gold: Britain, America and the Making of the Modern World*, New York: Vintage, 2007.

Mejías-López, Alejandro, *The Inverted Conquest: The Myth of Modernity and the Transatlantic Onset of Modernism*, Nashville: Vanderbilt University Press, 2009.

Menzies, Robert, *Afternoon Light: Some Memories of Men and Events*, London: Cassel & Co., 1967.

Millard, Candice, *Hero of the Empire: The Boer War, a Daring Escape, and the Making of Winston Churchill*, New York: Random House, 2016.

Milward, Alan S., *The Rise and Fall of a National Strategy: The UK and the European Community*, London: Routledge, 2002.

Misa, Thomas, *Leonardo to the Internet: Technology and Culture from the Renaissance to the Present*, Baltimore: Johns Hopkins University Press, 2011.

Miscamble, Wilson D., *George F. Kennan and the Making of American Foreign Policy, 1947–1950*, Princeton: Princeton University Press, 1992.

Moisi, Dominique, *The Geopolitics of Emotion: How Cultures of Fear, Humiliation, and Hope are Reshaping the World*, London: Anchor, 2010.

Moore, Laurence, and Vaudagna, Maurizio (eds.), *The American Century in Europe*, Ithaca: Cornell University Press, 2003.

SELECT BIBLIOGRAPHY

Murphy, Philip, *Empire's New Clothes: The Myth of the Commonwealth*, London: Hurst, 2018.

Naipaul, Vidiadhar Surajprasad, *The Enigma of Arrival: A Novel in Five Sections*, London: Picador, 2011.

Nichols, Thomas M., *The Death of Expertise: The Campaign against Established Knowledge and Why it Matters*, Oxford: Oxford University Press, 2017.

O'Connor, Brendon, and Griffiths, Martin (eds.), *Anti-Americanism: History, Causes, and Themes*, Oxford: Greenwood World Publishing, 2007.

Oldershaw, Lucian, *England: A Nation. Being the Papers of the Patriots' Club*, London: R. Brimley Johnson, 1904.

Persico, Joseph E., *Roosevelt's Secret War: FDR and World War II Espionage*, New York: Random House, 2002.

Peterson, John, and Pollack, Mark A. (eds.), *Europe, America, Bush: Transatlantic Relations in the Twenty-First Century*, London: Routledge, 2004.

Porter, Bernard, *The Absent-Minded Imperialists: Empire, Society, and Culture in Britain*, Oxford: Oxford University Press, 2004.

Powell, David, *The Edwardian Crisis*, Basingstoke: Palgrave Macmillan, 1996.

Quirk, Randolph, *The English Language and Images of Matter*, Oxford: Oxford University Press, 1972.

Read, Donald, *The Age of Urban Democracy: England 1868–1914*, London: Routledge, 1979.

Redwood, John, *Superpower Struggles: Mighty America, Faltering Europe, Rising Asia*, London: Palgrave Macmillan, 2005.

Renwick, Robin, *Fighting with Allies: America and Britain in Peace and War*, London: Palgrave Macmillan, 1996.

Reyn, Sebastian, *Atlantis Lost: The American Experience with de Gaulle, 1958–1969*, Amsterdam: Amsterdam University Press, 2010.

Reynolds, David, *Britannia Overruled: British Policy and World Power in the Twentieth Century*, London: Routledge, 2000.

Roberts, Andrew, *A History of the English-Speaking Peoples Since 1990*, London: Weidenfeld & Nicolson, 2006.

Roth, Michael S., *Memory, Trauma, and History: Essays on Living with the Past*, New York: Columbia University Press, 2012.

Runciman, David, *Politics: Ideas in Profile*, New York: Profile Books, 2014.

Scott, Jonathan, *When the Waves Ruled Britannia: Geography and Political Identities, 1500–1800*, Cambridge: Cambridge University Press, 2011.

Seeley, John Robert, *The Expansion of England: Two Courses of Lectures*, Cambridge: Cambridge University Press, 2010 [1880].

Shalev, Eran, *Rome Reborn on Western Shores: Historical Imagination and the Creation of the American Republic*, Charlottesville: University of Virginia Press, 2009.

Simms, Brendan, *Britain's Europe: A Thousand Years of Conflict and Cooperation*, London: Penguin, 2016.

SELECT BIBLIOGRAPHY

Smith, Anthony D., *Ethno-Symbolism and Nationalism: A Cultural Approach*, Abingdon: Routledge, 2009.

Sorel, Georges, *Reflections on Violence*, Glencoe, IL: Free Press, 1950.

Spiering, Menno, *A Cultural History of British Euroscepticism*, London: Routledge, 2015.

Steil, Benn, *The Marshall Plan: Dawn of the Cold War*, New York: Simon & Schuster, 2018.

Tadashi Wakabayashi, Bob (ed.), *Modern Japanese Thought*, Cambridge: Cambridge University Press, 1998.

Tharoor, Shashi, *Inglorious Empire: What the British Did to India*, London: Penguin, 2017.

Troitiño, David Ramiro, Kerikmäe, Tanel, and Chochiap, Archil (eds.), *Brexit: History, Reasoning and Perspectives*, Cham: Springer, 2018.

Vucetic, Srdjan, *The Anglosphere: A Genealogy of a Racialized Identity in International Relations*, Stanford: Stanford University Press, 2011.

Wadhwa, Vivek, *The Immigrant Exodus: Why America is Losing the Global Race to Capture Entrepreneurial Talent*, Philadelphia: Wharton Digital Press, 2012.

Ward, Stuart (ed.), *British Culture and the Empire*, Manchester: Manchester University Press, 2001.

West, Nancy Martha, *Kodak and the Lens of Nostalgia*, Charlottesville: University of Virginia Press, 2000.

Westen, Drew, *The Political Brain: The Role of Emotion in Deciding the Fate of the Nation*, New York: PublicAffairs, 2005.

Ziegler, Philip, *Legacy: Cecil Rhodes, the Rhodes Trust and the Rhodes Scholarships*, New Haven: Yale University Press, 2008.

INDEX

INDEX

INDEX

INDEX

Harry Potter (media franchise): 68
Harvard University: 83, 140; faculty of, 44
Hawke, Bob: 139
Hayden, Michael: 318
Henry VII, King: 76
Hinduism: 23, 35–6
Hitler, Adolf: 11, 57, 60, 71; death of (1945), 81
Hobbes, Thomas: 175
Hofer, Johannes: *Dissertatio Medica de Nostalgia, Oder Heimwehe* (1688), 25–6
Home Office: 122
Horthy, Miklós: 45; ideology of, 24–5
Howard, John: 89
Huffington Post: 138
Hundred Years War (1337–1453): Battle of Agincourt (1415), 76
Hungary: 45
Huntington, Samuel: 47

Iceland: 150
immigration: 4, 27, 34–5, 37–8; fears of, 20, 22, 47, 65; misconceptions of, 8, 28
Imperial Conference (1907): 88
Imperial Federation League: 97, 100; aims of, 94; founding of (1884), 94; shortcomings of, 97–8
imperialism: 17–18, 139, 145; British, 5, 7–8, 125–6; French, 146
India: 6, 18–19, 43, 98, 120, 123–5, 145, 148, 170; British Raj (1856–1947), 66, 122, 125–6, 158; economy of, 23, 126; Hindu population of, 35–6; Independence of (1947), 18; Muslim population of, 36; New Delhi, 124; Rebellion (1857), 89

Indian National Congress: members of, 125
Inglehart-Welzel Map: 144–5
INSEAD Business School: reports compiled by, 146
Institute of Chartered Engineers: 134
Instituto per gli Studi di Politica Internazionale (ISPI): ix
International Meridian Conference: 17
International Monetary Fund (IMF): 38
Ipsos MORI: polls conducted by, 77
Iran: political sanctions targeting, 167
Iraq: 23; Kirkuk, 23; Mosul, 23; Operation Iraqi Freedom (2003–11), 34, 164, 169
Ireland Home Rule: 88
Islam: 37, 96, 144
Islamism: 28
Israel: 125; Jerusalem, 167
Italy: 3, 48, 61, 115, 145–6, 155, 178; Florence, 113; Rome, 65

Jamaica: call for reparations from UK (2015), 31
Japan: 31, 34, 101, 125, 137, 146; Meiji Restoration (1868), 23, 52; Tokugawa Shogunate (1603–1867), 23
Jerome, Jennie: family of, 82
Jesuits: 93
jingoism: 3
Johnson, Boris: 8, 77, 109; Chatham House Speech (2017), 75; *Churchill Factor, The* (2014), 74; Mayor of London, 74; political rhetoric of, 11, 20, 81–2, 130–1, 134, 166; resignation

234

INDEX

INDEX

Venezuela: 101
Victoria: 77
Victoria, Queen: 91; reign of, 55
Vikings: 143
Village, The: 68

Wall Street Journal: 141
Ward, Joseph: 141
Washington, George: 82
Weale, Albert: 4
Westen, Drew: 78
Western Samoa: 18
Whigs: ideology of, 57, 82
Whorf, Benjamin Lee: 142
Whorfianism (linguistic relativity):
  concept of, 142
Wilhelm II, Kaiser: 11, 57

World Bank: Ease of Doing
  Business Index, 145
World Economic Forum (WEF):
  Davos Summit (2017), 33
World Trade Organization (WTO):
  167
World Value Survey: 123

xenophobia: 36–7, 72
Xi Jinping: 3; political rhetoric of,
  22, 31–3, 52

YouGov: polls conducted by, 19, 27

Zheng He, Admiral: exploration of
  Red Sea, 22–3
Zimbabwe: 18, 96